In Search of the New Old

In Search of the New Old

REDEFINING OLD AGE IN AMERICA, 1945-1970

RICHARD B. CALHOUN

Elsevier · New York

NEW YORK · OXFORD

ELSEVIER NORTH-HOLLAND, INC.
52 Vanderbilt Avenue, New York, New York 10017

Distributors outside the United States and Canada:
THOMOND BOOKS
(A Division of Elsevier/North-Holland Scientific Publishers, Ltd)
P.O. Box 85
Limerick, Ireland

Library of Congress Cataloging in Publication Data

Calhoun, Richard B.
  In search of the new old; redefining old age in
America, 1945-1970.

  Bibliography: p.
  Includes index.
    1.   Aged—United States.   2.   Retirement—United
States.   3.   Old Age assistance—United States.
I.   Title.
HV1461.C34   362.6'0973   78-17721
ISBN 0-444-99048-8

Manufactured in the United States

Designed by Loretta Li

Contents

Acknowledgments

The following study was funded by the Administration on Aging, U.S. Department of Health, Education and Welfare, under grant number 93-P-57618, and carried out under the auspices of the Center for Policy Research, New York City. Special thanks go the the project's principal investigator, Dr. Amitai Etzioni, Professor of Sociology at Columbia University and Director of the Center for Policy Research, Inc., for his encouragement, assistance and patience; and to Dr. Walter P. Metzger, Professor of History at Columbia University, for his attempts, mostly successful, to repress the excesses of the poet and to stimulate instead the orderly thought processes of the scholar. Where he did not succeed, the fault lies with the author's stubborn refusal to abandon bardic inclinations. In sum, whatever merit this work may possess derives in no small part from the efforts of these two gentlemen.

Introduction

Aging, no less than death and taxes, is one of life's certitudes—
a biologically determined tax upon human faculties which only
the grave can repeal. Some of us age faster than others; but the
process, whether rapid or snaillike, is inexorable. Not surprisingly, given the obsessively analytical temper of modern society,
aging has come to pose an existential crisis. As in matters of
faith and man's relationship to his fellow, the crisis provoked by
the process of aging is at once personal and philosophical. Personal, because it involves observable physical decrement, evident
in ways ranging from the mildly irritating to the distressing and
painful; philosophical, because it occurs in a society that has not
only stripped its older members of traditional functions but
added to their embarrassment by exalting and glamorizing
youth.

Yet there remains, in old age no less than in youth, a basic
need to find life continually affirmed. Though youth be fled,
existence in most cases is still preferable to its only empirically
verifiable alternative. This fact alone provides a powerful incentive to define the process of aging in terms as benign as possible.
Today, the terms once applicable to the aged—wisdom, experience, caution—are no longer especially relevant, and the aged
themselves more numerous than ever before; the imperative is

1

obvious. Both humanity and practical necessity have combined to demand that something be done to soften the negative implications of aging. Ignoring the process will clearly not achieve this end, if only because aging itself is an obtrusive chain of events. Thus, only direct and positive action will answer the requirements of the situation.

The following story tells how, in the post–World War II setting, various interest groups worked (if not always as allies) to institutionalize a new, more positive concept of the aging process. To illustrate the fact and magnitude of this development, we might use a family photo album as the appropriate analogy for what we shall present in the first two chapters. By looking at societal "snapshots" taken in two base eras—1945–1950 and 1965–1970—and comparing them, we can establish both the nature and degree of alteration in the image of America's older (over sixty-five) citizens in the postwar era. This alteration, as we shall note, is reflected in the "media" representation of the elderly, in the popular attitude toward aging as a personal phenomenon, and in the terminology applied both to the aged and to the process of growing older.

Before proceeding with this task, however, I shall attempt to justify the time frame I have employed. Admittedly, basic attitudes toward senescence do not date from 1945. Indeed, we can find many of the attributes of old age to which present day biological and social scientists subscribe in Cicero's *De Senectute,* written half a century before the birth of Christ. And in our own century, prior to 1945, a number of significant developments indicated that old age was becoming a matter of public concern. Some of the more important of these events include the publication of G. Stanley Hall's *Senescence* (1922), a Freudian description and explanation of the aging process; a report, *The Care of the Aged* (1931); initiated and financed by the Deutsch Foundation; the Social Security Act of 1935; the Macy Foundation-sponsored Wood's Hole Conference on Aging (1937), during which recent scientific research on biological aging was disseminated and discussed; and the subsequent publication by

Dr. E. V. Cowdry of the proceedings of this conference under the title, *The Problems of Aging.* (1938).[1]

Nonetheless, 1945 is defensible as a starting point for several reasons. To begin with, the demographic trend was apparent. The proportion of citizens over the age of sixty-five, constituted the most rapidly growing age group of our whole population. From 1900 through 1920 the figure was 5.4 percent; ten years later it was 6.8 percent; by 1950 it had reached 8.2 percent. People clearly were living longer lives in greater numbers than ever before. A man born in 1900 in the United States had an average life expectancy of 47.88 years; a woman 50.70 years. By 1950 newborn males and females could expect to live 65.47 and 70.96 years, respectively. Not only were numbers and proportions increasing, noted sociologist Ernest W. Burgess, but they were doing so against a backdrop of urbanization and industrialization that devalued the traditional social roles of older people. Policymakers were finding it more difficult to ignore such data, especially as all projections affirmed the continuation of these trends.[2]

In placing the problem of aging on the postwar agenda, social planners were also reacting to the socioeconomic implications of this demographic fact. As one physician, Dr. Frank L. Hinman, put it, progress in medicine had inaugurated "an age of elders unknown to history." Within a few decades, he predicted, old people will outnumber the young in the United States; yet businessmen, politicians, and social scientists have disregarded this fact so far. Lawrence K. Frank, an officer with the Macy Foundation, attacked this "almost brutal neglect or callous dismissal" of the nation's elderly, charging that it constituted an appalling "wastage of human resources." The ultimate response to this problem, he concluded, would be nothing less than "a crucial test of our democratic faith."[3]

Failure to integrate ever-growing numbers of older people into American society meant not only an increase in the number of economic dependents but heightened opportunities for political deviancy as well. Dr. Edward Stieglitz, of the newly formed

3

Gerontological Society, emphasized the "potential menace to national economic equilibrium" posed by large numbers of non-productive citizens; geriatrician Martin Gumpert saw "dynamite" in the fact of a rapidly aging population in a society that had traditionally made little provision for its relatively few older members. An editorial page columnist for the *New York Times* expressed reservations about having large numbers of idle oldsters "thinking up all sorts of strange new ideas which sooner or later the young people will try to put into practice." Such a situation, the columnist insisted, was "not conducive to social stability."

Writing in one of the nation's mass circulation periodicals, William L. Laurence foresaw the "kinds of social upheaval generated by those dispossessed by the industrial revolution" sweeping America if the problems of the elderly continued to be neglected. In New York State, the pioneering Joint State Legislative Committee on the Problems of Aging heard and accepted testimony that attributed great potential for political havoc to old people who were dependent, nonproductive, and thus, politically susceptible to demagoguery. Investigating the national scene, *Time* magazine focused on the "noisy prophets" of the West Coast whose specialty was "lead[ing] the aged in holy wars on the nearest State Treasury" and "mak[ing] pensions a permanent social issue." A chief proponent of these pension drives was the Communist Party, warned *Time,* particularly in Washington State, where the Washington Pension Union was openly headed by a "crafty and smooth-talking party-liner." In a speech before the National Conference on the Aged in 1950, Federal Security Administration (FSA) Director Oscar Ewing also warned, albeit obliquely, against allowing old people to be duped by various un-American forces.[4]

Finally, the science of gerontology reached maturity as a practical discipline in the postwar setting. Although the U.S. Surgeon General created a National Advisory Committee on Gerontology in 1939, that organization was dominated by a few members of the medical profession more interested in geriatrics, itself a

4

"poor relation" among medical specialties. By 1945, however, one worker in the field remarked that the growing interest in the aged and their problems was spreading from the realms of biology and medicine to those of sociology, economics, social work, and psychology. A small group of researcher–administrators had emerged, to speak out on behalf of older people. Thus the year 1945 saw the founding of the interdisciplinary Gerontological Society, and in January 1946, the first number of its organ, *The Journal of Gerontology,* appeared. The American Geriatric Society was also created during this period, giving added professional status to medical researchers in the field of aging, and the house publication, *The Journal of the American Geriatric Society,* was established. Subsequent convention–congress-style meetings supplemented fact-finding and dissemination processes initiated by the creation of these umbrella organizations. Most notable among these conferences was the 1950 National Conference on Aging held in Washington, D.C. One enthusiastic participant found fellow attendees "eager to help . . . feeling that we cannot let change evolve at its own pace while so many of the 11.5 million Americans who are sixty-five years old are living unproductive, unsatisfactory lives." And the sponsoring institution, the Federal Security Administration, pronounced the meeting an entire success in evoking "a driving sentiment . . . for fair play and an equal chance" for the nation's aged.

Thus, beginning in 1945, the scattered individuals within both the biological and social sciences who were interested in the aged steadily moved toward cooperation. The early going was not easy, but a start had been made. State Senator Thomas Desmond of the New York State Joint Legislative Committee on the Problems of Aging wrote of these men and women: "Ill-supported in their important work, and toiling in relative obscurity, the age fighters are hammering at different fronts, but driving toward a common goal: Better life in more years of life."[5]

Related to, indeed inseparable from, the issue of aging is that of retirement. Because of a long-standing social tendency to classify and define adults in terms of their occupational roles, no event is more apt to cause devaluation of an individual than retirement. With age the key factor in determining when an individual is to retire, advancing years become associated with the loss of this very significant social role. The logical sequence is unavoidable: Advancing age signals retirement; retirement means loss of occupation resulting in loss of social utility; therefore, the later years mean loss of social utility.

Thus, one cannot discuss the popular attitude toward aging unless one is prepared to confront the modern phenomenon of mass retirement, and to attempt to understand the impact it has had upon our society. Instituted to prune older workers from the labor force in favor of younger workers, retirement became a way of life during the Great Depression. Initially conceived as an economic rather than a social welfare policy, no effort was spent to portray mass retirement as anything other than what it was—a way of making a greater share of a contracting labor market available to younger workers who were presumably a more productive and certainly a larger and more volatile segment of society than that constituted by older Americans. The creation of the Social Security Administration in 1935, and the setting of an age—sixty-five—as the accepted retirement age made it possible to fix to the very day that point in an individual's life when he or she ceased to be economically productive. After one's sixty-fifth birthday, one could only be "old." Business did not help the situation any when it referred to this newly instituted policy as "superannuation."

Clearly, the redefinition of aging, to give it a more positive connotation, demanded a corresponding and precedential, rather than simultaneous, overhaul of the notion of retirement. Two decades of debate over the combined issues of retirement and retirement income and its relationship to the attempt to modify attitudes toward aging will be discussed in detail in Chapter 2. For the present, however, we shall confine ourselves to an examination of the case regarding 1945–1950 as the period which initiated society's efforts to redefine the later years and the ways in which they might be spent. Such efforts were forecast in the growing concern of the reasons for the retirement decision and the recognition that it was the result of a combination of highly complex factors. Management led the way in this recognition. Thus, as early as 1950, a *Business Week* staff writer tried to determine why fully 60 percent of those in the coal, steel, and automotive industries eligible for retirement on the generous benefits won for them by their unions, continued on the job. The writer found, first, that earnings were currently high. The discrepancy between the working income and the most generous benefits was still too great to tempt the majority into voluntarily leaving the work force. Second, in many of these pension plans, benefit levels depended upon the length of service (defined in terms of "credits"), and thus, workers felt the pressure to stay on simply to accumulate more "credits", ultimately with higher benefits. And finally, there was the psychological element—the fears of the "boredom of retirement," of "failing to stay busy"—fears felt by many workers, which resulted in an inclination to remain on the job past retirement age where variables in the interests of "manpower policy"—that is, by trading off adequate pensions for control of retirement age, and as we shall note in a subsequent chapter, introducing "retirement preparation" programs to help overcome workers' psychological resistance—had already evolved and were even then being put into practice.[6]

The FSA report for 1951 and a California state survey carried out by the University of California—Berkeley in 1952 illustrate a growing awareness of, and interest in, accumulating information on the reasons for the decline in the labor force participation rate of those over sixty-five (from 68 percent in 1890 to a low of 42 percent by 1950) (Table 1). The apparent irreversibility of this trend stimulated the careful analysis of such data.

The discrepancy in the finding of these two reports on voluntary retirement for reasons of health, explained Clark Tibbitts of the U.S. Office of the Aging in an accompanying essay, derived from the fact that fully 35 percent of the Old Age and Survivors Disability Insurance program sample reported that

7

TABLE 1
Reasons for Retirement of Males 65 Years Old and Over (1951–1952)

National Survey, OASDI Beneficiaries, 1951	All Benefici- aries	Unem- ployed Benefi- ciaries[a]	University of California Survey, 1952	Percent
Total[b]	100%	100%	Total[c]	100%
Quit Job	55.2	56.0	Voluntary Retirement	75.9
Unable to Work	41.5	44.2	Health	59.3
Other	13.8	11.8	Other[d]	16.6
Retirement Voluntary; Good Health	3.9	—		
All Other[e]	9.9	—		
Lost Job	44.8	44.0	Involuntary Retirement	24.1
Reached Retirement Age	10.9	—	Compulsory Retirement	13.7
Other[f]	33.9	—	Other[g]	10.4

Source: Henry Sheldon, *The Older Population of the United States* (New York: John Wiley & Sons, 1961), Table 18, p.99.
[a] Unemployed at least 6 months prior to end of survey year.
[b] Retired OASDI beneficiaries 65 years old and over.
[c] Males 65 and older with work experience but not in labor force.
[d] Includes those who retired for reasons of age, family decision, or other.
[e] Includes those who quit full-time covered job: hoping to find a different job; to take a part-time job, covered or noncovered; after a quarrel with boss or fellows; during a strike; because of un- willingness to adjust to another kind of work; because needed at home; etc.
[f] Includes those losing jobs because: of discontinuance of work; employer thought worker was no longer capable; fired for unknown reasons.
[g] Includes discharges for reasons of age, layoffs and subsequent inability to find work, and other.

they had returned to some form of employment subsequent to their initial qualification for benefits and thus could not reason- ably argue that they had originally left the labor force because they were too ill to work; whereas all of the California sample had been out of the labor force for at least six months and were being asked only about their most recent retirement. In addition, the California sample included persons not covered by OASDI— the self-employed, for example, who tended to continue work- ing until forced to stop because of physical disability. Much of the difficulty in interpreting data on retirement, he observed, was inherent in the nature of the OASDI sample typically used. This included older men and women who did not simply retire at sixty-five but embarked instead upon "a series of forays in and out of the labor market" before finally voluntarily leaving it or being forced to leave it for good. The percentage of voluntary retirement for reasons other than health was about the same in both samples, although a category for "voluntary retirement in good health" was included only in the FSA survey. In fact, the percentage for this category (3.9) was quite small. "Whether this preference [of healthy older workers to stay on the job] reflects a high value placed on work per se," Tibbitts wrote, "or a choice between the income implicit in continued employment and that implicit in OASDI benefits, is an open question." Within the two samples, about the same percentages—10.9 (OASDI) and 13.7 (California)—had been excluded by formal retirement rules. Tibbitts found this datum "somewhat surprising" in view of the large amount of attention "forced retirement" received in literature on employment problems of older workers. Yet, such concern was not entirely out of place, he continued, since "with the large-scale development of industry-wide pension plans, it is clear that formal retirement systems may considerably increase their contribution to the volume of retirement." The last major discrepancy between the two studies—the difference between the percentages of involuntary retirements other than formal retirement systems; that is, 33.9 percent of the OASDI to only 10.4 percent of the California sample—Tibbitts explained as the complement of the differences observed in the voluntary–poor health categories.[7]

If, as management desired, and analysts like Tibbitts suspected, retirement was to become a fact of life in modern industrial society, then the members of that society would have to learn how to prepare for it. Journalist Murray Teigh Bloom shared a sense of this inevitability: "The idea of retirement has become too much a part of tradition for men ever to revert to the old idea of working until the day they drop." At the same time, he pointed out, each year increasing numbers of healthy older men and women were ushered into "a strange world of overwhelming leisure, [in which] the exile feels guilty because he isn't working and futile because he doesn't know what to do." Rather than resisting the idea and ignoring the reality of retirement, Bloom suggested, the individual ought to prepare himself, mentally no less than financially, for the day he leaves the labor force. He recommended the counseling service established by the Marshall Field Corporation of Chicago as a model for employer–employee cooperation in this area. A national publication directed at high school students agreed: "Age 65 has become—rightly or wrongly—the signal for calling a man 'too old to work.' " Retirement, the article went on to point out, involved both emotional and financial problems which students ought to consider in order to understand the problems of the current retired generation and to help prepare for their own future retirements. As to calls for the elimination of involuntary retirement programs, the writer dismissed them as based upon wishful thinking: "That would be in the distant future, for the trend is still in the other direction, towards earlier retirement." Current policy, the article concluded, ought to focus on the financial problems of retirement, and strive to eliminate emotional dislocations by defining the retirement years in terms of usefulness and productiveness rather than those of boredom and decline.[8]

Adding to the volatility of the situation at that time was the specter of postwar military demobilization. Politicians, economists, and large numbers of older workers could recall vividly the prewar days when a depressed labor market had imposed an especially high unemployment rate on the aged and resulted in the passage of the Social Security Act. The accompanying trend toward compulsory retirement was a product of this scarcity of jobs and represented industry's response to the surplus labor situation. "When the economy is sick," noted one student of the aging process, "discriminations of all kinds flourish—against racial groups, religious groups, age groups, women in industry and the professions." The need for labor on the home front during the war had, however, temporarily reversed the move toward forced retirement of superannuated workers. According to Social Security Administration figures, more than 50,000 individuals had voluntarily forfeited old age assistance and social security benefits in order to go back to work; but with the inevitable decline in the need for manpower in the postwar era, a return to prewar employment practices seemed likely. In fact, the editors of an influential business periodical, anticipating demobilization in early 1944, referred to the twenty–sixty-four years group as "our manpower backbone" and advocated social policies—schooling for the young and pensions for the old— designed to restrict employment opportunities to this "backbone" group.

Unlike the depression era, however, when all age groups faced job scarcities, the postwar environment promised a better employment picture, thus, greater opportunities for all segments of the labor force. Older workers and their social and political patrons, then, would look unfavorably upon policies designed to exclude them from the labor market. Consequent efforts to ensure full employment opportunities for the older person provided yet another means through which society's attention was being drawn to the problems of its aging and aged members.[9]

This then was the social and economic situation facing those concerned with the plight of the aged at the close of World War II. By 1945, all the incentives to action had fallen or were falling into place. The number of older people, their economic plight, and the irreversible realities of modern industrial society were "givens," to be ignored only at the risk of gravely damaging America's democratic institutions. Beginning with a small group of biomedical and social scientists, the first efforts at correcting this unfortunate situation were begun. In the chapters which follow, I will examine the roles of the various interest groups taking part in this reformist movement and attempt to show what these groups have contributed to the overall change in social climate as well as the varied—social, political, and economic—motives for involving themselves in the process of guided social change. Leaders from the fields of gerontology (biomedical and social scientists), social work, education, advertising, mass media, organized labor, and the business community have all worked—at times more in conflict than in cooperation— to renovate the popular conception of the later years of life; to make growing older more positive, less menacing, to those already in sight of their three-score-and-ten and to all of their juniors who will one day face a similar situation. Even more than a record of efforts to achieve a certain end, what follows ought also to interest all students of social change; for it tells us as much about the reformist style in a pluralistic society as it does about the substance of the specific reform under consideration.

NOTES

1. Good background on pre-1945 interest in aging is given by Clark Tibbitts in his introduction to Henry Sheldon, *The Older Population of the United States* (New York, 1955), pp. 1–2.
2. Population figures (totals) by age (to 1957) from *Statistical History of the United States* (1967), Series A23–33, p. 8; figures on proportions of +65s in total population in M. W. Riley and A. Foner, *Aging and Society,* 3 vol. (New York: 1968), I, Exhibit 2–6, p. 21; expectancy figures, Exhibit 2–13, p. 30; Burgess. "The Growing Problem of Aging," in C. Tibbitts ed., *Living Through the Later Years* (Ann Arbor, 1949); projections based on 1950 census data from Sheldon, op.cit, tables 6 and 7, pp. 21, 23; see also the contributions by Wilbert E. Moore and H. S. Shyrock to J. D. Brown, C. Kerr, and E. E. Witte, *The Aged and Society* (Industrial Relations Society, 1950).
3. Frank Hinman, M.D., "The Dawn of Gerontology," *Journal of Gerontology* I (1946): 416–417; Frank, "Gerontology," ibid.: 10.
4. Stieglitz, "Gerontology Comes of Age," *Science Monthly* 62 (January–June 1946): 82; Gumpert, "The Future of Old Age," *Science Illustrated* I (June 1946): 40; *New York Times* (June 21, 1947), 16:4; Lawrence, "You're Going to Live Longer Than You Think," *Saturday Evening Post* 222 (April 29, 1950): 28; first report of the joint legislative committee, doc. 61, *New York State Legislative Documents,* 1948; IX; "Nothing's Too Good for Grandpa," *Time Magazine* 54 (September 5, 1949): 16–17; Ewing, quoted in *Man and His Years* (Washington, D.C., 1950), pp. 1–2.
5. Lawrence Frank, "Gerontology," loc. cit., p. 1; E. J. Stieglitz, M.D., "Gerontology Comes of Age," *Science Monthly* 62 (January–June 1946): 81–82; Marion Robinson, "Magna Charta for the Aged," *Survey;* 86 (1950): 448; National Conference on Aging; *Aging* (published by the FSA), June 18, 1951, p.4; Desmond, "The Promise of Geriatrics," *Today's Health* 28 (June 1950): 46. A good short history of the origins of modern gerontology is found in Milton L. Barron, *The Aging American: An Introduction to Social Gerontology and Geriatrics* (New York: 1961), chap. 1.
6. "Old Hands Snub Pensions," *Business Week* (November 18, 1950): 124–126; a study

by Banker's Trust in 1950 revealed that between 1943 and 1947, 35% of all plans investigated had a service requirement and an additional 50% tied pensions to age as well as service. Similar figures for the 1948 and 1950 period were 30% and 51%. See *A Study of Industrial Retirement Plans* (New York: 1950).

7. Sheldon, op. cit., 46–53 (Table 18), and Tibbitts' commentary. Part of Tibbitts' objective in this essay was to persuade researchers that the retirement decision was not ordinarily a purely personal or purely social one, but rather one involved in both these categories.

8. Bloom, "Retirement Doesn't Have to be Exile," *Rotarian* 74–75 (October 1949): 15+ "Will You Enjoy a Ripe Old Age?" *Senior Scholastic* (November 30, 1949): 8–9.

9. Grace Rubin-Rabson, "What's Wrong with Growing Old?" *Hygeia* 26 (1948): 278; SSA figures reported and commented upon by J. C. and Helen Furnas, "Old Folks Aren't Useless," *Saturday Evening Post*, 217: (January 13, 1945): 86; editorial in *Business Week* (February 5, 1944): 144; see comments of Clifford Kuh, a physician with H. J. Kaiser's Permanente Foundation, on the war's beneficial influence on the employment opportunity for older workers and, as a result, their future in the labor market, "Selective Placement of Older Workers," *Journal of Gerontology* I (1946): 313–318.

1

The Emergence of the Senior Citizen: 1945–1970

> He had lost interest in other people's affairs and
> seldom attended when they spoke to him. He was
> fond of talking to himself but often forgot what
> he was going to say, and even when he succeeded,
> it seldom seemed worth the effort. His phrases
> and gestures had become stiff and set, his anec-
> dotes, once so successful, fell flat, his silence was
> as meaningless as his speech. Yet he had led an
> active, healthy life, and worked steadily, made
> money, educated his children. There was nothing
> and no one to blame; he was simply growing old.
>
> E. M. Forster, "The Road from Colonus"

Literary statements about old age as a physical and emotional
condition have been, more often than not, exceedingly negative
in tone. From Shakespeare's description of life's last stage as
"second childishness and mere oblivion, sans teeth, sans eyes,
sans taste, sans everything," through Forster's less brutal, if no
less depressing, assessment, the concept of old age has not been
treated kindly. Such literary statements have their origins in the
recognition that old age has been as much abhorred in real as in
fictional societies. Such indeed, Simone de Beauvoir assures us,
is the case. Moreover, she insists, never in an unrelentingly dis-
mal history has the condition of old age been less desirable than
it is in this modern industrial society. Even while transfixed by
the ideal of youth (a legacy of Nineteenth-Century Romanticism), western civilization has witnessed significant shifts in the

age distribution of its population toward the older end of the continuum. The resulting conflict features the cult of youth, which bids one to ignore, if not deprecate, the existence of older people, opposing the increasing number of older men and women who seek to establish that the elderly are an active and useful part of the social structure.[1]

Against this backdrop, however, emerging concern with the social and economic problems faced by the nation's elderly, in conjunction with a growing body of scientific facts about the processes of aging, has increasingly encouraged action upon behalf of the older segment of our population. At least two options, each rooted in recent American experience, suggest themselves as possible models for ameliorative action.

The first and most traditional option open to policy makers involves material intervention and institutional reform. In the New Deal rhetoric and legislation of the 1930s, America had provided perhaps the most extensive test of this formula in the history of the republic. Opinions of its success or failure notwithstanding, activists could not ignore such a massive precedent.

The second option (most recently and extensively undertaken in the various propaganda campaigns attending the prosecutions of World War II) involves approaching and treating problems through the medium of public relations. Madison Avenue, Hollywood, and the broadcast–print media played no small role in promoting the fortunes of "Dr. Win-the-War." Ad men sold the virtues of democracy and the American sense of fair play; Donald Duck encouraged the public to buy war bonds; the media convinced the public of the righteousness of the allied cause. Under these assaults, America's residual insularity and pessimism evaporated.

Each approach, of course, had its proponents, but from the outset the public relations option was dominant. Arguing for the importance of imagery, geriatrician Martin Gumpert observed in 1946: "Our whole attitude toward the problems of old age must change from the negative and charitable to the positive and productive . . . so that a new generation can grow up to a fuller,

16

wiser and more mature life." Geriatric social worker, Grace Rubin-Rabson, writing in 1948, implicitly rejected massive material intervention on behalf of the elderly in favor of long-range changes in the social climate designed to improve the position of the older citizen. She went so far as to argue that scientists control the pace of life-extending discoveries in order to provide "ample time to effect the necessary changes in our social structure." Speaking before the first University of Michigan Conference on Aging in 1949, psychologist Wilma Donahue, a pioneering figure in social gerontology, called transformation of society's view of old age, with its roles and goals, the most important and most difficult task facing her and her colleagues. Finally, Frank J. Hertel, general director of the Family Service Association of America, one of the most important private social agencies operating in the field of aging, indicated an agency preference of this option in a speech delivered in May 1950, when he called for "concerted action by professional and community groups to help alter some popular attitudes and prejudices toward older persons."[2]

This preference for a nonmaterialistic approach raises the question of why this, rather than the materialist option, seems to have shaped reformist thought and action. The similar problems faced by wartime propagandists and gerontologists provides one possible explanation of this phenomenon. As Americans adopted a habit of insularity during the course of their history, and as early lack of success on a battlefield breeds pessimism, so the elderly were insulated from society-at-large and beset by pessimism concerning the problems of old age. As massive public education had overcome these disadvantages in the first case, there was every reason to expect that the public relations approach would be similarly effective in the second. On a more specific level, this choice might also have originated in a conviction that change in the social definition of old age would not only make selected institutional reforms easier to achieve but would help to alter the self-conception of the older person as well. Such an argument might be especially persuasive to social

17

scientists who generally tend to agree that expectations, both societal and personal, play a key role in shaping human behavior.

However it is explained, the triumph of the public relations approach to the problems of the elderly was clearly a triumph for the pragmatic temperament. New Deal architect Harry Hopkins once allegedly defended an administration welfare measure by remarking that people "don't eat in the long run." This was certainly a pragmatic response to those conservative interests counseling gradualism. Considering the problems of the elderly, and here one might aptly remark that people do "age in the long run," Hopkins' short range methodology is inapplicable. But his brand of pragmatism is most appropriate. Aging, unlike economic depression, is neither a short term nor an occasional phenomenon. It demands more than ad hoc, stopgap solutions. Thus, the social reformer of New Deal vintage could accept quite readily the pragmatism of the 1930s, yet not feel bound by the specific approaches employed in that particular social and economic setting.

Selection of this option signaled the emergence of a new sort of social reformer—one retaining the traditional conscience and activist inclinations, but sensitive as well to political considerations, social and economic costs, and bureaucratic custom. This awareness of the larger social context further represented a New Deal heritage in its recognition that successful change required agreement among the largest number of interests, not only upon objectives, but upon methods. With the maturing of gerontology as a discipline, these sensitivities were refined and sharpened and, as I will attempt to show, touched an ever-broadening coalition of interests. Ad men, educators, social workers, and labor leaders all joined in the effort to alter the image of America's elderly citizens in the shared belief that beyond this lay improvement in economic and social position as well.

Leaving aside for the moment all considerations of motive and method, let us consider the validity of the premise underlying this entire study—that is, that there has been significant change in society's conceptions and expectations of the elderly during

18

the past twenty-five years. In attempting to demonstrate the tenability of this premise, we will, in the remainder of this introductory chapter, review the treatment of older people (defined for our purposes as those over the "retirement age" of sixty to sixty-five) in the print media during two base periods—1945–1950 and 1965–1970—with respect to the societal and self-images which they project and report. The differences in treatment will indicate the extent to which traditional negative images have given way to views more conducive to the reformist goals of gerontology.

When New York State Senator Thomas Desmond's vanguard group, the Joint State Legislative Committee on the Problems of Aging, presented its first report to the Governor in 1948, it emphasized the needs to "reorient our thinking . . . so that we begin to realize that the elderly deserve not so much sympathy as sympathetic encouragement," and to cast off the arbitrary definition of old age which had relegated too many old people to "the dump-heaps of neglect." The United States, remarked German-born Dr. Martin Gumpert, was surely "one of the bleakest places in the world to be old. . . . You cross a street a little bit slower than a Boy Scout and he grabs your arm and gets credit for a good deed." According to a vice president of the International Ladies' Garment Workers Union, the age of sixty-five seemed to automatically place the American working man in the categories of incapacitated and dependent. In truth, the socially accepted model of older persons in the immediate postwar environment stressed their dependency as well as their need for sympathy and assistance. Although no one officially echoed Shakespeare's "second childishness" observation, it seemed a most apt description of those on the far side of the "retirement age."[3]

The model of old age as a "barren, tragic time of decline and frustration," wrote gerontologist Lawrence Frank, "was a legacy of the Industrial Revolution." Technocrats had replaced wise old men as the repositors of knowledge; the aged no longer served as the medium by which skills were transmitted from one generation to another. Without any overtly cruel intention, society had passively adopted a kind of pitying attitude toward the functionless older person. There was also an inevitability about the aging process which, when coupled with its negative image, contributed to a pessimistic, if not outrightly repressive attitude toward it. Paraphrasing a position he frequently encountered, Dr. E. J. Stieglitz wrote: "There are too many old people already; why should we try to prolong life?" Nor were such attitudes restricted to unthinking laymen. Dr. Howard Rusk reported that at a medical conference on chronic diseases among older people, the gallows humor of participants gave rise to discussion of euthanasia and moratoria on wonder drugs as possible solutions to what seemed an insurmountable problem. There could be no doubt, insisted Dr. Gumpert, that the tendency to define old age solely in chronological terms, combined with the widespread belief that "progressive decline as the unavoidable companion of aging" was at the root of the "economic despondency and social discrimination" which many older Americans had to face. Such a state was, he concluded, "nothing to look forward to with happy expectation."[4]

Concerned individuals argued that the accepted societal view of aging had a self-fulfilling quality; that negative expectations generated negative responses. Popular writer–biographer Rollo Brown, for example, wondered how people could prepare for later life if they expected that their "only appropriate occupation will be 'fussing around a little.' " All preparation, psychologist George Lawton noted, was in fact negative in impact. "Most of us," he wrote, "are so afraid of old age and so hostile toward it, we assume 'aging' means decline and that 'change with age' is another way of saying 'loss.' " This attitude led many people to regard the inevitable cosmetic changes and physical decrements of age as having a much greater significance than was actually the case. Such beliefs resulted either in an unhealthy, self-imposed withdrawal from society, or in an equally unhealthy denial of the aging process.

Dr. Gumpert poignantly described his own conversion to geriatrics from an early specialization in dermatology–plastic surgery as the result of his dealings with aged clients. "The old people who came to us were frightened. They recognized that their sagging skin, their hairy growths, the glandular lumps on their necks were symptoms of old age, and they were ready to endure painful operations to get rid of them. Their terror moved me deeply."[5]

Aging Americans themselves recognized the strain which current social values placed upon them. According to the director of the Family Service Association of America, older clients of his organization often complained of being "set adrift by family and society," of the "group attitudes . . . [of] business, labor, and government" toward older citizens and about the widely held belief in the chronological basis of age, the cultural primacy of youth, and the conservatism of the aged. The essentially negative character of the existing image of old age was outlined by older writers, even as they counseled their peers to resist it. Writer Melville Cane, for example, celebrated his seventieth birthday by informing his elderly countrymen that growing old was "a normal, continuous process" and that success or failure in aging depended upon one's state of mind. Thus he advised them to avoid the phrase "old age" and never to describe their state of health as "pretty good for an old man" or pine for "the good old days." He also pointed out the necessity of staying on good terms with children and grandchildren as an invaluable link with youth. Another aging writer, a woman, reviewed the panic with which many of her friends regarded the approach of old age and wondered at her own exemption from it. Her own lack of concern, she decided must stem from a respect for age learned in her youth. Because of this she could see clearly the causes of fear among her friends. They were captives in a culture that defined youth as "a trade or a caste or, at the very least, a brilliant accomplishment . . . an extremely select secret society instead of . . . a temporary condition." Significantly, she did not attack the cultural emphasis on youth, pointing out instead that modern medical, dental, and beautification techniques had succeeded in removing most of the "real terrors"—that is, those associated with physical decay—caused by advancing years. Today, she concluded, there was no reason why older people should not deny the stereotype and "play children's games, start a new business, square dance, or get married again." Rube Goldberg, whose schematical asides on modern technology constitute a unique contribution to American humor, took occasion on his sixtieth birthday to proclaim: "Old age is a myth . . . loaded down with regret, resignation and uselessness . . . [and] prefabricated in a mesh of false dignity and artificially colored memories." Describing aging as an ascent rather than a decline, Goldberg advised his contemporaries, when facing the various losses imposed by time, to "take a leaf from the book of the young squirts and liquidate self-pity by keeping busy . . . latch onto something connected with tomorrow."[6]

It is worth noting that these older writers proposed no alternative definition for old age. Rather, they seemed, by implication, either to deny old age itself, or at least, to deny that it constituted any special status within the total population that justified its exclusion from a youth-oriented environment. In sum, they seemed to argue that modern elders required no separate social niche; that they were perfectly capable of enjoying, perhaps even more intensely than youth, the roles that society provided. Of course, not all elderly writers agreed. For example, Samuel Hopkins Adams, having himself achieved a respectable age, denied that older people ought to emulate their juniors. "Why in the name of all that is reasonable cannot the respectable citizen who has successfully cheated the graveyard of ten or twenty years be content with that achievement instead of struggling to retain the butterfly charm of youth?" In fact, he conceded, the lack of model was responsible for some of the more absurd excesses of elderly behavior. "Age," he complained, "is thrust upon us [by modern medicine] with no blueprint for making a go of it." Given society's generally hostile attitude toward its older members (even among the older members themselves), the solution of how to use the added years was squarely up to each individual. For Adams and others sharing his view, old age was obviously a confusing status.[7]

22

If there was nothing to indicate the existence of a general, positive model of old age in the immediate postwar environment, the impressionistic evidence reviewed up to this point strongly suggests that there was a negative model. The small amount of hard data available tends to confirm this. This data comes from a 1953 survey by psychologists Jacob Tuckman and Irving Lorge of a number of graduate students at Columbia University Teachers College. Starting from the premise that the cultural emphasis on "youth and speed" forced old people out of active roles in social and economic life, Tuckman and Lorge proposed to investigate the "misconceptions" about old age that had grown to bolster the exclusionary system and to measure the durability of these erroneous impressions. To this end, they questioned a group of 147 students, ranging in age from twenty to fifty-one, most of whom had, not only a firm grounding in psychology, but had also been interested enough in the subject of aging to have taken a course on it regarding their agreement or nonagreement with 137 stereotypical statements about a chronologically nonspecific "old age." Even among this supposedly highly sophisticated sample, Tuckman and Lorge found "substantial acceptance of the misconceptions and stereotypes about old people." For example, 34% of the sample thought that "old people" were absentminded; 61% that they tended to repeat themselves in conversation; 41% that they talked to themselves; 57% that they were forgetful; and 57% that they "like to doze in a rocking chair." Upon analysis of the responses to all 137 statements, Tuckman and Lorge found "old age" being perceived by their subjects "as a period characterized by economic insecurity, poor health, loneliness, resistance to change, and failing physical and mental powers." Thus, they concluded, with cultural expectations tending toward self-fulfillment, this negative image of old age ultimately lessened the average person's chance for successful adjustment.[8]

Leaping an interval of twenty years in this discussion of society's attitudes toward the aging process and the aged, the observer is struck by the sense that old people have actually gained a collective identity. This can be noted in any number of specific ways; some of which I will discuss in detail below. The emergence of old people as a socially-defined group is most simply and neatly illustrated by the development of a special symbolic vocabulary. In all the earlier material, old people were called "old people," the "aged," or the "elderly"—all of them vague, valueless, essentially neutral terms. How surprising to step into the 1965–1970 period and discover that "old people" have become "senior citizens," "golden agers," or the "new leisure class," and are now enjoying, instead of "retirement": "active retirement," "Modern Maturity," "Harvest Years," or "Best Years" (the last three being the names of popular "senior citizen"-oriented periodicals). In contrast to the bland phraseology of the 1945–50 period, these modern terms fairly crackle with relevance, optimism, vigor, and inspiration. Nowhere are the attempted changes in the societal definition of old age more openly exhibited than in the apparently wide acceptance of these symbols, both by older people themselves and society-at-large.[9]

Language is, to be sure, as much effect as cause—that is, as Jung suggests, language only gives symbolic status to ideas or "archetypes" already existing in the abstract. The conferring of this status, in turn, permits such ideas an ever-broadening public acceptance. Thus a term like "senior citizen" could not exist until older people were recognized as a potentially productive and useful segment of society. Twenty years before, most of the incentives given for mounting an effort on behalf of the aged had been generally negative, such as avoiding widespread economic dependency and political deviancy among the aged. By 1965–70, however, there were new incentives to action as reflected in the new vocabulary being applied to the nation's aged. Laying aside detailed discussion of these incentives and approaches for the present, we will examine the characteristics of the older person which present day vocabulary suggests and encourages.

In 1965, a writer in the *New York Times Magazine* suggested that older people were "the most visible group of Americans today." Although many of them remained isolated in the "separate, often frightening world of the aged," he saw cause for optimism in a new sense of activism among the elderly. "Most of them who are alert and mobile look to their own organizations, clubs and unions for human contact," he wrote, citing as an example the one-million-member American Association of Retired Persons. Even more exemplary was the National Council of Senior Citizens, an unabashedly political organization claiming two and one-half million members. In an attack on the National Council in 1966, Kenneth Gilmore charged that the organization served as a Democratic Party front, "a well-oiled pressure machine" which had been created to lobby for passage of President Johnson's Great Society programs. Though philosophically opposed to social welfare programs like Medicare or to increased social security benefits, Gilmore's outrage betrayed a grudging admiration for the Council's success. The President's admiration, hardly grudging, was expressed in remarks made before representatives from the National Council of Senior Citizens, the National Council on Aging, and the National Farm Union in the spring of 1968. Noting that older persons in previous decades had routinely suffered from dependency, sickness, and fear, Johnson proclaimed: "Things have changed since then, largely because of the leadership which people like you provided," particularly in getting the Older American Act (1965), Medicare/Medicaid (1966), an age anti-discrimination bill (1967), and increased social security benefits. Joining in this praise was his successor in the White House. In his proclamation of May 1968 as "Senior Citizens' Month" (a national practice initiated in May 1965 by Johnson), President Nixon remarked: "Significantly, older persons themselves have frequently provided the moving spirit to start senior programs of projects being proudly displayed this month." Finally, *Forbe's* magazine expressed surprise at the political clout recently demonstrated by the nation's elderly. "The over-sixty-fives are no longer a doddering, ineffectual group. The American Medical Association has learned that. It was the over-sixty-fives, massed in the 2.5 million-member National Council of Senior Citizens who beat down the lobbyists for the AMA and pushed the Medicare bill through Congress."[10]

The activism of older people was highly newsworthy. Citing one such example—the picketing by oldsters of a San Francisco restaurant which had boosted the price of its "Senior Citizen's lunch"—*Newsweek* reported on "the latest pressure group to appear on the American scene—Senior Power," and quoted William Hutton, director of the NCSC: "Political action makes old people feel important again. It gives them a psychological uplift." Ray Nordheimer, chairman of the Chicago Area Commission of Senior Citizens, felt that group action had not merely revolutionized old people's self-image but had improved their societal image as well. "Two or three years ago," he remarked, "we used to go hat in hand to Springfield and beg them to introduce a bill for us. Now they call us up to tell us they're introducing legislation and ask for our support." Former fears of political deviancy had all but evaporated since politicians increasingly recognized, as Ned Linegar of the American Association of Retired Persons put it: "Older people are very patriotic. They believe in the system—in fact, they helped create it." Candidates in the New York City Mayoralty contest in 1965, for example, certainly recognized the emerging political importance of older voters, as Republican–Liberal Lindsay and Democrat Beame unveiled elaborate programs for older citizens during the course of their campaigns. If, however, any single politician serves as a barometer of the heightened seriousness with which old people as a group were being regarded, Barry Goldwater, the blunt, conservative Republican from Arizona, is that man. No friend to social welfare programs, Goldwater was nonetheless heard, in September 1969, advocating favorable senatorial action on legislation designed to strengthen the Older Americans Act of 1965. His reasoning was uncharacteristic of the man who had always insisted that fighting paternalistic, big government was more important than courting political advantage: old people vote. "Let no one mistake it," he intoned, "this means that our senior citizens are going to be able to make their desires known in a way elected officials will have to answer." It is then clear that old people in the 1965–70 period possessed a group identity sufficient to confer the political significance usually accorded to population "blocs." Both among themselves and among politicians (and by extension, those they represented), a new activist model of old age had emerged, and like other forms of "liberation," senior power was an increasingly visible phenomenon.[11]

The individuals in this new, politically important group were hardly the broken down, dependent, miserable, and socially isolated older citizens of twenty years before. That the latest generation of older Americans was the subject of considerably more social and political concern can be in part attributed to the broadening acceptance, at least among professionals, of Erik Erikson's definition of old age as being yet another stage of growth in the life cycle. "Old age," remarked a writer in the monthly journal of the Federal Administration on Aging, "need no longer loom like a spectre at the end of life. It can become, and it is now for many, a time of life to do the things a person always wanted to do—a time of fulfillment." The same article noted that only 4 percent of the nation's 18.5 million over-sixty-five population were institutionalized, and that the "great majority" of old people were "capable of leading lives that are interesting to themselves and valuable to the community." As Donald Kent, head of the Administration on Aging put it: "The problems of earlier generations centered around survival itself; those of today center on making life richer." When compared to the stereotyped oldster, insisted social worker Mae Rudolph, "the majority of older people are stable, at ease with themselves, less anxious about their health, and considerably less isolated." Moreover, they "feel happier and more satisfied with themselves and their way of life than the self-questioning middle-aged." This new optimistic view of the older person's capacities was given strong support by such surveys as that carried out among a number of older welfare recipients in Los Angeles by a student at the

University of California–Berkeley School of Social Work. Even among this sample, which might be expected to include the most hopeless victims of the aging process, the study indicated a general rejection of institutional living, an inclination toward social involvement, and a tendency to be embarrassed by the need for public assistance. The profile which emerged was hardly that of the depressed, dependent, resigned, and apathetic older person so often described twenty years earlier—and the more striking for being drawn upon a sample of the least economically and socially favored among the aged population. Based on extensive analysis of data on health, economic and social expectations, self-conception, housing preferences, and similar indices of social adjustment in old age, Matilda W. Riley and her colleagues at Rutgers (*Aging and Society*) concluded that the "typical older person seems to have a strong sense of his own worth, to minimize his self-doubts, and not even to regard himself as old . . . [and is] at least as likely as the young person to feel adequate and to have a sense of satisfaction in playing his various marital, parental, occupational or housekeeping roles." If this assessment were correct, yesterday's "exceptional" has become today's "typical" older person.[12]

The link between changing social expectations and self-image seemed apparent when the views of older citizens on the subject of age were aired. In contrast to his or her 1945–50 counterpart, the senior citizen circa 1965–1970, harbored definite and positive attitudes about life styles and self-worth. When a number of leading older Americans were asked their views on old age during the first Senior Citizen Month celebration in 1965, their responses were confident and assertive. Classicist Joseph Wood Krutch, for example, called the postretirement years "an inheritance of freedom which few young people enjoy"; dramatist Conrad Aiken bid older people disregard the wrinkled visage in the mirror: "It is really the boy who still looks at you there, he has not changed; or if he has, it is only in the fact that he has all his life been gathering an inestimable treasury of memory, his own great poem to the universe"; while Lewis Mumford, the philosopher–urban planner, demanded that society stop regarding and treating older people as "invalids and outcasts"—they were neither—and he added, cease calling them "senior citizens," a phrase that he felt connoted "second-class citizenship." There was the uncelebrated, but delightful nonagenarian who hoped to contribute to society's understanding of the aging process by detailing his own progress through the seventies and eighties. He concluded that at the age of ninety-three he had "a totally different attitude than young persons have, a happier attitude" since for him there were no more uncertainties. With science steadily increasing the span of good health, this old gentleman expected that most older citizens would feel as he did. "Young persons," he wrote, "often get the erroneous impression that old persons are in misery, creeping along, helpless, and on their last legs with nothing to live for and just waiting for death." Of course, he admitted, there were frailties and losses associated with aging, but far from being elements of a negative stereotype, they were disguised blessings. Hearing loss meant no longer having to hear everything ("Half of what is said is not worth hearing anyhow."); impaired visual powers dictated that he would no longer see everything going on around him ("Thank God for that!"); and lack of physical stamina meant a slower pace, thus lessening the possibility of exhausting his limited store of energy. However, his most important attributes—mental acuity and zest for living—remained undiminished by the aging process.[13]

Of course, not all older people subscribed to the image of postretirement living which, as we will see, was largely popularized by Madison Avenue. This did not, however, mean that their view of old age was a survival of the 1940s pessimism. With the nonagenarian quoted above, many older people tended to accept the losses of age as blessings in disguise rather than as evidences of irreversible decline. Old age was, in this view, a time for individualism; freedom from the social restraint operating against younger people. Thus a novelist approached old age in the Eriksonian vein: "Far from regretting the decline of some appetites, I would like to have them sped on their way so that having done with them, others, neglected until now, might take their place." Jonathan Daniels, after an active sixty-five years in politics, diplomacy, and journalism, reported looking forward to his retirement as a well-deserved rest. "I am ready to be honestly, and I hope happily, old," he wrote, contrasting his intention against those "who tried to dodge oldness," and concluding: "I doubt that the full life can be lived without testing the qualities of all ages. And all have their virtues." Weare Holland, writing in the *Atlantic Monthly*, fondly recalled a time when old age meant repose "and a man's (65th) birthday did not automatically unveil a vista of unlimited leisure." He assailed those communities of "so-called retired people" engaged in daily whirls of activity and proclaimed that he would never engage in activity for activity's sake. For Holland, old age meant doing nothing at all; he expected his "declining years" to be tempered only occasionally by the vaguely remorseful recollection that "alertness is supposed to be one of the primary qualifications of senior citizenship." He too expected to be blissfully happy.[14]

In the forefront of this movement were the biological and social scientists. Their work constituted the foundation upon which others would build; their empirical research provided the information upon which the new conception of the later years would be based. Such findings had been discussed by professionals in periodicals like the *Journal of Gerontology* and at their various conferences in the late 1940s, but it does not appear that this data had much public impact before the 1960s. The Duke University Center for the Study of Aging and Human Development was an exemplary gerontological institution. Since 1954, the Center had been extensively studying old people, during which time its researchers, in the words of Director Carl Eisdorfer, M.D., "found that a lot of information in the literature about aging simply isn't true." The promulgation of these findings, Dr. Eisdorfer observed, was a major contribution toward a better social understanding of both the aged and the aging process. Older people were more likely, because of the emerging revision of concepts of aging, to be considered among the nation's resources—a distinct improvement over the immediate postwar definition of older workers as economic liabilities. In the past, noted the Administration on Aging, rare individuals have shown themselves capable of leading productive lives in their eighties and nineties; today, such cases are increasingly frequent because "when modern medicine extended the life span, it also extended the potential for active lives." A respected business journal described the older American in terms both succinct and encouraging: "The over-sixty-fives are not people without a future, waiting only for the grave. . . . With the life span in the United States steadily increasing, by the end of this century people will be spending one-fourth of their lives in retirement."[15]

Then, there was the marketing system's growing recognition of the aged as a potential consumer group. This was a most significant step in the development of a new social image for old people. In the immediate postwar environment, with its emphasis on the physical and economic liabilities of age, old people had scarcely been approached as potential consumers of anything, save public beneficence. As their numbers grew through the 1950s and 1960s, and as public and private pension funds multiplied in number and value, the market potential of pensioners became a topic for discussion. One writer, analyzing "one of the coming markets of this century" for *Dun's Review,* noted the appeal of the older market, emphasizing its generally debt-free status and spend-rather-than-save orientation. Stating that the assets of pension funds would reach one hundred billion by 1970, he called the over-sixty-fives "an irresistible target for the more aggressive merchandisers." Thus far, older consumers had been neglected by business; but there were signs "that this obscurity is coming to an end . . . as manufacturers seek to tap a $40 billion market."[16]

A common tactic of market creators involves the use of flattery to get potential consumers to identify with the group whose patronage is being sought. In keeping with this, retirement residence merchants talked about "golden years" of health, independence, activity, and happiness in retirement. What reasonable older person would not be responsive to such a projected future? Thus, in a society where mass communications and entertainment media play important roles in defining or redefining many social roles (i.e., the competent housewife vs. the ham-handed husband, the streetwise urban black cop vs. the rural southern sheriff), older Americans began in the 1960s to gain some advantages. Where formal schooling and more traditional avenues of social education proved laggard in disseminating a bright view of aging, market researchers seemed to enjoy a surprisingly substantial influence in shaping the popular profile of the older American. To note that the actions of these particular image-makers were typically self-interested, or that the models they created were generally, if not always, regarded in intellectual circles as banal and inaccurate, is not to deny their importance as an educational force. Social engineers, having resigned themselves to a culture addicted to information in sixty-second capsules, would have to learn to live with the consequences and might perhaps even turn the situation to a social profit.[17]

The change in image of the elderly during the 1945–1970 period is obvious: on some levels even striking. So fundamental, in fact, has been this alteration in perspective that an investigation into its causes cannot help but be informative—both as a means of explaining an observed phenomenon and, on a more general plane, as a study of what the sociologist would call an exercise in "guided social change." Not only for answers to specific questions does man continue to look for ways to organize and control his environment. Thus the efforts of an amalgam of interests during the post–World War II era provide us with a unique opportunity to watch the social engineers in action. At the outset—and this is a point that will be repeated hereafter perhaps more often than will seem necessary—let me disavow any intention to treat the architects of this particular change as monolithic in either structure or attitude. Motivations and methods ranged as widely as might be expected in a pluralistic society—a mixture of idealism and self-interest; a melange of truth and buncombe—

but the effect sought, for whatever reason, was the same: an upgrading of the image and status of the elderly in American society.

N O T E S

1. Simone de Beauvoir, *The Coming of Age,* tr. Patrick O'Brien (New York: 1972), gives a poignant account of the older person in western societies, particularly Western Europe and the United States where the youth cult is strongest. Another French scholar, Philippe Aries, argues that the "technological idea of preservation" continues to displace "the biological and moral idea of old age," because the idea of youth so dominates society. Thus, old age has become not simply negative, but a time to be denied recognition altogether. See *Centuries of Childhood,* tr. Robert Baldick (New York: 1962).

2. Gumpert, "The Future of Old Age," *Science Illustrated* I (1946): 37–40; Rubin-Rabson, "What's Wrong with Growing Old?" loc. cit., 278; Donahue, "Changes in Psychological Processes with Aging," C. Tibbitts (ed.), *Living Through the Later Years* (Ann Arbor: 1949), pp. 63–84; Hertel speech reported in *New York Times* (May 7, 1950), 74:1.

3. Document 61, *N. Y. State Legislative Documents,* IX (1948): 2, 5: "Profile—Martin Gumpert, Geriatrician," *New Yorker* 26 (June 10, 1950): 34; Julius Hochberg, "The Retirement Myth," *The Social and Biological Challenge of Our Aging Population* (New York: 1950), p. 131.

4. Frank, "Gerontology," op. cit., p. 10; Stieglitz, "Geriatrics," *Journal of Gerontology* I no. 2 (1946): 160; Rusk's comments reported in *New York Times* (July 31, 1949), 30:1; Gumpert "Recharting Life for an Aging America," *New York Times Magazine* (August 13, 1950): 12.

5. Rollo W. Brown, "Growth in Years," *Atlantic Monthly* 178, no. 5 (November 1946): 86; George Lawton, "Old Age: Minus and Plus," *Science Monthly* 64 (January–June 1947): 53–54 [his position developed more fully in his book *Aging Successfully* (1947), of which this article is an adaptation]; Gumpert Profile (Part 1) in *New Yorker* (June 3, 1950), p. 36.

6. Family Service Association director quoted in *New York Times* (May 7, 1950), 74:1; Cane, "Stray Notes at Seventy," *Good Housekeeping* 129 (October 1949): 113; Margaret Widdemer, "It's Wonderful Not to be Eighteen," *Good Housekeeping* 130 (February 1950): 49, 237–238; Goldberg, "On the Privilege of Being Sixty," *Rotarian* 76–77 (October 1950): 12–14. For an example of "denial approach to old age, see Kyle Crichton's report on life in St. Petersburg, Fla., the home of the "ancient actives"— "Life Begins at Sixty," *Collier's* 119, no. 13 (March 29, 1947): 22+.

7. Adams, "Old Age: I Spit in Its Eye," *Saturday Evening Post* 222 (May 27, 1950): 31, 132.

8. Tuckman and Lorge, "Attitudes Toward Old People," *Journal of Social Psychology* 37 (1953): 249–260.

9. On the importance of language and vocabulary in social engineering, with particular reference to models of aging, see A. Etzioni, *The Active Society* (New York and London: 1968), pp. 156–160; a similar treatment of the changing European model

and the language alterations accompanying it found in Aries, *Centuries of Childhood*, pp. 31–32.

10. Julius Horowitz, "This is the Age of the Aged," *New York Times Magazine* (May 16, 1965), 25, 82; Gilmore, "Let's Stop Exploiting People Over 65," *Reader's Digest* 89 (September 1966): 229–38; President Johnson quoted in *Aging* (April 1968): 5; Nixon, ibid. (May 1969): 3; first Senior Citizen's Month proclaimed, see *Times* (April 12, 1965), 26:3 "The Forgotten Generation," *Forbes' Magazine* 103 (February 15, 1969): 23.

11. "Senior Power," *Newsweek* 76 (October 12, 1970): 101; Beame–Lindsay programs reported in *New York Times* (October 20), 1:2; (October 27), 34:2 (Lindsay); and (October 28), 38: 1, 5 (Beame); "Goldwater Plea for the Elderly," *America* 121 (September 13, 1969): 149.

12. Erikson's theory as presented in "The Problem of Ego Identity" in *Identity and the Life Cycle* (Pschological Issues Monograph No. 1) (1959), and in *Youth Identity and Crisis* (New York: 1968), especially pp. 139–140, will be discussed in Chap. 4 in greater detail; "A New Day Dawns of Older Americans," *Aging* (May 1966): 1–2; Kent, "Social Services and Social Policy" in J. C. McKinney and F. DeVyver, *Aging and the Social System* (New York: 1966); Mae Rudolph, "Sense and Nonsense About Growing Older," *Reader's Digest* 97 (September 1970): 23–24; "Some Seniors Value Being 'On Own' Even at Risk of Death," *Aging*, (May 1967): 22; Riley and Foner, *Aging and Society*, 1, p. 7.

13. Views of notable elders from "Harvest in May: The Promises of Age," *American Education* 1–2 (May 1965): 20; Adolph S. Hopp, "My Life after Ninety," *Aging* (January 1967): pp. 2–3.

14. Views on aging among gerontologists have, as we shall discuss later, tended to favor the activist model of aging, although a school of "disengagement"—i.e., old age as withdrawal—has been developed to explain such views as entertained by the older people quoted in this paragraph. Gabriel Fielding, "The Splendid Old," *Harper's* 230 (February 1965): 105; Daniels, "I'm Old and Glad of It," *Saturday Evening Post* 240 (February 25, 1967): 8, 14; Holland, "Escalating the Lease on Life," *Atlantic Monthly* 220 (August 1967): 89–90.

15. Duke University Center described in Theodore Irwin, "How to Handle the Problems of Aging," *Today's Health* 47 (July 1969): 28–31, 58; "Older People as a Resource," *Aging* (May 1969): 19; "The Forgotten Generation," op. cit., 23.

16. Leon Morse, "Old Folks: An Overlooked Market," *Dun's Review*, 82–83: April 1964, pp. 45–46, 88.

17. Speaking before a Federal Conference on Aging in 1967, Wilma Donahue reviewed the progress of the educational establishment in contributing to a revised popular conception of old age. On the primary and secondary school levels, she saw little being done to introduce material on aging into the curriculum and indicted the nation's "teacher training institutions" for their failure "to make aging an important aspect of the training of young teachers." See Donahue, "The Common Body of Knowledge," *Aging*, October 1967, p. 5. On the importance of Madison Avenue techniques in modern education. Perhaps the approach of programs like "Sesame Street" best illustrates the attempt to take advantage of the market researcher's findings and successes.

2

Building a Retirement Ethic: 1945–1970

Mass retirement, based on a fixed age, is a relatively modern phenomenon. In the sense of giving up "business or occupation in order to enjoy more leisure or freedom," the Oxford English Dictionary first example of this usage comes from a 1667 entry in Samuel Pepys' diary, and makes clear, by reference to the sine qua non of "pensions" or "competences," that it was a status available only to the nobility or mercantile elites. Working folk in Pepys' England did not "retire" in the sense that a nobleman left government service or that a merchant turned over the direction of his fleet or counting house to his son. The typical mechanic or agrarian worker lacked access to the requisite "pensions" or "competences." (Indeed, in Pepys' time "pensions," as R. H. Tawney pointed out, referred to royal grants made out of public monies.) In addition, however, to the economic impossibility of widespread retirement opportunities, the emerging capitalist order, as Max Weber and Tawney have persuasively argued, had actually sanctified the notion of work. The secularization of the ethics of rebellious Protestantism by this new economic order, they argued, served capitalism well by giving work a spiritual as well as an economic dimension. Not only was retirement economically unavailable to those at the base of the social pyramid; it was not even morally or emotionally healthy for them. To this view, a number of durable folk sayings attest: "Arbeit macht das Leben suess" (Work makes life sweet); "Busy hands are happy hands"; "The devil makes work for idle hands."[1]

The idea of work as an emotional necessity, as a major source of human dignity, was well implanted by the church and the workshop and remains to this day, as we shall see, a factor of some potency in the labor market. Yet, it is an idea which has become increasingly outmoded in the twentieth century. Technological progress; population growth; the accompanying contraction of manpower needs relative to availability; and an increasing understanding of and ability to control the business cycle fostered a rethinking of the traditional concept of an infinitely expandable labor force. The product of this rethinking has been designated "manpower policy," and the need for devaluation of the time-honored "work ethic" recognized as a prerequisite for its implementation.

The issue of "superannuation" or retirement, crucial as it is to "manpower policy," has always been inseparable (as the OED definition suggests) from that of pensions, even though the meaning of pensions has changed drastically from its seventeenth century sense. The key change in the meaning of pension, and by extension, in the meaning of retirement, has occurred within the past one hundred years. Pensions, as we commonly understand them today (i.e., as payments by an employer to retired or superannuated employees) date from the last quarter of the nineteenth century. During this period, the great paternalistic entrepreneurs (Pullman, Ford, et al.) initiated the practice of "pensioning off" older workers. Such payments were part of a paternalistic philosophy of labor relations. Beyond being a means of rewarding long and faithful service, pensions also promised to secure a measure of employee loyalty against a backdrop of growing labor union activity. But paternalism is one-sided; what father gives, he can also take away. Thus, such pensions were both discretionary and revocable.

During the 1920s continuing attempts were made to redefine

36

pensions as a right of the employee and a duty of management, based on the "human depreciation" theory of labor usage. However, despite some governmental encouragement in the form of tax incentives, reformers enjoyed little success in altering the concept of pensions to suit this new theory; nor did the number of workers covered by such pension plans increase. The Great Depression, with its devastating economic impact, created the necessary pressure for a reevaluation of the concepts of retirement and pensions. The resulting unemployment had an especially devastating effect upon older workers, who tended to be among the first expelled from the labor force—either to widen the number of jobs available to younger workers, or simply to thin out the ranks of employees in the face of production cutbacks. In response to this situation, the federal government passed the Social Security Act of 1935. The influence of this piece of legislation on the whole question of retirement and pensions would be impossible to overestimate. It established the principle of a guaranteed "floor" income as a right bought by the continuing contributions of employee and employer over the span of an individual's working life. It gave added impetus to demands for the extension of private pension coverage based on the "human depreciation" or the increasingly resorted-to "deferred wages" interpretation of employer pension liability. It provided a much needed standard age by which one could define "superannuation." In the very extremity of its departure from the idea of individual responsibility for maintenance in old age, it signalled a completely new era in financial arrangements for life after retirement.[2]

The ultimate victory of this view, however, came with the mobilization–demobilization cycle of World War II, which sharply expanded, then just as sharply, contracted the labor market; raising, then dashing the employment expectations of American's over-sixty-five workers. The reversion to a peacetime economy threatened large numbers of older workers (including those who had continued working past the OASDI "normal retirement age" of sixty-five and prewar pensioners who had returned to action on the home front) with unemployment. Demobilization thus gave the issues of retirement and postretirement income a special significance; first, because of the numbers and ages of those facing ejection from the labor force; and second, because of the loyalty and efficiency with which this group had served during the wartime emergency. Thus, in the late summer of 1945, a major business publication reported that many of the nation's more than twenty million older—that is, over forty-five—workers "are wondering, and with good reason, whether they and their contemporaries won't bulk largest in the breakdown of postwar statistics." Such expectations were well-grounded in experience. According to a United States Labor Department statistician, the percentage of gainfully employed American males over the age of sixty-five had steadily declined from 62.8 percent in 1900 to 42.2 percent in 1940. Although the war halted and even reversed this trend for a time— in 1945 the gainfully employed of this population stood at 48.8 percent—by 1950 the employment fortunes of the over-sixty-fives were once more on the wane. The census for that year showed that only 45.1 percent were still in the labor force. Beginning in 1945, the fate of America's older workers became the subject of an intense and continuing debate. The points of contention involved the definitions of retirement (when, how, and at whose discretion) and the structure of pension funds (adequacy, source of funding, portability and vesting, and eligibility requirements).[3]

Before pursuing these arguments in detail, however, we ought to be familiar with the complexities of the issue, especially the varieties of retirement and the postwar interest in retirement income. The two basic types of retirement were "involuntary" and "flexible." This simple dichotomy was complicated by the number of subvarieties used by the architects of retirement policy—that is, "fixed," "mandatory," "automatic," "normal," and "compulsory." The confusion resulting from the use of these terms was as much semantic as substantive. "Compulsory retirement age," for example, sounds as if it meant that age at which a worker must retire; in fact, it is defined by the Labor Department, as well as in most collectively bargained retirement plans, as that age at which a worker can be involuntarily retired by reason of age alone on full pension. This compulsory retirement age, "c.r.a.," in turn, might or might not have been the same as the "normal retirement age," or that age (typically sixty-five) at which a worker can elect to retire on full pension. In addition, under many plans, the "c.r.a." is topped by an "automatic retirement age," or the ultimate, unexceptionable retirement age. Ideally, the "involuntary" retirement system would be a mandatory, fixed retirement plan with one "automatic retirement age;" whereas the "flexible" system would offer "normal" and perhaps "compulsory" (subject to waiver) retirement ages, but no "automatic" age, with each worker's retirement being the result of voluntary withdrawal or administrative decision based upon consideration of the individual case. In practice, however, such clarity seldom exists, and few retirement plans can be called either purely voluntary or purely flexible. Nor are those using this descriptive terminology overly precise; thus, "fixed" retirement might as easily mean mandatory and involuntary as refer to the "automatic retirement age" used under a quasi-flexible system.[4]

Besides the bewildering terminology confusing the subject of retirement age, the issue of retirement income further complicated the dialogue over the proper role of the older worker in the labor force. The emergent interest in "adequate" pensions, both public and private, and the growing efforts to define and win such pensions muddied the waters of the debate by insinuating ideological overtones: Were demands for adequacy realistic? Was the movement socialistic? Was it dominated by the Communist Party? Were demagogues taking advantage of the legitimate needs of older people? Concerns such as these often overshadowed and confused this aspect of retirement policy debates. When the Mineworkers' and Steel Unions succeeded in winning generous monthly benefits for their members in 1950, for example, spokesmen for the business community decried the precedent set. Peter Drucker, the management consultant and author, argued that high-cost pensions imposed "tremendous additional handicaps" on older workers wishing to remain in the labor force, since the rate of contributions of management on behalf of workers over forty-five was (allegedly) much higher than that for younger workers. The editors of *U.S. News & World Report* reported that Drucker's hunch was correct, even though his facts were not. Based on interviews with management representatives in San Francisco, New York City, Baltimore, and Washington, D.C., they found that pension costs appeared to constitute a "psychological barrier" to the hiring of older workers. "Employers seldom sit down and calculate the pension liability on older men as compared with a young man," they noted; "They just feel that a man who will be eligible for a pension in twenty years, for example, is not as good a risk for them as the man who won't be able to collect a pension for forty years." Yet, their own calculations revealed that in the "vast majority" of plans, pension costs were the same for older and younger workers—older workers simply collected smaller pensions. "Employers have a big crop of younger people to choose from," the article concluded; "Pressure is on to cut costs. If an employer thinks older workers might add to pension liabilities, he is likely to slam the door on applicants over forty, except in special cases."[5]

Conservative spokesmen, returning to the public arena for the first time since 1929, charged that the pension demands of organized labor presaged a drift towards the welfare state. For example, Dr. Roger I. Lee, past president of the American Medical Association and a staunch opponent of socialized medicine, detected in labor's agitation for an "adequate," universally available retirement income (based upon a combination of total OASDI coverage and private employer-contributed pension funds) some dangerously socialistic tendencies. He equated such pensions with "handouts" and warned against any concession to the "something-for-nothing" mentality. The editors of *Saturday Evening Post*, a very influential mass circulation periodical at the time, lent their authority to this counterattack by alerting readers, in strongly colored language, to the "inflationary possibilities of the pension epidemic." *Life* magazine mingled the issues of retirement age and generous pension settlements in assailing "the dangerous illusion that no one over sixty-five should work and that everyone at sixty-five should get a $100-a-month pension." If geriatricians succeeded in lengthening the average life span to 120 years as they predicted, *Life* advised the productive (under sixty-five) segment of the population that they would be obliged to sustain the retired on high pensions for as long as fifty-five years. And when, in 1950, United States steel workers, following the United Mineworkers' example, won $100 per month benefits (including social security), *Newsweek* pronounced the settlement an "economic disaster," calling it socialistic, subversive of individual initiative, and inflationary (i.e., increased pension costs would ultimately be footed by the consumer).[6]

Then too, the pension movement admittedly elevated to public prominence, leaders whose methods were questionable and whose objectives seemed at times broader than the welfare of the aged. This group of leaders attracted a disproportionate amount of attention and thus helped to move the debate over retirement policy even further afield. In the immediate postwar era, the West Coast seemed, as it had in the 1930s (with the Townsend, EPIC, and Ham and Eggs movements), an incubator for a number of bold, but economically unsound pension schemes. *Time* magazine editorialized on the alleged influence of "party-liners" in the pension movements in the states of California and Washington; and yet another of Henry Luce's magazines, *Life,* reviewed the machinations of California's flamboyant "pension preacher," George McClain. An advocate of old age pensions after the example of Dr. Townsend and a practitioner of emotional demagoguery on the model of Huey Long, McClain cleverly engineered a state-wide referendum on a bill to grant the state's older (over sixty-three) population a monthly pension of $75 (per couple). Aided by the heavy support of his older constituency and the apathy of those in opposition, he won. For this success, he gained nationwide attention. The ease with which a subsequent referendum, spearheaded by the California Chamber of Commerce, the League of Women Voters, and the Parents-Teachers Association, repealed this law indicates that the media had initially taken him far too seriously. Nonetheless, Alfred Q. Maisel was disturbed enough by McClain's alleged national aspirations, to write, in *Look* magazine (1950): "Outside of California, the idea of this sharp-suited swami sitting in Roosevelt's chair and sleeping in Lincoln's bed may seem more ridiculous than terrifying. But it is just the other way around to many a thoughtful citizen of California." Given such overreactions, it did not take many McClains to divert the retirement policy dialogue down blind alleys.[7]

With these diversionary and extraneous issues and complexities put into context, we can now consider the positions of the chief participants in the retirement policy debate—management, organized labor, and social reformers. Each group shared the assumption that labor force participation rates of older workers depended upon both the structure of the retirement system (voluntary versus involuntary) and the availability of "adequate" pensions. Beyond this common belief, however, they differed over whether retirement policy ought to be (indeed, whether it could be) administered flexibly, and whether or not current policy trends were advantageous to both the older worker and the national economy. Moreover, each group had its own view regarding the role of "adequate" pensions—as a quid pro quo for control over retirement policy (business); as a right of the worker (organized labor); or as an extraneous issue being used to justify the exclusion of the older worker from the labor market (social reformers)—in the often highly charged discussion of the issue of retirement.

Business spokesmen in the postwar era did not contest the legitimacy of old age pensions. The 1935 Social Security Act generally established an income floor as the right of every covered American of sixty-five years or older and, by setting up a contributory fund, the concept of pensions as "insurance" (as in

OASDI) or deferred wages. Once businessmen accepted this, the arguments for the paternalistic approach (pension as reward) and management's denial of responsibility for retired workers disappeared. Moreover, pressures for the establishment of private pension plans by organized labor and by a security-conscious work force were irresistible. The federal government's amended policy (initiated in 1926) providing tax incentives to companies establishing employer-funded pension plans further smoothed the way; as did corporate recognition, showing that interest in older and retired employees was both good personnel policy and good public relations. Thus, after about 1945, management viewed privately funded retirement plans not only as the price but as the very basis of a manpower policy on which to manipulate the size of the labor pool. A key element in the success of this policy involved control of the retirement system and the consequent ability to expand or contract the labor force by being more or less rigid in defining retirement age and conditions. So, while assuming a responsibility to make up the difference between the OASDI floor and an "adequate" (50 percent of working income) retirement income, business would insist that the power to set retirement age was a management prerogative.[8]

The idea of "manpower policy" emerged in response to the postwar economic downturn. As we have seen, older workers were the major victims of demobilization. Speaking before a state legislative committee investigating employment opportunities for older workers, Carroll E. French, director of Industrial Relations for the National Association of Manufacturers (NAM), defended a management-controlled compulsory retirement age on four accounts. First, he noted, industry recognized that older workers were often physically incapable of productive performance in modern industry; second, they were more accident-prone, thus making their compensation insurance costs higher; third, state compensation laws tended to discourage the retention of older workers by explicitly tying premium rates to age; and four, effective retirement planning required a compulsory retirement age. P. C. Wolz, the Industrial Relations officer for Eastman Kodak, long a leading corporate voice in the discussion of retirement policy, seconded these views. If management lacked the power to retire less productive older workers, he argued, profits could be imperiled and the whole economic system threatened. Wolz affirmed industry's responsibility to prepare the worker for the time "when . . . productive capacity and earning power will decline;" in return he asked that society permit industry to define that time. In an essay summing up the business position on retirement, Princeton economist and director of the University's Industrial Relations Section, J. Douglas Brown, expressed it even more strongly than Wolz: ". . . to thrust upon private industry the obligation to employ or compensate older worker under conditions which lead to loss or even bankruptcy, is to impair the function of the private corporation as a highly important institution in our national economy." John M. Convery of the NAM pointedly warned a 1950 gerontological conference that continued attempts to force industry to retain older workers (that is, deny it the right to retire older workers) could only limit job opportunities for younger workers and by "discouraging business from taking the risks that make for an expanding economy, tend to lessen job opportunities for everyone." Moreover, in a small pamphlet prepared to alert its membership to labor's drive to establish pension plans, the NAM exhorted corporation executives to stand fast on the issue of "compulsory retirement age," declaring that unless management was the sole arbiter of retirement age, a "principal benefit" of such a plan—"the orderly, nondiscriminatory separation of superannuated workers"—would be lost. Optimally, the pamphlet asserted, a managerially fixed, unexceptionable retirement age was best; but where flexible plans could not be forestalled by management efforts, businessmen should at least demand the final say on all exceptions.[9]

As part of its Personnel Series, the American Management Association prepared, in 1951, a guide to retirement preparation plans. A contributor to this handbook, A. D. Marshall, a General Electric executive, began by repudiating the extreme positions on retirement: Dr. Townsend's belief that everyone should be retired at sixty with a pension of $200 per month, and Harvard economist Summer Slicter's position that the demand for labor was infinitely expandable and thus no one need be retired against his wishes. Retirement, in fact, was a useful tool in a changeable economic environment. When the economy was booming (World War II), and the demand for labor was high, Marshall pointed out, there was no barrier to extending work lives beyond arbitrary retirement ages; but when production dropped off (demobilization), "all would agree that the older worker who has a reasonable retirement income should be retired in order to give an opportunity to the young men and women knocking at the gates of our industrial plants." There were, he noted, other arguments but the crucial one involved "manpower policy." Doubtless, Marshall conceded, management's definition of "compulsory retirement ages" as "automatic retirement ages" had cost industry many capable hands; he felt, nonetheless, that "this is a small price to pay for the advancement [of younger workers] afforded by the program."[10]

While business spokesmen conceded adequate pensions to be the price of manpower policy and preferred to emphasize the issue of retirement age, organized labor reversed these priorities. The Congress of Industrial Organizations (CIO) particularly focused its attention on pensions and tended to neglect the issue of retirement age save for vocal opposition to "mandatory retirement." The same circumstances responsible for management's quiet accommodation to the spread of the private pension plans motivated labor's loud crusade upon their behalf. Of particular importance were the actions of the Wage Stabilization Board during the war and in the immediate postwar era, the interpretation of the Labor–Management Relations Act of 1947 by the National Labor Relations Board (NLRB), and the Supreme Court's validation of that interpretation in the Inland Steel case of 1949. The influence of wage stabilization policies in limiting wage raises by legally restricting them to a fixed percentage opened up a new area of collective bargaining. The area was "fringe benefits" with pensions constituting one of the major "fringes." But were pensions subject to the collective bargaining process? According to the Labor–Management Relations Act of 1947, the NLRB ruled they were; in 1949 the Supreme Court sustained this ruling in the Inland Steel decision. With the way legally cleared, the issue of retirement pension systems would occupy an increasingly important place in union contracts.[11]

The United Mine Workers served as the cutting edge of organized labor's postwar involvement in the issue of retirement income. As early as 1946, with wage rates frozen, John L. Lewis made the establishment of a noncontributory "welfare fund" a major objective in contract negotiations. The innovative aspect of the United Mine Workers' plan was the financing process, depending as it did upon contributions from mine owners on a "royalty" basis—that is, a certain fixed amount, a nickel or ten cents—per ton of coal mined. This system had not only the potential to provide retired miners with generous $100 monthly benefits (including social security); it also made the relationship between wages and pensions somewhat less obvious by using the device of a "fixed royalty" and thus seemed to separate pension contributions and wages into two distinct bargaining issues. The autoworkers' union leadership, for example, discovered the necessity of differentiating pension from wage demands in the interest of progress on both fronts, when the rank and file at United Auto Workers–Ford splitting along age lines, voted down a 1947 pension plan in favor of a straight wage increase. Lewis emphasized his insistence on this plan by taking strike action during 1949–50 and winning his point. With the mineworkers' example to inspire them, the United Auto Workers and the United Steelworkers (also CIO affiliates) took up the pension crusade. Within this vanguard, however, little was said on the issue of retirement age. With adequate pensions (according to labor's definition of adequacy) provided, these unions felt that their members would be quite content to retire, and so they made little of management's desire to control this aspect of retirement policy.[12]

The skilled "aristocrats of labor" were more restrained than the CIO both in rhetoric and approach. As Federation President William Green wrote in a letter to Desmond's New York State Legislative Committee: "Organized labor is concerned in developing an economy that will make it possible for working people to look forward to old age with confidence—not with the haunting fear of being discarded or with the dread of dependency." The American Federation of Labor (AFL) position thus included demands for universal social security coverage; social security benefit schedules more responsive to inflationary pressures and "more realistic" private pension benefits. Clarence W. Campbell of the Typographers Local No. 6 (NYC) told the Desmond Committee that his highly skilled union's chief problem was "not so much in finding work for our older workers as it is to find enough money for them to retire on . . . to take them out of the labor market." Even so, the Federation was more likely than the CIO to resist employer attempts to impose retirement ages upon the rank and file. Here, seniority (especially important to the highly graded structure of skilled crafts) was the desideratum. In the view of Federation Director of Research, Sol Barkin, management offered labor a Hobson's choice on retirement—either permit breaches in the seniority system by making pay cuts and job reclassifications (which Barkin saw as a demotion) as the price of retaining older, "less efficient" workers, or give the employer the exclusive right to determine and enforce retirement age upon the worker. Barkin answered the challenge put to labor by the NAM's John Convery: employers should "carry the additional cost of retaining such [older, less efficient] workers in order to discharge their responsibility to long service employees." The AFL's opposition, however, was mainly vocal; in practice the Federation saw the initiative on setting retirement age slip to management, leaving union leaders like Green and Campbell to concentrate on the issue of adequate pensions.[13]

Reform-oriented social scientists—whom we will hereafter refer to as "social gerontologists"—were in a somewhat disadvantaged position in this debate. As business leaders conceded their responsibility to provide for retired workers, and as organized labor focused its attention on the issue of adequate pensions at minimal cost to the rank and file, gerontologists became increasingly isolated in their assaults on forced retirement. Agitation for liberal pensions, they argued, made the elderly, along with many of those pleading upon their behalf, seem irresponsible. For example, as the war neared its end, an otherwise liberal opponent of forced retirement made the pragmatic argument that postwar economic planning could forestall a repeat of the "crackpot schemes for old age pensions", which had marked the 1930s, by providing employment opportunities for older workers. In 1950, the Gerontological Society found itself, as an organization specifically dedicated to the interests of the elderly, in the unlikely position of commending California's voters for their decision to repeal the generous old age pension law passed the previous year. "The current setback for those favoring liberal payments to the aged," observed the editors of the *Journal of Gerontology,* "serves to highlight the other ways in which the ideal of social security may be attained, and to emphasize the need for industry to take the lead in abolishing compulsory [meant in the sense of forced or involuntary retirement] retirement ages, and in keeping older people gainfully employed according to their functional capacities."[14]

When they could ignore the pension issue, and deal solely with retirement age, gerontologists and those within labor and the academic community who shared their views attacked forced retirement for ignoring the capacities, preferences, and needs of the elderly. Fixed, involuntary retirement ages, they argued, perpetuated certain misconceptions about the aged. These views, in turn, limited employment opportunities for the older worker. Looking into this discriminatory cycle in 1948, the Desmond Committee uncovered four "erroneous" conceptions of the older worker, allegedly common among employers. After querying representatives from business, labor, and government, the committee declared that its investigation had shown; first, that

State Workman's Compensation Insurance rates did not rise as a function of the age of the covered employee; second, that workers over forty-five had fewer accidents than the younger group; third, that where physical strength was not involved (that is, most jobs in modern industry), advancing age appeared to have no adverse effect upon productivity; and fourth, that older workers were not more conservative nor unresponsive to proposed changes in routine than younger workers. Geriatrician Dr. Edward Stieglitz ridiculed the notion that a man's fitness to work could be determined on a chronological basis. "Is it not utterly ridiculous," he asked, "that a man sixty-four years and 364 days old is perfectly competent to carry on the immense responsibilities of an important post, and the next day he is too old to carry them?" George Lawton, as a psychologist, condemned forced retirement as the legacy of the "pseudo-scientific . . . almost entirely fallacious" view that human abilities decline with age and the supposedly humane conviction that by the age of sixty-five a man has "done his duty" and deserves a chance to relax, whether he wants to or not. Speaking before the American College of Surgeons in late 1946, Dr. Harvey Agnew assailed the trend toward the establishment of forced retirement policies, precisely at a time when "medical science promises longer, healthier lives in which calendar ages will become less important." The example of the older workers on the home front during the war, however, provided one of the strongest (as well as most poignant) arguments available to opponents of mandatory retirement policies. As Dr. Clifford Kuh of Kaiser Permanente Foundation put it: "Since the aged have proved their worth during the war, it is hoped that the future will see a great proportion of them kept in industry and properly placed on work they can do."[15]

Social gerontologist critics not only contended that forced retirement contributed to an economically disadvantaged status for the elderly; they also argued against it on humanitarian grounds. Compulsory retirement schemes, they held, could actually hasten the disintegrative processes of aging. "Death comes at retirement," charged Dr. Roger I. Lee. The retirement of workers at the ages of sixty and sixty-five, he asserted, often "cut short the very life of productive individuals." Geriatrician T. G. Klumpp concurred: "Have you seen, as I have, the faithful employee 'retired' to the boneyard by some compulsory retirement scheme? I believe I understand why many die so soon after retirement." The Desmond Committee's 1948 report noted, of the well-intentioned desire to provide the older worker with a deserved respite from toil: "we provide no security, no interests that enable them to relax . . . We say 'retire'—and we little understand that useless vegetating on a rocking chair means, as the geriatricians tell us, early death." Desmond further underlined this view in the pages of a prestigious religious journal: "Old age without occupation is not only tedious, but dangerous," and cited the expert view that the best way to kill many otherwise healthy older men was to retire them. One of the most outspoken foes of fixed retirement, a vice president of the International Ladies' Garment Workers Union (ILGWU), insisted before a Health Education Conference that mandatory retirement schemes were "little better than the savage practice of killing off the old people as soon as they become a burden to the tribe." This, he argued, was a product of the entirely false notion that "men of sixty-five and over are incapable of providing for themselves and must therefore be supported by society." Reporting on a recent Gallup poll on the problems of old age, a team of financial writers gave special mention to the finding that "one of the surest ways to die before your time was to retire without having an interest in some other pursuit." This datum reportedly disturbed Dr. Gallup. " 'The evidence was so overwhelming,' he says, 'that I immediately decided that I would die with my boots on and at my desk.' "[16]

Fewer and fewer Americans, however, enjoyed Dr. Gallup's choice between retirement or continued employment. The Columbia Broadcasting Company (CBS) dramatized a more common situation on October 28, 1947. "Fear Begins at Forty" told the story of a man who had reached the compulsory retirement

50

age of sixty in 1939. Without sufficient financial means and unable to find another job, the retiree and his wife moved into the four-room apartment of their son and daughter-in-law. The normal tensions of propinquity, accentuated by generational differences over child-rearing philosophies, made the experiment an unpleasant one. The outbreak of war, however, gave the father an opportunity to return to work. Soon he and his wife were reestablished in a separate household, and he was earning money and regaining self-respect. Then came the end of the war, demobilization, and again his forced retirement—this time complicated by his wife's ill health. Unable to afford in-home treatment or private institutional care, the old man eventually had to commit his wife to a public institution, while he himself took up residence in a dingy boardinghouse room rented for him by his son. According to CBS, the wages of retirement were estrangement from family, loss of independence, and ultimately a miserable and lonely death. The Gerontological Society publicly commended CBS for "courage in presenting this important problem to the people of America." New York State Senator Desmond also praised the network. "The facts," he declared, "were not the fabrication of some imaginative script writer's mind. They were real. They were close. They could not be denied. . . . It drove home the obvious but often overlooked point, that there are such things as discriminatory age barriers in employment, and that they are causing untold grief."[17]

But, in the end, the leading critics most often based their objections to involuntary retirement plans upon the alleged universality of the work ethic in American culture. The majority of older workers, they argued, simply did not want to retire. Thus, two sociologists declared after having investigated elderly workers' attitudes: "No one would propose that the old be kept in the harness of regular employment until they drop; but it is no less cruel to place a barrier in the way of those to whom work is the breath of life." When the The New York Times' "Topic of the Times" column briefly reviewed Walter Pitkin's book on retirement, The Best Years, the writer took special note of Pitkin's "startling predictions" of shortened working days, weeks, and lives. Financial writer, A. B. Comstock, in a letter to the editor, sought to rebut Pitkin's assertions. The average worker, he argued, "is happier with his work than he could possibly be with leisure after premature retirement. . . ." The 1950 National Conference on Aging, sponsored by the Federal Security Administration (FSA), provided a good reading of gerontological opinion on the issue of retirement in the postwar era. Directed by President Truman to give particular attention to existing retirement policy trends, the conference reported "that the predominant feeling of the section [on employment] as a whole was against compulsory retirement based on age. . . Retirement for a worker able to afford it and prepared for it was not opposed. But 'the guillotine approach' with compulsory retirement cutting off man's productivity and possibly shortening his life, they vigorously condemned." Conference participants based their reasoning on the generally accepted view of work "as a fundamental human need." As one labor delegate put it: "There are deep emotional reasons why workers want to continue to work; it's more than a means of making a living, it's a way of life, life itself." Later, a conference observer wrote that some of the delegates "wistfully supported the idea of leisure and freedom [in retirement], but they were a small minority."[18]

James Michener, in a short story written for *Nation's Business,* tried to point out what he felt to be the dominant attitude toward involuntary retirement (or, in his tale, retirement in general) among American workers. The story involved John Bassett's last day at work as the head accountant at J. C. Gower and Company, and the bizarre form of revenge he meant to take upon his employer for forcing him into an unwanted retirement "simply because he was sixty-five." At quitting time, he had promised himself, he would walk into Mr. Gower's office and "spit in the boss's eye." However, the perceptive employer was aware of his accountant's devotion to work and his paucity of outside interests. Concluding that forced retirement might well kill Bassett, he waived the company's sixty-five-and-out rule.

Thus, Bassett was able to stay on his job, though now at half pay. By portraying Bassett's grateful acceptance of this arrangement, Michener obviously wanted to emphasize the nonmonetary significance of work to many older employees facing forced retirement and the cruelty of simply expelling them, even on generous pensions (as Bassett's was), from the labor force. Michener also expressed his own sense about the tenacity of the work ethic by having Mr. Gower present Bassett with a set of woodworking tools in an effort to inspire his employee with a nonvocational interest. Bassett, of course, rejected this kindly intervention, and on his way home that night after working late, determined to give the tools to his grandson. Without any attempt at subtlety, the author let his hero deliver the lines which he felt summed up the dominant attitude among American workers: such substitutions for paid employment, Mr. Bassett snorted, "are for kids; what a man needs is a job!"[19]

Michener's conviction that the work ethic had a crucial significance in shaping the attitude of the average worker, whether white or blue collar, toward retirement, had strong backing from other quarters. In attempting to buttress this conviction, however, opponents of evolving retirement policy sometimes made questionable inferences from the facts at hand. New York State Senator Thomas Desmond, for example, a firm opponent of involuntary retirement system, used a Federal Security Administration report to support his contention that most able-bodied men sixty-five years of age and older did not wish to retire. Ignoring the relatively small number of workers with access to supplementary private pension plans and the insufficiency of OASDI benefits alone, Desmond cited the finding that nearly 900,000 of the 1.6 million individuals sixty-five and older eligible for social security had elected to defer acceptance of these benefits and continue working. Again, the Desmond Committee polled 130 employers in New York on the tendency of older workers reemployed during the war to leave the labor force on their own volition at the end of the emergency. They made much of the fact that sixty of these companies reported no such trend. The report said nothing of what the remaining seventy companies reported and gave no attention to what the kinds of retirement policies in operation were in the sample companies. Although such omissions weakened the committee's case, the legislators did admit that the allure of "a decent-sized paycheck" might share responsibility for the decision to remain on the job. Still, they attributed paramount importance to the influence of the work ethic.[20]

The data on the incidence of voluntary retirement of workers supplied by the International Ladies Garment Workers Union and Amalgamated Clothing Workers Union provided a more credible argument for the work ethic's influence on the average worker than that supplied by the FSA, because retirement benefits won by these unions were so much more generous than social security. With supplemental monthly benefits of $65 available—meaning monthly incomes in excess of $100 when social security payments were included—and retirement voluntary, an ILGWU vice president reported no rush to retire among those eligible. Only 23 percent of 6,250 ILGWU eligibles and 33 percent of 9,000 in the ACWU. This, the official asserted, proved how much work, even when income was not a problem, meant to the majority of older men and women. One might, however, question the typicality of this sample and argue that these garment workers, who were predominantly immigrant, Eastern European Jews, represented a portion of the most highly motivated, upwardly striving and work-oriented of all the great ethnic migrations to the United States. The seemingly small number of voluntary retirees (assuming health was not a factor in their decisions) might, in fact, have been inordinately large, and thus as much an indication of the work ethic's deterioration as of its strength. But even if such were the fact, few observers within the gerontological community were prepared to preceive it as such.[21]

The position of business, organized labor, and concerned social reformers on retirement policy in the immediate postwar era can be summarized as follows: for management, the goal was the evolution of a "manpower policy" designed to help cope with business cycles; for organized labor, it was "bread and butter," meaning the gaining of "adequate" pensions; for gerontologists, it was the welfare of the aged, which included the freedom to work as long as one was able and desirous of doing so.

In the twenty years after midcentury, however, new attitudes toward retirement developed, and by 1965–1970 a changed outlook was apparent in the growing assertiveness of older people themselves and in the dominant themes sounded both by the popular press and within the gerontological community. The labor movement which had, to a large extent, given in on the issue of retirement age in preference to the issue of pensions during the 1945–1950 period, ultimately took the position that retirement was the inalienable right of every worker, and bargained as fiercely over pensions and retirement ages as it had over working hours and wage rates. Retirement had become a popularly accepted part of the life cycle and, as time passed, was increasingly invested with positive qualities. Nathan Shock, one of the founding spirits of the Gerontological Society, agreed: "Ten years ago it was generally assumed that retirement was looked upon as a threat by many people." However, he continued, recent research more and more tended to disprove "the assumption that all older people wish to continue work" and to suggest "that retirement is becoming an acceptable way of life for an increasing proportion of the population." As sociologist George Maddox observed, "the general environment in which retirement takes place is changing. . . . Clearly it is easier than it once was for a man to accept retirement gracefully if an adequate income is maintained." He linked this change in environment to a "change in our philosophy of aging" which offered a more positive view of old age by defining it as "the consummation of life."[22]

In the immediate postwar environment, as we have observed, the business community served as the chief proponent of involuntary, fixed age retirement programs. Yet, twenty years later, management was silent. Retirement age was no longer an issue. A quick survey of popular and gerontological opinion explains this situation. Business simply no longer needed to defend the notion of retirement; it required no defense. It had become a part of life and was widely accepted as such. The small vanguard group which had argued in 1950 that the trend toward superannuation of workers was inexorable had been correct. Indeed, they had, if anything, underestimated the swiftness with which labor unions would embrace, and the rank and file accept, the idea of retirement apart from the issue of pensions. In 1945–1950, the retirement age being debated was sixty-five; twenty years later, thirty-years-service-and-out by age fifty-five was a typical union demand. In a lengthy article in 1965, one business writer pointed out this shift in union emphasis toward earlier retirements and explained it as a policy offering something for everyone. To unions, it provided room for younger workers; for management it represented a painless means of eliminating, by attrition, marginal jobs; and to workers, it gave an opportunity to collect that "dividend of leisure that our affluent society can so well afford to declare." For example, the UAW's 1965 "supplement" plan had the effect of reducing retirement age to sixty. Under this plan, an auto worker aged sixty with thirty years of service retired on a monthly pension of $400 (a regular pension plus a "supplement," designed to keep income level at $400 until such time as the worker qualified for full social security benefits—that is, at age sixty-five). "In five more years," predicted Charles Odell, the UAW's director of Older and Retired Workers, "there will be very few workers over sixty in the Big Three [GM, Ford and Chrysler] companies."[23]

According to *Business Week,* early retirement programs won by the UAW in various Big Three plants constituted "one of the most exciting social discoveries of recent years." Employers and unions were learning "that given livable financial arrangements, production workers are far more eager for early retirement than anyone had imagined." Corporate and UAW officials freely predicted that one-third to one-half of the thirty thousand eligibles would opt for early retirement when the plan went into effect. Much was made of comments like that of one fifty-five-year-old Chrysler employee who told his local president: "All I want to do is get the hell out of here. I'm tired of working." Or the fifty-nine-year-old production worker who called early retirement "one of the finest things that ever happened to me." Or the Ford workers, a UAW spokesman reported, who thought the plan "terrific." Douglas Fraser, head of the UAW's Chrysler Division, awarded much credit to the corporation's "preretirement" educational program which, he said, actually stimulated worker response by "removing the mystery" from retirement in the course of six two-hour classes on such topics as social security, living arrangements, and uses of leisure time. Successes like these, in fact, led some respected gerontologists to conclude that "when we provide adequate income for retirement prior to age sixty-five, and even prior to age sixty," there seemed little worker resistance to retirement. Nor did early predictions fall short of the mark, as manufacturers reported themselves "swamped" by applications for early retirement. Money, observed knowledgeable officials of both management and labor, appeared to be the key element. But in analyzing early retirement applications, these observers found, surprisingly considering long-standing assumptions, that better paid skilled workers were more likely to stay on the job than lower paid production workers. Economic need was not the sole desideratum after all; it appeared that the nature of one's job was more critical than had been thought when considering incentives to retire early. Still, one reporter, after interviewing a number of General Motors' early retirees, reported that these men were unanimous in the conviction that early retirement would have been unthinkable "if it had not been for the bonus or supplemental allowance as it is officially called."[24]

This trend toward earlier retirement, with its implications of a new, positive attitude toward life in the later years and a growing acceptance of leisure pursuits as acceptable substitutes for work, appeared to overturn some once-unassailable assumptions. Seeking explanations for this, social scientists went into the field to gather data on the early retirement phenomenon. Caroline E. Preston, of the University of Washington School of Medicine's Psychiatry Department, for example, tested the hypothesis that the older person's view of life, (shaped by "frustrations" and "gratifications," varied with employment status), using two separate samples—one composed of 190 retired men and women with a mean age of 76.2, and the other consisting of 106 working men and women and spouses employed by the University of Washington or the Bell Telephone Company with a mean age of 63.8. Each subject filled out a questionnaire, expressing agreement or disagreement with 110 statements; some positive, some negative, on the general topics of social interaction, health and intellect, mood, attitude toward the future, past experience, current interests, and activities and mobility. After establishing that no relationships of responses and of sex, marital status, educational level, and occupation existed between the samples, Preston reported that employed people in their mid-sixties did not "perceive or report significantly more gratifications or fewer frustrations than retired subjects in their mid-seventies." Citing earlier studies by I. Banay and Ruth Aisenberg, she suggested that the older person of the mid-1960s, as opposed to those of a decade earlier, "may indeed be representative of changing attitudes" and that "a positive outlook on the conditions of being is more possible than has been previously assumed for the aged, retired members in current society." In a follow-up to this study, Preston focused on a sample of recently retired or soon to be retired people from the faculty or staff of the University of Washington—ninety-nine men and women whose mean age was sixty-eight, seventy being the automatic retirement age at the University—to see whether the fact of impending retirement strengthened one's tendency to regard himself/herself as old. Again, the findings suggested that assumptions routinely made twenty years earlier were no longer possible. "Contrary to expectations," Preston reported, "their status of retirement versus nonretirement was unrelated to thinking of oneself as 'old.' " Data such as this provided further insight into the early retirement phenomenon. If older people no longer considered old age to be an inseparable component of retirement, they faced one less psychological barrier to voluntary exit—early or late—from the labor force.[25]

Failing health was another negative element long associated with retirement, particularly when compulsory retirement plans forced active, able-bodied men and women out of the labor market. The phenomenon of early retirement certainly ran counter to this assessment, and vindicated the earlier conclusions of researchers, like Ethel Shanas of the University of Illinois and Wayne Thompson and Gordon Streib of Cornell University, in which they dismissed as a factual distortion, the linkage of deteriorating health with retirement. As Shanas observed, this popular association derived from the "fact" that "so many retired people were in poor health." A 1957 cross-national study, however, led her to the conclusion that poor health much more often was the cause rather than the result of retirement. Results on the self-reporting of retired older subjects relative to their health, compiled by Thompson and Streib in 1958, further suggested that given the high incidence of poor health-related retirement, quitting work had the immediate effect on an individual's health of improvement rather than deterioration.[26]

Americans had long associated retirement and advancing age with ill-health, and not unreasonably so, given the degenerative processes of aging. In this respect too, there was evidence of change. Perceptions, sociologist John W. Riley argued in a 1968 article, simply had not yet caught up with reality. Society, he observed, in large part "defines the conditions under which a person is to be considered well or ill" as a means of maintaining a "good health" norm. This social approval or disapproval could have great impact on the behavior of the individual. Riley offered the condition of pregnancy as an example of a condition which society had once defined as a "sick role," but did so no longer; with a corresponding difference in female behavior during pregnancy the result of this altered definition. "Some of the concepts involved in the changing response to pregnancy," he argued, "may be applied to the health problems of an aging population. For," he continued, "is it not true that our society *tends* to define old age as a state characterized by ailments and chronic ill health?—a sick role, as it were, from which old people are not expected to recover." Biological decrements, Riley emphasized, were an undeniable part of aging; nonetheless, a case could be made that society encouraged older persons to behave as if they were sick, by regarding and treating them as such. Medical science and therapeutic techniques have done much to increase the span of a healthy, active life, but the inclination to withhold from the elderly those social roles associated with good health (i.e., most normal social functions) persisted. Retirement, Riley suggested, was a condition which stripped the older person of social roles and thus reduced the number of social controls operating to keep him or her healthy and well-adjusted. Added to the accepted poor health–advancing years equation, the rolelessness of retirement (and its own association with old age) made an individual's assumption of the sick role, even when not physically warranted, that much easier. Besides medical progress, Riley concluded, upgrading the health status of the elderly depended upon redefining the later years as a "normal, dynamic aspect of life" and reevaluating retirement to emphasize the potential of leisure time and the need to develop new, positive social roles. The growing acceptance of early retirement indicated that, in fact, many of these associations had fallen by the wayside—that retirement was no longer necessarily regarded as the threshhold of a degenerative biological process.[27]

Early retirement also called into question the conventional belief that the cultural bias against leisure made separation from the work force a traumatic event and resulted in a resistance to it. In fact, Riley's recommendation that the leisure time potential of retirement receive more emphasis was finding broader and broader expression in the retirement village phenomenon. Two researchers—Gordon Bultena, an Iowa State University sociologist and Vivian Wood, a University of Wisconsin Professor of Social Work—working on an HEW–funded retirement study project, found in the multiplication of such facilities "dramatic

expression of the changing perspective of the aged toward leisure." Using a sample of 322 retired midwesterners living in
four different Arizona retirement communities, they attempted
to show how the retirement village setting both capitalized upon
and legitimized new attitudes about leisure. On one key issue—
the alleged desire of older people to stay busy and involved in
the affairs of the larger society—Bultena and Wood reported
that, although 28 percent felt such a desire in the form of an
obligation, 19 percent said that it was a matter of individual
preference and 53 percent reported feeling no such desires or
obligations. Admitting to limitations on their conclusions because of the atypicality of the sample (midwesterners of higher
social, economic, and educational attainments than the norm),
they nonetheless felt that the promotional efforts of retirement
villages in stressing leisure values were having a broader social
impact: "These leisure values appear to be meeting increased
acceptance among our aged population," they concluded, "and
may eventually comprise the core of a more general aged sub-
culture in American society." Another gerontologist, writing on
the increasing trend toward retirement for leisure, argued, much
as Bultena and Wood, that while it was not yet a widespread
tendency, "the good life" promised in future generations to become an acceptable and common retirement motive.[28]

As conditions improved (greater financial security, better mental preparation, improved health, heightened opportunities for
social involvement and activity), society adopted an increasingly
optimistic view of retirement. The recognition that modern
technology was decreasing rather than expanding industry's
manpower needs, in tandem with improving socioeconomic
prospects in retirement, made such an attitude unfashionable.
Discrimination in employment on account of age—a cardinal sin
in the immediate postwar era—had not disappeared; but it had,
with the assent of business, labor, government, and increasingly,
those in the gerontological community lost much of its iniqui-
tous quality. The emphasis had shifted, to make the best of retirement by redefining it in terms that almost commanded a
positive orientation. To the thoughtful proponent of such a pos-

itive orientation, the task was how to soften the transition from work to retirement for the older person in today's society and how to educate present and future generations to a view of the retirement years as a time for creative self-expression, richer personal relationships, and increased service to others.

We might easily overstate such findings as these. The earlier views of retirement and its effects were based upon impression rather than empirical data. Gerontologists of the immediate postwar period did not, after all, have access to the sophisticated survey techniques used to gauge the modern, more positive image of retirement. Had these techniques been available in 1945–1950, one might argue, early gerontologists might have espoused a more optimistic assessment, based on hard quantitative data rather than on impressionistic evidence. Such an argument, however, ignores the improved financial status of today's retiree, relative to his counterpart of twenty years ago, and fails to take into account the general increase in the variety of social services available to the nonworking older citizen. At this point we are dealing in the realm of perceptions. The description of "reality" is obviously an important research objective, but considering the nature of the topic with which we are dealing, it is perhaps less immediately important than the semblance of reality. We are studying a continuing process, and thus it is difficult to discuss "reality." Too much unfinished business remains. We can, however, discuss the blueprints of a contemplated or half-completed reality—that is, the ideas which reformers hope, ultimately, to translate into concrete achievement. With this caution in mind, let us turn to a consideration of the various architects of change in the concepts of aging and retirement in attempting to answer the obvious questions: who did what—and why?

N O T E S

1. Weber, *The Protestant Ethic and the Spirit of Capitalism,* T. Parsons, ed. (New York: 1958); Tawney, *The Acquisitive Society* (New York: 1958), are the basic statements of this thesis. On the cautionary side, there is a tendency among the exponents of

this view to present this partnership of religion and capitalism as conspiratorial. A more realistic view, I think, is provided by Erikson's biography of Luther, in which the compulsive aspects of Protestantism (and here one might also include Calvin and Wycliffe) seem naturally, if unintentionally, to lend themselves to an acquisitive, goal-oriented economic order. See Erik H. Erikson, *Young Man Luther* (New York: 1962).

2. Dan M. McGill, *Fundamentals of Private Pensions* (Pension Research Council, 1955) and James E. McNulty, *Decision and Influence Processes in 'Private Pension Plans* (Pension Research Council, 1961); Abraham Epstein, *Facing Old Age* (New York: 1922) is a good statement of the "right" concept of pensions; O. Pollak, *Social Adjustment in Old Age* (New York: 1948), section entitled, "Old Age and Making a Living," for an account of the effect of the depression on the labor market.

3. "How Old is Old?" *Business Week* (September 1, 1945): 104–107; statistics from Henry Sheldon (compiler), *The Older Population of the United States,* Table 19, p. 54; n.b., the steadiness of employment among the 45–54 group and the less than 6 percent decline among the 55–64 group.

4. The various types of retirement discussed and defined by E. K. Rowe, *Pension Plans under Collective Bargaining* (Washington, D.C.: Bureau of Labor Statistics Bulletin No. 1147, 1953); Geneva K. Mathiasen, *Flexible Retirement* (New York: 1957), pp. 23–24; James Hamilton and Dorrance C. Bronson, *Pensions* (New York, 1958), pp. 53–54; Lowell E. Gallaway, *The Retirement Decision* (Washington, D.C.), HEW Research Report No. 9, 1965, pp. 3–8; Fred Slavick, *Compulsory and Flexible Retirement in the American Economy* (Ithaca: Cornell University Press, 1966).

5. Drucker, "The Mirage of Pensions," *Harper's Magazine* 200 (February, 1950): 31; "Pensions versus Jobs for Older Workers," *U.S. News & World Report* 28, pt. 2 (May 5, 1950): 18–19.

6. Lee speech quoted in *New York Times,* June 18, 1947; "Who'll Carry the Pension Load by 1980?" *Saturday Evening Post* (September 18, 1948): 180; "Beware of Age Categories," *Life,* (June 19, 1950): 34; High pensions, as business defined them, were those in excess of one-half of working income; see Folsom statement in *Vital Speeches,* 16:184; "What to do about Old Folks?" *Newsweek,* (March 20, 1950): 58–61.

7. "It Pays to be Old in California," *Collier's* (March 26, 1949): 28+; "Nothing's Too Good for Grandpa," *Time,* (September 5, 1949): 16–17; "The Battle for Pensions," *Life,* (October 17, 1949): 41–45; Maisel, "The Pension Preacher: He Wants to be President," *Look* (January 31, 1950): 21–25. In an historical appreciation of the McClain movement, F. A. Pinner et al. points out from the outset the media's view of the man was "decidedly negative", and that this contributed to his national image as a "self-seeking, arrogant exploiter of his aged consitutents." See *Old Age and Political Behavior* (Berkeley and Los Angeles: 1959), p. 46.

8. McNulty, *Decision and Influence Processes:* Rowe, *Pension Plans Under Collective Bargaining;* H. Folk, *Private Pension Plans and Manpower Policy* (Washington, D.C.: Bureau of Labor Statistics Bulletin No. 1359, 1962); "How Old is Old?" *Business Week* (September 1, 1945): 104–107, related retirement to manpower policy by predicting that, in providing reduced OASDI benefits at age 60, the government could encourage the departure of as many as 1.5 million workers from the glutted postwar labor market.

9. French, "Industry Views Its Elderly" and Wolz, "The Practical Side of the Old Age Problem in Industry," in N.Y. State Joint Legislative Committee, *Never Too Old* (Albany: 1949); Brown, Kerr, and Witte, *The Aged and Society;* Convery, "How Industry Looks at the Employment of Older People," Tibbitts and Donahue, *Plan-*

ning the Older Years (Ann Arbor: 1950), 223, NAM, *Management Faces the Pension Problem* (October, 1950), pp. 14–15.

10. American Management Association, *Preparing Employees for Retirement* (AMA Personnel series no. 142, 1951); see also Helen Baker (Assistant Director of the Princeton Industrial Relations Section), *Retirement Procedures Under Compulsory and Flexible Retirement Policies* (Princeton: 1952), in which she argues that management control over retirement age is a necessary check against the stagnation potential of the seniority system; Slicter, whose views on the expandability of labor demand were frequently assailed by the advocates of "manpower policy," gives his position on the cruelty of forced retirement coupled with inadequate pensions in "The Pressing Problem of Old Age Security," *New York Times Magazine* (October 16, 1949): 9+, and on the expandability of markets for labor in "Retirement Age and Social Policy," in Brown, Kerr, and Witte, *The Aged and Society,* pp. 106–114.

11. Factors contributing to spread of private pension plans detailed by the NAM, *Management Faces the Pension Problem;* Rowe, *Pension Plans Under Collective Bargaining;* McGill, *Fundamentals of Private Pensions;* Hamilton and Bronson, *Pensions;* and McNulty, *Decision and Influence Processes in Private Pension Plans.*

12. Lewis' plan described in an interview conducted by *U.S. News & World Report* (November 14, 1948): 33–41; UAW–Ford setback on a conventional contributory pension plan. ibid. (September 26, 1947): 32; UMW's successful strike over this issue discussed in "Old Age Pensions: How Big? Who Should Pay for Them?" *Time* (May 22, 1950): 26. Historical appreciation of UMW campaign given by McGill, *Fundamentals of Private Pensions,* pp. 14–15; the CIO's general rejection of the idea of a "work ethic" discussed in "Old Hands Snub Pensions," *Business Week* (November 18, 1950): 124.

13. N.Y. State Legislative Committee, *Never Too Late,* 101 (Green letter) and 97–98 (Campbell testimony); Barkin, "Union Policies and the Older Worker," in Brown, Kerr, and Witte, *The Aged and Society,* pp. 84–85, and "Jobs for Older Workers," *Journal of Gerontology* 7 (1952): 426–430.

14. Margaret W. Wagner, "Mental Hazards of Old Age," *The Family: Journal of Social Casework* 24, no. 4, (1944): 132–137; "Current Comment," *Journal of Gerontology* 5, no. 2 (1950), 177.

15. Doc. 61, *N.Y. State Leg. Documents, 1948,* IX, pp. 21–27; Stieglitz, "The Personal Challenge of Aging," in Tibbitts (ed.), *Living Through the Older Years,* p. 51; E. W. Burgess, "The Growing Problem of Aging", ibid., for results of research showing no loss of productive efficiency with age; Lawton, "When Should a Man Retire?" *New York Times Magazine* (April 27, 1945), 12, 52; Dr. Agnew quoted in *New York Times* (December 20, 1946), 22:3; Kuh, "Selective Placement of Older Workers," *Journal of Gerontology* I (1946): 313–318; similar arguments made by J. C. and H. Purnas, "Old Folks Aren't Useless," *Saturday Evening Post* (January 13, 1945): 17+; and in "Experience, Loyalty, Skill—Come with AGE," *Occupations* 27, no. 5 (February, 1949): 301–302.

16. Dr. Lee quoted in *New York Times* (June 18, 1947): 28:1; doc. 61, *N.Y. State Leg. Docs.,* 1948, p. 1; Klumpp, "Care of the Aged and Chronically Ill, *Hygeia* 25 (1947): 298; Desmond, "America Must Age Successfully," *Christian Century* 65, pt. 2 (1948), 828; Julius Hochman, "The Retirement Myth," *Social and Biological Challenge of Our Aging Population* (New York: 1950), pp. 131, 145; A. B. Comstock and Sydney Morrell, "Need 65 be Time to Retire?" *Nation's Business* 37 (June, 1949): 69.

17. Comments on program from *Journal of Gerontology* 3, no. 1: (1948) 61–62; N.Y. St. Leg. Comm., *Never Too Old,* p. 94.

18. M. T. Wermel and Selma Gelbaum, "Work and Retirement in Old Age," *American*

Journal of Sociology 51 (1945–1946): 21; *New York Times,* June 6, 1945, 20:5; Truman's message to conference in the *Times* (August 15, 1950), 31:8; FSA, *Man and His Years,* 74, 76–77; impressions of the conference position on retirement from Marion Robinson, "Magna Charta for the Aged," *Survey* 86 (1950): 450.

19. Michener, "Out to Pasture," *Nation's Business* 37 (April, 1949): 30, 70–74.
20. Desmond, "America Must Age Successfully," *Chrisitan Century* 65: 829; doc. 61, *N.Y. State Legislative Documents,* 1948, p. 153; a more detailed consideration of retirement incidence by an OASDI bureau official stated that a recent FSA survey of beneficiaries showed that "only 5% had stopped working because they wanted to." The roles of health and involuntary retirement plans in retirement were not indicated in this statement nor was the factor of low benefits introduced, thus giving perhaps a disproportionate influence to the alleged psychological resistance to retirement—see speech of OASDI director, R. M. Ball, quoted in *New York Times* (May 7, 1950), 34:3.
21. Clothing workers data from Hochman, "The Retirement Myth," *The Social and Biological Challenge of Our Aging Population,* p. 137; the suppositions about Jewish attitudes have been introduced merely to serve as a counterweight to Hochman's rather rigid rejection of the whole idea of retirement for anyone with strength left to wield a needle.
22. Shock, "Aging with a Future," *Gerontologist,* 8, no. 3 (1968): 147; Maddox, "Adaptation to Retirement," ibid. 10, no. 1, pt. 2 (1970): 14–18; see also the comments of Dr. Carl Eisdorfer in F. W. Carp, "The Retirement Crisis," *Science* 157 (July 7, 1967): 102–103.
23. Indeed, by 1971, businesses like GMC were actually resisting union demands for increasingly liberal early retirement programs since, according to one executive, these new demands involved cutting into the "peak productivity" periods of the workers' life cycle; see "Thirty and Outers Opt for Late Retirement," *Business Week* (October 9, 1971): 82–83; E. K. Faltermayer, "The Drift to Early Retirement," *Fortune* 71 (May, 1965): 112–113, 222; Faltermayer himself was not enthusiastic about early retirement as a consistent policy, but it is not clear that he spoke for any business group. A similar analysis of the situation is "The Dilemma of Retirement," *Dun's Review* 86 (October, 1965): 81+.
24. "Early Retirement Plan Scores Big," *Business Week* (May 22, 1965): 166–167; "Early Retirement Gets a Big Push," ibid. (September 11, 1965): 170; Tibbitts quoted by Faltermayer, loc. cit.: 114; A survey taken by the NICB of companies offering early retirement plans antedating the UAW supplement experiment revealed that two-thirds of these 554 companies could get only a 5% response, while another 20% could report only 5–10% of eligibles electing to retire early. The response to the UAW plan, demonstrates the importance of money against the traditional 'work ethic' argument—see "The Dilemma of Retirement," loc. cit.; 81. The article on GM workers, "How Workers Like Early Retirement," *U.S. News & World Report* 59 (October 18, 1965): 96–100.
25. Preston's findings reported in "Self-Reporting Among Older Retired and Non-Retired Subjects," *Journal of Gerontology* 22 (1967): 415–420, and "Subjectively Perceived Agedness and Retirement," ibid. 23 (1968); other studies in which her data appear to confirm are those of I. Banay and R. Aisenberg, reported in Robert Kastenbaum (ed.), *New Thoughts on Old Age* (New York: 1964).
26. Shanas, *The Health of Older People* (Cambridge, Mass.: 1962); Thompson and Streib, "Situational Determinants: Health and Economic Deprivation," *Journal of Social Issues* 14 (1958): 18–34. The issue of health in later life will be treated in greater detail in the following chapter.

27. Riley, "Old Age in American Society," *American Society of Life Underwriters' Journal* 22 (1968): 27–32.
28. Bultena and Wood, "Leisure Orientation and Recreational Activities of Retirement Community Residents," *Journal of Leisure Research* 2, no. 1, (1970): 3–15; L. Cain, "Age Status and Generational Phenomena: The New Old in Contemporary America," *Gerontologist* 7 (June, 1967): 83–96; other studies that refer to the new legitimacy of leisure and its effect on retirement patterns—i.e., more voluntary and early retirement—include E. Shanas, *Old People in Three Industrial Societies* (New York: 1968); E. Palmore, "Retirement Patterns" (a comparison of data from 1951 and 1963 Social Security Administration data) in Epstein and Murray, *The Aged Population of the United States,* pp. 101–112; R. Barfield and J. Morgan, *Early Retirement: The Decision and the Experience* (Ann Arbor: 1959); M. F. Lowenthal, "Perspectives for Leisure and Retirement" in R. Brockbank and D. Westerby-Gibson (eds.), *Mental Health in a Changing Community* (New York: 1966), pp. 118–126.

3

Biological and Social Scientists and the Problem of Aging Stereotypes

> Gerontology, as it emphasizes growth and devel-
> opment, and the correlation of data concerning
> physical and emotional maturation, must bring
> into close relationship previously isolated species.
> As the anatomist, physiologist, sociologist, and
> philosopher convene from time to time in a single
> forum to exchange ideas, the understanding of the
> problems of later life should be greatly clarified.
>
> E. L. Bortz, "New Goals for Maturity," *Journal of
> Gerontology*, 9(1954), p.72.

The intellectual substance for the broad changes in the images
of and attitudes toward, old age and retirement outlined in the
preceding two chapters originated largely in the efforts of an
amorphous group of biomedical and social scientists working in
the field of gerontology. Coined to describe "the scientific study
of old age and the process of aging," the word "gerontology"
came into general usage just prior to World War II. The *Readers'
Guide to Periodical Literature* first used it as a subject heading in
1940, while the OED's 1972 supplement provides a quote from
Time magazine of September 22, 1941, as the earliest of its usage
examples. While we recognize that scientists pursued the interests encompassed by this term years before its appearance, we
may conclude that the emergence of a specific word at this time
indicates a certain degree of maturity in the field. From this point,
at least, we can begin to consider the various practitioners in
different research disciplines as members of an increasingly in-

tegrated coalition focusing on the problems of old age and their resolution.

On the other hand, we would be reading too much into the gerontological movement if we were to view it as a monolithic, organized group with the conscious objective of altering the physical, social, and economic condition of the aged. To be sure, biomedical and social scientists were participants—perhaps the most important participants—in the movement to improve the lot of the older citizen. We should not, however, presume from this that they were proponents of a vast social engineering project. They showed, in fact, no tendency to view themselves as agents of social change. Some especially among the biomedical scientists, occupied themselves exclusively with the collection of data and the examination of specific aspects of aging, leaving to others the task of translating their findings into socially useful information. Others, particularly the social gerontologists who became active in the 1960s, undertook to fuse the processes of deriving and applying research findings. It would be tempting to focus on this latter group, but it would distort the nature of the gerontological contribution. Primarily, gerontologists "made" knowledge. A significant number went on to use, in a practical context, the knowledge they had produced—but gerontologists concerned themselves for the most part with providing the data which, properly presented, might constitute the basis of social change.[1]

One of the earliest contributions to the biomedical aspects of aging was Dr. Edmund V. Cowdry's 1938 volume, *The Problems of Aging*. After introductory discussions of aging in plant and lower animal life, this seminal work went on to analyze the effects of aging on various systems of the human body. Each chapter, written by experts in such fields as endocrinology, cardiology, neurophysiology, and so forth, stressed the need for more knowledge about the phenomenon of aging. In a concluding chapter, geriatrician Edward J. Stieglitz discussed the "Social Urgency of Research in Aging" by focusing on the role of the knowledge maker: "Little intelligent and farseeing planning is possible in the social fields," he wrote, "until we know more about the changing capacities, the limitations, the weaknesses and strengths of older persons, and learn how to measure them." By the late 1940s and early 1950s, such views had become more common within the medical profession. Thus, writing in another forum, Dr. John E. Kirk of the Washington University (St. Louis) Medical School observed: "I cannot help feeling that since aging is a biological phenomenon, progress in sociology, economy and welfare of the aged must be ultimately dependent on the advances made in the biologic approach to aging." The special targets of this kind of research should, he thought, include those misconceptions about health, based on purely chronological measurements, which underlay the popular tendency to underestimate the physical and mental capacities of the elderly. Psychologist George Lawton called for similar researches in the area of mental ability. "In the next decade or two," he predicted in a 1943 collection of essays, "the study of mental abilities in the aged will be almost as common as that of children today, and vocational guidance based on a knowledge of when old people are weak and when strong will be possible."[2]

Dr. Cowdry defined the emerging biophysical conception of the aging process in a dialogue with his colleagues at the 1948 Macy Foundation Conference on the Problems of Aging. Regarding the traditional definition of aging, he observed: "I cannot agree. This definition is in terms of failure. We can't define aging as anything more than change with time." Before the New York State Joint Legislative Committee on the Problems of Aging, Dr. Stieglitz conceded that aging was inevitably associated with increasing physical disorder. However, he argued, not all of this disorder was inevitable. Much of it, in fact, resulted from "the abuse of the machine which is our body." This abuse, he continued, could be prevented if the educational system could be induced to teach "the average layman . . . what makes him tick." Health in the later years, he concluded, was not a universal given, but it could be earned by good personal hygiene and access to preventative medical facilities. The New York State Commissioner of Health, Dr. H. E. Hillboe, addressing the same forum, called for an end to public ignorance of the health needs of older people. He assailed the assumption that such needs were the unavoidable companions of old age, and the tendency to approach them on a wholesale basis on the grounds that the elderly shared, as a group, common problems. "I think," Dr. Hillboe declared, " . . . that very often the older person does not begin to deteriorate physically and mentally until he is told that his usefulness is past and he is asked to retire." Thus, the much alleged decline of health in the later years might stem as much from social as from biological forces. He too emphasized the potential role of preventive medicine in slowing and in some cases halting the progressive loss of faculties with age.[3]

The National Conference on Aging, sponsored by the Federal Security Agency in 1950, devoted a section to health maintenance and rehabilitation. The report of this section defined aging as biological change resulting in modifications of organic structures and functions, and impairment of vigor and recuperative powers. But, the section insisted, these modifications and impairments were highly individual matters. One simply could not associate any particular age with the collapse of physical vigor and mental competence, and a rapid plunge thereafter into ill-health and senility. Nonetheless, a paucity of data on the process led the section to define aging in terms of decline and limitation. The physical handicaps of age were very real, noted an editor of the *American Journal of Public Health,* but they were in many cases, reversible. Such simple interventions as eyeglasses or hearing aids, he observed, could restore an older person to active life. Similarly, the physical and emotional health of the elderly had in documented cases been substantially revived by enhancing their social opportunities or inspiring them in some new creative interest, suggesting again the nonbiological basis of many of the physical and psychological problems of aging.[4]

In the postwar era, physicians and biological researchers became increasingly familiar with this new view of aging. A number of influential spokesmen had emerged to disseminate fresh opinions on the subject. One of the most influential of these was Dr. Edward L. Bortz of Philadelphia, president of the American

Medical Association in 1947. A prolific writer and lecturer in the field of geriatrics, he continually sought to impress upon his colleagues the idea that aging constituted but one more stage in the developmental processes of life, stressing its special characteristics of growth and maturity. Another seminal figure, Martin Gumpert, a German-born surgeon, moved easily between the medical and lay worlds in his own crusade to gain a more positive social appreciation of the physical and mental capabilities of older people. The visible nature of his ministry, in fact, gained him a profile in the *New Yorker* in June, 1950. Dr. C. Ward Crampton, chairman of the Geriatrics subcommittee of the New York County Medical Society and tireless advocate of his medical interest, coined the phrase "de-aging" to describe how a properly informed medical profession could remove some of those burdens of aging that doctors had only recently begun to consider potentially reversible. Dr. Theodore G. Klumpp, a physician and pharmaceutical industry executive from New York, was similarly active in the intraprofession movement to revise conceptions of geriatric health status. His own theory prescribed continuing vigorous physical and mental activity into the later years as the best means of preserving health. He cited experiments showing a positive relationship between activity and endocrine secretions as proof of his theory. Klumpp expressed his confidence, in a 1952 biographical sketch, that his profession was about to enter upon "a golden age of research on the medical problems of the aging." These men comprised the vanguard of an expanding medical specialty. Indicative of the growing interest in this field, the American Geriatric Society increased in size from 400 in 1950 to 7,500 in 1961. Older people no longer appeared to represent hopeless medical prospects in the eyes of at least a substantial portion of the medical profession.[5]

In addition to Drs. Cowdry and Stieglitz, other members of the Macy Foundation-sponsored Club for the Study of Aging promoted the more positive view of aging through their various deliberations and debates. For example, British clinician Marjorie Warren, during an interchange with colleagues at a Foundation conference in September 1951, charged that within the medical profession "there has been in the past a defeatist attitude toward the problems of aging persons." Yet, she continued, experience had taught her "that most conditions among elderly people are remediable to a certain extent." When others on the panel, nonetheless, sought to define aging as depletion of reserves or loss of efficiency, Dr. Frank Fremont-Smith offered a less negative assessment. "The other side of that picture ought to be added," he remarked, "because simultaneously with the lowering of functional efficiency in certain activities, there is an increase . . . with respect to other activities. It is terribly important that we emphasize the positive side as well as the negative." Diffusing such views even more widely, Nathan Shock, in his 1951 *Trends in Gerontology* challenged those within and without the medical profession who held chronic disease and old age to be synonymous by pointing out that while many of those over sixty-five were healthy, just as many younger people were victimized by long-term sicknesses. Further, he argued, the disabilities and impairments afflicting the elderly did not represent the sudden result of the old age, but rather a culmination of disintegrative processes (in many cases, preventable) begun in one's forties and fifties. The Federal Security Administration (the nation's social security agency) adopted this view early on, insisting in a 1952 public information pamphlet that "far from being a process of deterioration or regression, aging can (provided proper care of one's health is taken) be literally a period of further development." To support this view, the Administration referred to biological studies indicating that, if not foreshortened by inattention to personal hygiene, the average duration of physical and mental competence was much longer than commonly imagined.[6]

Between the biologists and doctors on the one hand, and the social science community on the other, the exchange of data and information became increasingly common. As a result of this interchange, the tendency within the medical profession to define aging solely in biomedical terms disappeared. Through the medium of "gerontology" the data compiled by biological and medical researchers were passed on to social scientists who evaluated, refined it, and made them available for use in practical contexts. More and more often, the words "social" and "economic" found their way into the biomedical lexicon when the topic of aging was raised. As one physician put it: "The social side of aging can no longer be neglected, and requires first of all scientific study . . . studies of social disciplines of elders should stimulate investigation in other social sciences which to date are almost negligible . . . " Conversely, the social gerontologists began to delve more deeply into the issues of physical and emotional health, and by offering plausible nonbiological interpretations, helped to strip away the pessimism traditionally associated with the process of growing old. The initial stages of biomedical–social science cooperation involved the simple recognition by both sides of the mutual importance of the biological and social aspects of aging. A sociologist strongly stated the need for a partnership between the social and medical disciplines. Noting that increasing numbers of medical specialists had come to the conclusion that, given "suitable adjustment to aging," a surprising amount of the "pathology" of aging could be forestalled by preventive medicine or minimized by therapeutic techniques, he continued: " . . . this is not a medical problem in the narrow sense of medicine. It is one for constructive medicine of a sociomedical character, requiring the cooperative contributions of, not only the social scientists, but also of the educator and the administrators of social and industrial policy."[7]

The process of developing "medicine of a socio-medical character" had in fact begun well before the coining of this phrase. Its progress was slow, and communication between the camps often unclear. But steadily, the biomedical and social scientists forged an alliance. As Dr. E. J. Stieglitz noted in his contribution to Cowdry's monumental *Problems of Aging,* the science of gerontology included three branches: first, biological; second, clinical; and third, socioeconomic. Progress in any one of these areas, he declared, depended upon and reinforced progress in the others. In the same collection, psychologist George Lawton empha-

73

sized the interdisciplinary nature of research in the field of aging. "The science of gerontology," he wrote, "requires many types of workers, but it demands most of all 'social engineers' of imagination, ingenuity and courage, who will manipulate community resources, and when necessary, devise new instrumentalities." Lawrence Frank, writing in the first issue of the *Journal of Geronotology* (January 1946), also focused on the need for cooperation between professionals in various fields, biomedical and social. "It [gerontology] is not . . . the latest addition to the . . . ever-lengthening list of 'ologies' . . . nor is it merely applied science . . . which takes over and utilizes the basic research of others." Rather, it represented a multifaceted approach to the problem of aging in such diverse areas as "human growth, development and aging, ecology and regional planning, mental hygiene, human conservation, [and] cultural change." Robert Havighurst, one of the earliest proponents of "social gerontology," argued that within fifty years the phenomenon of aging will profoundly affect society, and in consequence, social institutions would have to be modified. "The speed and vision with which these modifications are made will depend largely upon the development of the new science of gerontology—the study of aging. This science, if properly supported and developed, will do much to help us make the kind of social changes that are healthful for our society."[8]

One of the pioneering research groups, the Macy Foundation-sponsored "Club for Research on the Problems of Aging" became an early (and, in the case of several club members, reluctant) convert to this approach. Created in 1940, the club had traditionally invited to its annual conferences only biological and medical scientists. In 1950 this policy changed and a number of social scientists including Havighurst, Wilma Donahue, and Ollie Randall were asked to attend the yearly discussion. Introducing the opening paper, Dr. Roy Hoskins, a Harvard endocrinologist, warned his fellows that former Macy Foundation vice president Lawrence Frank's "approach may be different—that he will talk primarily about the nature of human nature, and the problems arising from that." In the course of his presentation, entitled "Interpersonal Aspects of Gerontology," Frank asked how many of the problems commonly associated with aging resulted from the aging of the physical organism and how many from personal stresses and morale failures due to the social situation. In response, a charter member of the Club, the well-known University of Chicago physiologist Anton Carlson, spoke for perhaps a majority of the natural scientists present when he observed: "I am a little confused by your language, Mr. Frank." Havighurst, a professor of educational sociology, also at the University of Chicago, translated for the "confused" club members: "Mr. Frank has offered the proposition that these changes are not due simply to biological deterioration or biological change, but they are also due to the way the person is treated by the significant persons in his life." Despite the language barrier, most agreed by the end of the two-day meeting that a fruitful dialogue had begun.[9]

Increasingly aware that the process of aging had a social as well as a biological dimension, gerontologists began to consider the potential sources of the "personal stresses" and "morale failures" which Frank asserted were of such crucial significance to any understanding of that process. The most important initial contributions to the search were theoretical rather than empirical. A key figure in the evolution of a social geronotology, Yale University anthropologist Leo W. Simmons treated aging as a cultural pheonomenon. His 1947 volume, *The Role of the Aged in Primitive Society,* had great influence upon those disposed to accept the idea of the social dimension. He provided a philosophical framework within which the status of the elderly could be envisioned as a cultural variable. Although Simmons wrote of societies with no similarity to those of the western industrial world, his essential argument that cultural definitions of aging shape both the behavior of older people and society's treatment of them provided the empiricists with a thesis to test. Another anthropologist, Margaret Mead, placed the Simmons contribution squarely in the context of nonprimitive societies by describing the burdens which modern industrial civilization placed upon its older members. Such a culture, she pointed out; assigned a high importance to autonomy, while it associated old age with the loss of autonomy; it placed great emphasis on growth and success, while it defined aging in terms of decline and failure; it idolized youth and denigrated, openly or by implication, advanced years. Addressing herself specifically to those concerned with improving the social position of the elderly—testifying before Senator Desmond's New York State Legislative Committe—Mead stated that two basic options were available to social gerontologists. They could either attempt to alter social institutions such as the family, the factory, and the economy; or they could try to redefine aging in such a way as to minimize the issues of dependency and loss. The first, Mead suggested, was impractical; the complexity of modern society and its continuing evolution bid defiance to such planned interventions. The second, however, offered a feasible means of improving the lot of the aged. Gerontologists, she concluded, must accept the need to concentrate upon altering public opinion rather than social institutions. She labeled this option "cultural reorientation."[10]

The eminent University of Chicago sociologist David Riesman also made the link between cultural definition and social status. In a contribution to a special 1954 issue of the *American Journal of Sociology* devoted to the problem of aging, Riesman used the personality typology that he had developed in *The Lonely Crowd* to explain the disadvantages under which the older person labored. He left aside consideration of the two relatively rare extremes, the "autonomous" and the "anomic," and concentrated on the "adjusted" personality type. This group, which included the vast majority of people, could adjust comfortably to the process of aging, he argued, "so long as the cultural conditions remain stable and protective." Riesman called these conditions "cultural preservatives," and included among them such components of social status as work, power, and position. Yet, he suggested, these were precisely the components which the process of aging, denied to the individual. Thus he viewed the process as a kind of Chinese box enigma; the conditions required to ensure adjustment to old age were precisely those destroyed by the process of aging. The question, then, was how to facilitate individual adjustment to aging. Riesman's theories about aging tended, like those of Simmons and Mead, to focus attention on the need to alter the ways in which aging was defined. Until there was some inquiry into the origin and extent of the negative definitions attached to aging and the degree to which these definitions were warranted, such a prescription, no matter how eminent its formulators, would seem but a hopeful echo of Dr. Coué.[11]

The theorists were, however, striking a responsive chord among their more empirically oriented colleagues. Thus a physician, writing in the official publication of the American Geriatrics Society in 1952, submitted a nonbiological diagnosis of the aging process. Apparently influenced by these theoretical speculations, Dr. Raphael Ginzburg added his opinion that the disadvantaged status of the elderly in American society derived in part from society's "negative attitude" toward them. This negative attitude, he continued, had its source in the widespread conviction that older people were as a rule "lost causes . . . doomed to regression and degeneration." This conviction, Ginzburg asserted, limited the social and economic opportunities for the elderly, thus frequently consigned them to inactivity before any loss of physical vigor or mental competence. The key premise of his argument was that the loss of these characteristics was more often assumed than proved. To his mind, the overbroad gap between assumption and reality would have to be eliminated in the social appreciation of aging; otherwise, "there is no door open to a constructive solution of their problems." Milton L. Barron, a sociologist was, with Ginzburg, a partisan of the social interpretation of aging. He went further, however, by offering one of the earliest models for understanding aging as a social phenomenon. He suggested that gerontologists treat the elderly as a "minority group." Barron supported his proposition by arguing that all the elements of prejudice, including fear and stereotyping, figured in society's group image of the older pop-

77

ulation. This group image in turn contributed to the feeling that older people represented a political and social menace because of their alleged susceptibility to demagogues like Townsend or McClain. The components of this group image, including slowness, physical and mental incompetence, inability to learn, and crankiness—like color or race—denied the aged opportunities for social participation. They responded to such treatment in the classical minority group mode, exhibiting "bitterness, resentment and self-hatred." The use of this analogy, Barron asserted, allowed gerontologists to consider invoking the same kind of ameliorative actions that had applied in the past to racial and ethnic minorities (i.e., antidiscrimination, equal opportunity, and housing legislation).[12]

Barron's arguments were open to some rather obvious criticisms. Two definitive differences between the elderly and the racial or ethnic minority were; first, that everyone had personal contact, even if only within the family context, with representatives of the aged population; and second, that old age was a status, unlike, for example, blackness or Jewishness, which everyone expected to achieve. One could argue, that however vague, this awareness of aging as a personal as well as a social phenomenon, would tend to discourage some of the more virulent expressions of prejudice. On the other hand, this same awareness created perhaps some special problems for those seeking to improve the social lot of the aged. Such problems would derive from an often unwarranted assumption of familiarity with the social and personal situations of the elderly, and their responses to those situations. As gerontological empiricists would find, prejudices against the aged expressed in the form of negative stereotypes, although less powerful and overt than those characteristic of Negrophobia or anti-Semitism, tended to be more widely accepted and to cut across age, educational, regional, and professional divisions. In this view, the aged were not, as Barron would have it, typical of the minority group member in a social situation. Focusing as it did on negative stereotypes and provoking criticisms, his thesis, which for the first time proposed empirical research into the extensiveness and sources of the stereotypes, was an influential one in the evolution of social gerontology.[13]

Amid such theoretical speculation, gerontological investigators began at last to examine the bases upon which traditional attitudes toward aging rested. If, as they suspected, many of these attitudes proved to be either exaggerated or completely unfounded, the "cultural reorientation" processes suggested by the theorists could be put into effect and new, positive images of the age evolved. The potential impact of a more optimistic view of the later stages of the life cycle would be twofold. First, society-at-large would become more sensitive to the needs and the aspirations of the elderly, and the institutionalized opportunities or social roles available to them would be expanded to reflect this heightened sensitivity. Second the destruction of the negative stereotypes upon which existing attitudes were built would ultimately result in a higher level of social expectations for the aged. The critical import of this second potential benefit derived from the causal link made by social scientists between expectation and behavior. These researchers felt that in stripping away the mythology associated with the processes of aging, they could reshape social expectations and, beyond that, the all-important self-image and behavior patterns of the elderly themselves. This, they argued, merely constituted a reversal of the present cycle by which low levels of expectation, based on negative stereotypes, resulted in the adoption by the aged of self-images and behavior patterns which, in turn, reinforced the negative stereotype and justified the low expectation level. If society defined old age as a time of ill-health, deviancy, and dependency, the social gerontologists were saying, older people would be encouraged to behave as unhealthy, deviant indigents. Conversely, if the later years could be purged of their negative associations, the elderly person would be more likely to behave as a healthy, socially useful, and independent individual.

Sociologist Robert J. Havighurst, speaking in 1951 on the relationships of sociology, psychology, education, and religion in the interdisciplinary approach to aging research, placed heavy emphasis on the use of sociopsychological methods and concepts. The methodological tools which he recommended to his fellow members of the Macy Foundation-sponsored Club for the Study of Aging included sampling techniques; the evolution of tests designed to measure objectively the degree of decline attributable to age; the use of interview schedules to obtain subjective, self-reporting data; and the development, based upon data so collected, of rating scales to provide a usable index for determining the effects of aging upon the individual. The conceptual tools which he advocated were: (1) "social roles," meaning, according to Havighurst, "any defined pattern of behavior which carries with it certain expectations by society"; (2) "age grading," or the way in which social roles are assigned; (3) "defense mechanisms," defined as those ways in which the individual defended himself against the insults of aging; (4) "adjustment," a measure of the "competence" shown by the individual in facing the circumstances of agedness; and (5) "constriction of self," i.e., how the individual's sphere of interactions was contracted to accommodate the fact of old age. Beyond providing his colleagues with a methodology and a set of tools, Havighurst listed what he felt to be the main objectives of gerontological research. He called upon empiricists to evolve a valid, nonchronological scale to measure individual changes in ability and to relate these changes to the process of aging, or to the reactions of the individual to that process; to determine the degree to which value systems change with passing years; the way in which the self reacts to the stresses imposed by advancing age and how social roles are distributed—that is, to what degree the assignment of roles is a personally and socially determined phenomenon. The importance of understanding role assignment procedures, particularly as they operated in the latter part of the life cycle, Havighurst emphasized by asking: " . . . can the society, through its institutions change the social roles that are available to older people, and thus make life better or worse for older people?" If they could, as Havighurst felt, then here was the mechanism by which Mead's theoretical "cultural reorientation" could be accomplished.[14]

Investigations into the nature and pervasiveness of stereotypes about older people provided the necessary basis for "cultural reorientation" efforts. As researchers repeatedly found, these stereotypes, however obliquely or apologetically expressed, were both deep-seated and widespread. Two pioneering surveyors of social attitudes toward older people, Jacob Tuckman and Irving Lorge of Columbia University's Teachers' College, designed a questionnaire including 137 statements about old age which were divided into thirteen categories—statements on physical condition, finances, conservatism, family, attitude toward future, insecurity, mental deterioration, activities and interests, personality traits, best time of life, sex, cleanliness, and interference in lives of others. With this questionnaire, they spent almost a decade documenting the extent to which people, especially better educated individuals and professionals, accepted negative assessments of the status and capacities of the elderly. For example, they used this questionnaire in 1951 on a group of 147 (92 men and 55 women) Teachers' College graduate students, all of whom were enrolled in a class on the psychology of the adult. The age range was twenty to fifty-one, with a mean age of 30.9 years. When this sophisticated sample of well-educated, professionally oriented individuals had finished filling out the survey form regarding old people, Tuckman and Lorge found that; 90 percent agree they were "set in their ways"; 78 percent, they were "conservative"; 80 percent, they were resistant to change; 77 percent, they were more interested in religion than younger people; 66 percent, their coordination was poor; 65 percent, they needed glasses; 53 percent, they were hard of hearing; 50 percent, they were very talkative; 67 percent, they liked to gossip; 61 percent, they tended to repeat themselves in conversation; and 57 percent, they were forgetful. While these figures represented substantial acceptance of negative stereotypes, Tuckman and Lorge also pointed out that, considering the elite nature of the sample, the fact that 33 percent felt older people to be meddlesome; 41 percent, that they often talked to theselves; 34 percent, that they were absentminded; 42 percent, that they always felt sorry for themselves; and 34 percent, that they were "bossy," indicated the strength and depth of the negative imagery surrounding old age. The two surveyors called such results "a reflection of cultural expectations regarding the activities, personality characteristics, and adjustment of older people" and of "a social climate which is not conducive to feelings of adequacy, usefulness and security and to poor adjustment in their later years.[15]

Showing a remarkable ability for making use of their captive sample of Teachers' College students in the psychology course, Tuckman and Lorge produced a series of assessments of the problems created by old age stereotypes. A battery of twenty-one questions designed to measure sample opinion as the "best years of life," for example, yielded the data shown in Table 2.

TABLE 2
Period of Life

Criteria		−12	13−19	20−29	30−39	40−49	50−59	60−69	70
Health	+	24	23	47	5	1	0	0	1
	−	2	0	0	1	1	2	2	93
Ambition	+	0	24	58	16	2	0	0	1
	−	0	2	1	0	0	0	0	97
Ability to Learn	+	43	29	21	2	1	2	1	2
	−1	2	0	0	0	0	0	0	98
Happiness	+	35	12	27	14	8	3	0	0
	−	2	9	2	5	2	2	7	43

Source: Excerpted from Tuckman and Lorge, "The Best Years of Life: A Study in Ranking," *Journal of Psychology* 34 (1952), 140 (Table 1).

In these areas and others represented on the survey, Tuckman and Lorge found "most favorable" (+) sentiments dropping off sharply after the 50–59 period. This, they suggested, resulted from "the conditioning, by cultural *stereotype,* that aging is always accompanied by physical and mental decline." Going perhaps a bit beyond the warrant of the survey, the two researchers attributed this "negative attitude" toward aging to an "unconscious acceptance of decline, with the corresponding changes in self-concept, in behavior, and in aspirations of an aging population."[16]

They polled the same group on its attitudes toward older workers using a fifty-one question survey developed by the researchers for this purpose, and again the responses indicated widespread acceptance of stereotypes: 58 percent thought that older workers "resist new ways of doing things"; 68 percent, that they "look to the past"; 66 percent, that they are slow; 59 percent, that they "need longer rest periods more often"; 77 percent, that they "take longer in getting over illness" and 78 percent," . . . in getting over injuries"; 58 percent, that they "dislike to work under younger supervisors"; 74 percent, that they "need more time to learn new operations"; and 51 percent, that they "are slow to catch onto new ideas." Finally, the team of researchers attempted to ascertain the effects of the adult psychology course on these attitudes by retesting the group upon completion of the course, using forty selected statements from the two (older persons and older workers) original questionnaires. Oddly, they found the general tendency of the course was to harden negative attitudes. Stratifying the class into two age groups (20–29 and 30–51), Tuckman and Lorge found that both groups increased their percentage of agreement with twenty of these statements, that the older group was more prone to agreement on twelve additional statements, and the younger group on three others. The remaining five statements either registered no change, or the proportion of agreement was slightly reduced. Tuckman and Lorge explained the apparent failure of this course in encouraging a positive reassessment of the aging process by theorizing: "Since these students accepted the cultural stereotypes about age even before instruction, the objective course material on physiological and psychological change may only have served to reinforce the concerns or fears that they may have had about their own aging, and offset any of the positive aspects of the material presented with the result that they view the future with misgiving."[17]

Although this catalogue of papers does not exhaust the uses

that the two Teachers' College psychologists found for their graduate student sample, they did query other groups about attitudes. Thus, along with Albert J. Abrams, special counsel to Senator Desmond's New York State Legislative Committee on the Aging, they surveyed the feelings of 533 students, aged twelve to twenty, in the Junior and Senior High Schools of Newburgh, New York. Grouping the sample into six subdivisions, aged thirteen through eighteen and over, this trio found that almost all the subjects defined old age chronologically, although they were also given a choice of five different non-chronological definitions. None of the thirteen-year-old subjects selected a non-chronological definition; 5 percent of the fourteen-year-olds did so; 11 percent of the fifteen-year-olds; 16 percent of the sixteen-year-olds; 5 percent of the seventeen-year-olds; and 6 percent of these eighteen or over. For the bulk of those students opting for an age-based definition of old age (stated in quintiles, from under forty through ninety to ninety-four), their choices clustered between fifty to fifty-four and seventy to seventy-four with the most frequently cited of these being sixty to sixty-four and sixty-five to sixty-nine. The responses of these students to a battery of statements generally reflective of old age stereotypes (i.e., older people are grouchy, old-fashioned, hard of hearing, lonely, often sick, nuisances to others, poor workers, and so forth) demonstrated that the adoption of many of the erroneous bromides about age were fixed early in life and were probably related to the nearly universal tendency to define old age as a certain number of years lived. In another study, carried out upon another student sample, this one consisting of fifty undergraduates and their parents at a Connecticut state normal school, Tuckman and Lorge along with George A. Spooner of the Connecticut State Department of Education, tested the potential influence of in-family attitudes upon opinion formation. The attitudes, measured as percentages of agreement with the 137 statements on the Old People questionnaire, of all three sample groupings—fathers, mothers and children—were noticeably similar. Thus, on the thirteen statements under the heading of "Family," the three samples showed mean agreement percentages of 61, 58, and 51, respectively; on the twenty-seven statements under "Physical," similar figures were 60, 57, and 48 percent; on the 14 listed under the heading "Conservatism," the percentages were 80, 80, and 84; for "Mental Deterioration," (fourteen statements), 49, 49, and 39 percent; and for "Personality Traits" (also fourteen statements), 57, 60, and 63 percent. The absence, according to the author's undefined standard of significant variation, of any marked variation in the views of parents and children, stemmed from "the tendency of both parents and children to think of old age in terms of disability rather than ability," and suggested a "need for an educational program to emphasize the normality of the aging process and its positive aspects," and to communicate this information to young and old alike. In conclusion, they argued that whatever could be done to lessen the influence of negative stereotypes in the classroom could be undone if the supporting environment (that is, the family unit) was oriented toward acceptance of them.[18]

Tuckman and Lorge looked, in addition, into the attitudes of professionals who had experience with the aged. In an article in *Science* in 1952, the two men declared that a poll of thirty-five individuals from the fields of business, medicine, social work, and labor relations, all delegates to a conference on the problems of older workers, showed that they too needed to agree with a large number of old age stereotypes. Arguing that the sample was too small on which to base generalizations they gave no statistical account of their results. Nonetheless, the data seemed surprising, and one apparent relationship worth pointing out was stated by Tuckman and Lorge as follows: "The representatives from universities, government, and labor who, in their daily work look for and are impressed with the positive rather than the negative aspects of aging, subscribe less to the stereotyped opinions that the management, social work, and medical groups, which tend to see the negative rather than the positive aspects of aging." Recognizing the crucial influence of these last three groups upon public opinion as a whole, Tuckman and Lorge argued that subscription to stereotypes by these professionals was based upon their day-to-day experiences with the small minority among the elderly who were most in need of their services. This exposure helped to perpetuate unwarranted attitudes. A more statistically defensible statement of this view appeared under the Tuckman–Lorge imprimature in a 1958 comparative study of attitudes toward old age and the older worker by several groups, among which was a sample of "experts" drawn from a 1953 lecture group on aging sponsored by the Federation of Protestant Welfare Agencies of New York. Exposing this group to a 40 statement condensation of the 137-statement Old People and the 51-statement Older Worker questionnaires, 54 percent of the ninety-two "experts" thought older people repetitious in conversation; 26 percent thought they were burdens to their children; 36 percent, that they always felt sorry for themselves; 42 percent, that they were typically touchy; 35 percent, that they had poor coordination; 88 percent, that they disliked changing the way they did things; and 54 percent, that they liked to gossip. As to older workers, the same sample felt them to be slow (69 percent), unable to keep up with changes in work methods (41 percent); unsure of themselves (43 percent); unsettled under pressure (70 percent); and in need of more time (than younger workers) to learn new operations (67 percent). Finally, an inquiry by Theodore Arnhoff and Irving Lorge into the attitudes of thirty-six fellows at a 1958 interuniversity summer institute in gerontology revealed that at least one-half of these respondents felt that older people worried more, tired easily, were forgetful, more religious, more conservative, resistant to change, gossip-prone, resentful of younger people, and without many friends. The durability of such attitudes, which these researchers had consistently branded as exaggerations, "means that their activities will tend to be palliative rather than positive."[19]

Many of the most widespread and harmful of the stereotypes documented by surveyors were those which associated aging with unavoidable and irremediable biological degeneration. This popular tendency to equate ill-health with old age had a number of unfortunate consequences. First, it tended to lower social expectations of older people, based upon an assumption of declining competence and to lessen the number of social and economic opportunities open to them. Second older people, while they often denied aging as a personal liability, tended to accept such social judgments as being generally valid, consenting, thereby, to often unwarranted limitations upon the number and types of social rules available to them as a group, and to uncalled-for decrements in social status. Finally, it was, as geriatrician Lester Breslow insisted in the pages of the *Journal of Gerontology*, "the harmful, illogical notion of degenerative disease" as the inevitable companion of age, which continued to retard the establishment of widely accessible health services. Such services, by providing lifelong health maintenance, could enable each individual to capitalize an inherent potential for good health, well into later life. Thus, if the notion of old age as biological "shipwreck" could be eliminated and replaced by one stressing each individual's potential for continuing good health, a formidable barrier to the establishment of these services would be overcome and, beyond this, a higher level of social expectation vis à vis the aged would come to be accepted.[20]

How widely accepted were such notions about health in the later years? Tuckman and Lorge found large-scale subscription to the degenerative image among their various sample groups. For example, 84 percent of the original Teachers' College graduate student sample, asked to locate the "best years" of life, using health as a variable, thought that the first three decades was the healthiest time of life, while 93 percent tabbed the oldest choice given (over 70) as the least healthy time of life. The same sample was asked to respond to twenty-seven statements classified as relating to the health of the aging. Their mean percentage of agreement on this part of the battery was 48 percent. Looking at the sampling of Connecticut normal school students and their parents, the mean percentages of agreement on the twenty-seven statements were 60 for fathers, 57 for mothers, and 48 for children. Looking at the percentages of agreement expressed upon various "significant" physical stereotypes within the various samples used, we can represent Tuckman and Lorge's overall findings in Table 3.

TABLE 3

Statements About the Physical Condition of the Aged	1953 CUT C Students	1953 Sample of Elderly[a]			1953 Conn. Sample[b]			Experts
		A	B	C	A	B	C	
Walk slowly	87							
Poor coordination	66	19	25	63				35
Always cold	44							
Stay indoors during bad weather	77	57	85	81				
Need less food	72	48	45	83	80	80	56	
Poor eaters	23	38	20	48	54	46	12	
Need to watch diets	80							
Lost most teeth	79							
Chronic constipation	46				72	62	40	
Sensitive to noise	54	62	70	83				
Suffer much discomfort	42							
Die soon after retirement	42				58	50	24	
Die of cancer/heart disease	54	33	50	54	58	58	36	
Need glasses	65	76	84	95				62
Hard of hearing	53	57	75	90				36
Can't taste food	11	43	15	56				
Voice breaks	42	52	30	63				
Need less sleep	42	33	50	73				
Go to bed early	32	52	40	67				
Need daily nap	35				62	54	40	
Tired most of time	34	43	45	75				29
Have many accidents at home	43	19	45	56				
Don't recover from broken bones	34							
Sick in bed often	29	33	30	63				20
Develop infections easily	51	29	30	56				
High care accident rate	36	19	30	52				
Die after major operations	35				58	53	30	

[a] Sample of elderly includes: (1) independent older persons (2) older persons in an old age apartment complex and (3) older persons in an institutional setting.
[b] Connecticut Normal School sample includes: (1) fathers (2) mothers (3) students/children.

Unfortunately, Tuckman and Lorge did not reveal statistics for all categories in all samples, thereby limiting the impact of the foregoing table. Particularly in those investigations stressing comparative attitudes, streamlined questionnaires were used; in many cases, only those statements for which "significant" variation existed within the survey population were cited. For the most part, these data are self-explanatory and indicate a generally low estimate of the physical capacities of the elderly. One relationship worthy of note is the generally high percentage of agreement expressed by the institutionalized older people (column 3C). If we can assume that this reflects a confession of the physical incapacities which place older people in institutional settings, and if we can further assume that this type of older person is most frequently in contact with medical and welfare "experts," then the origins of the "expert" biases noted by Tuckman and Lorge (and admitted to by Drs. Mullan, Butler, and Kastenbaum in cited articles) may seem a littler clearer.[21]

Attempts to revise popular attitudes about health in later life provide not only an example of the basic means by which gerontologists hoped to improve the lot of the aged in American society, but a model of the type of interdisciplinary cooperation upon which such means depended as well. Three significant contributions to this reassessment effort were the localized studies of a sample of 151 over-sixty-fives in Grand Rapids, Michigan (1953), a sample of 500 elderly from the Kips Bay section of New York City (1953) sponsored, respectively, by the University of Michigan Insitute for the Study of Human Adjustment, and by the Russell Sage Foundation–Cornell University Medical School–New York City Department of Health; and the cross–national study (1957) carried out by Ethel Shanas and her associates on 1,734 subjects under the aegis of the National Opinion Research Council (NORC) and the University of Chicago. Shanas, a sociologist, best stated the motivating rationale for such compilations of factual data: "Much of what is presented to the public as 'facts' about older people today are not facts, but impressions gained from small, selected groups in our older population." The designers of each of these investigations thus went to great pains to ensure that their samples were representative. All of them used data compiled in direct contact with their older samples, and one (the Kip's Bay project) also constructed a "Physical Health Index" based on clinical evidence against which to test the realism of self-reporting. Both the two local studies, to varying degrees, broke down the sample by differences in age (from sixty to eighty plus), while the NORC survey included all those over sixty in one category.

Allowing for widely different and often flawed methods of arranging data (the Grand Rapids study, for example, had only two classifications for ailment reporting: "no ailments" or "one or more"), the composite picture suggested a much healthier older population than the stereotype indicated. The New York City study, compiling information on the incidence of chronic complaints among older residents in Kip's Bay, found that from its whole sample, 23 percent reported no such conditions, 54 percent reported having one or two, and 23 percent reported more than three. Broken down by age groups (as in Table 4), the corrective data were the unexpectedly small increase in the number of chronic ailments reported as a variable of age.

TABLE 4
Percentage of Illness by Age

No. of Complaints and Health Designation	60–64	65–69	70–74	75–97	80+
None (excellent)	26	29	20	18	15
1–2 (good)	57	48	58	56	49
3+ (3–5: fair) (6+: poor)	17	23	22	26	36
Total no.	117	139	115	82	47

Source: Bernard Kutner et al., *Five Hundred over Sixty* (New York: 1956), p. 133 (Table 42)

The Grand Rapids study was far less precise on this point, but it found that 17.2 percent of its entire sample reported themselves free of chronic conditions, and 82.8 percent reported one or more. There was no age breakdown. Orthopedic (56 percent) and circulatory (44 percent) ailments headed the list within this group. Adding up the percentages reporting ailments of any kind (including the 38.4 percent citing poor eyesight and the 32 percent listing poor hearing; both of which are usually remediable to some extent), the average number of complaints per individual subject was three. The NORC study data on chronic condition incidence was out of line with that provided by the other two—only 24 percent of the sample reported having one or more such conditions. Moreover, using the indices of dependence and expenditure on health aids, Shanas and associates found only 21 percent admitting to the use of such aids and 33 percent reporting an outlay of cash connected with their health during the month preceding the survey. Perhaps the discrepancy between the NORC findings and those of the Michigan and New York surveys rested upon variant definitions of "chronic" conditions; in any case, the data, even with plenty of margin for upward revision, taken with that of the other two studies, were instructive.

How many of the elderly could be classified as "very sick"? By such criteria as number of ailments, days in bed, hospital visits, and medical services required, the New York City project so designated 17 percent of its sample (85), while the NORC reported that 17.3 percent, or 264 of its subjects could be identified as such. Based on self-reporting, the incidence of serious impairment was somewhat less, or just under 10 percent in each study. Another significant relationship was that existing between mobility and age. Did advancing years limit one's physical environment? In the Kip's Bay report, analysts eliminated the 23 percent reporting none and the 23 percent reporting three or more ailments, on the grounds that among the first group activity limitation would be abnormally low, and within the last, abnormally high. Of all those reporting one or two chronic conditions, 44 percent reported no serious curtailments of activity; 13 percent said that they were kept at home; 18 percent that physical activity was limited; 4 percent that social interaction was reduced; 13 percent that they could no longer work; and 8 percent that they were limited in all the above ways. The NORC researchers reported limitations from two viewpoints—that of the whole sample and that of the 408 (24 percent) reporting at least one chronic impairment.

RESTRICTION	PERCENT OF TOTAL	PERCENT OF IMPAIRED
Unable to work	9.6	40.7
Unable to go out without help	7.1	30.1
Kept to bed/wheelchair	4.9	20.8

Source: Ethel Shanas et al., *The Health of Older People: A Social Survey* (Cambridge, Mass.: 1961), p. 11 (Table 3).

The Grand Rapids survey also examined the mobility factor, adding a consideration of the criterion as a function of age.

RESTRICTION	TOTAL	65–69	Percent 70–74	75–79	80+
None	81.5	93.3	80.4	73.1	57.9
Confined to bed/house/ wheelchair	17.2	6.6	17.4	26.9	36.8
No information	1.3	0.0	2.1	0.0	5.3

Source: Woodrow W. Hunter and Helen Maurice, *Older People Tell Their Story* (Ann Arbor: 1953), p. 130

This project also included a note on self-reporting of the number of activities limited by health: 51.7 percent reported none; 45.7 said they had had to curtail at least one activity as a concession to health; and 2.7 percent gave no answer. The research report observed, in this context: "Nearly all . . . mentioned the fact that it was necessary to adjust activities to lessened physical strength and vigor. At the same time, most of them appeared to accept this adjustment as a natural concomitant of aging." Thus, although lessened vigor could be associated with old age, this association should not be expanded to include general and systematic limitations on activity.

Other random details turned up in the course of these investigations included an assessment of senility and advancing years. Using an unexplained three-criteria senility index developed by the Cornell Sociology Department for use in the earlier Elmira,

New York Mental Health Survey, the Kip's Bay project laid the groundwork for an alternative opinion as to the mental competency of the aged, even among the "very old."

CRITERIA (No.)	TOTAL	60–64	Percent 65–69	70–74	75+
0–1	74	79	80	71	66
2	20	15	15	23	28
3	6	6	5	6	6

Source: Kutner et al.: Five Hundred Over Sixty, p. 133 (Table 41).

Data from Grand Rapids suggested that older people, as individuals, did not assess their personal health as bad. Of the entire sample, 53 percent considered their health good; 33.8 percent felt it to be fair; and only 13.2 allowed that they were in poor health. Self-reporting as a function of age yielded the following information, flawed by the lumping of Fair and Poor together:

SELF-RATING	65–69	Percent 70–74	75–79	80+
Good	63.3	54.3	38.5	36.8
Poor/Fair	33.7	45.7	61.5	63.2

Source: Hunter and Maurice, Older People Tell Their Story, p. 14.

If self-reporting seemed at variance with popular notions about the health of the elderly, their sense of fatalism about degeneration was apparently in congruence with that of the larger society. The Grand Rapids survey asked its subjects to express an attitude on the improbability of health in old age. Sharing society's negativism on this point, only 24.5 percent said that health could be improved in the later years and 73.5 said that it could not; 2 percent expressed no opinion. This data disturbed the study's directors. "Actually," they wrote, "geriatricians and other medical experts maintain that much can be done to prevent illness and disability in old age and to rehabilitate those already disabled. There appears to be a need to educate older people to this philosophy and to implement ways to create better health during old age." Beyond this, however, all the evidence provided by these studies suggested that society consistently underrated the health of the aged. The Kip's Bay project called the health of older people "generally sound," though by no means free of minor ailments and major chronic complaints. Such ailments and complaints were not, however, nearly as disruptive to the life style of the older person as was popularly supposed. As Ethel Shanas put it in the conclusion to her NORC-sponsored study: "The American stereotype of the elderly—as sick, infirm, and indigent—is not validated by this study. These people look first to themselves and to their own resources, and then to the programs of the federal government for the means by which they may live out their lives in dignity and respect."[22]

N O T E S

1. The job of translating research findings into accessible information, as we will discuss in subsequent chapters, was most widely performed by educators, the media, marketers, social welfare agencies, and the business and labor communities.

2. Cowdry, *Problems of Aging*, Stieglitz quoted on p. 906; Kirk comments from the Macy Foundation's *Conference on the Problems of Aging, (September 7–8, 1951)* (New York: 1952), p. 55; "Aging, Mental Abilities and Their Preservation" in Lawton (ed.), *New Goals for Old Age* (New York: 1943), p. 29.

3. *Conference on the Problems of Aging: Transactions of the 10th and 11th Conferences, February 9–10, 1948 and April 25–26, 1949* (New York: 1950), p. 6; Stieglitz, "Aging, Today and Tomorrow" pp. 195–202, and Hillboe, "Geriatrics and Our Elderly," pp. 211–216, in the NYJSLC, *Birthdays Don't Count* (Albany: 1948); see also Stieglitz, "The Personal Challenge of Aging," in Tibbitts (ed.), *Living Through the Later Years* (1949).

4. FSA, *Man and His Years*, chap. 6, pp. 103–127; "Emotional Problems of the Aged," *American Journal of Public Health* 40 (September 1950): 1140–42. As we shall note in a subsequent chapter, activities in golden age clubs and centers were widely credited with reestablishing good health.

5. Bortz, "Geriatrics—New Light on Old Folks," *Clinics, Philadelphia*, I (1942), pp. 385bb.; "Geriatrics as a Specialty," in *Health in the Later Years: 3rd Annual Southern Conference on Gerontology, January 26–27, 1953*; "New Goals for Later Maturity," *Journal of Gerontology* 9 (1954): 67–73; Gumpert, "The Shock of Aging," *American Scholar* 19 (Winter 1949–Autumn 1950): 67–72; "Martin Gumpert—Geriatrician," *New Yorker* (June 10 and 17, 1950); also "New Developments in Geriatrics," in NYJSLC, *No Time to Grow Old* (1951), pp. 218–221; Crampton, "Medical Benefits and Aids at 40, 60 and 80," in NYJSLC, *Young at Any Age* (1950), pp. 118–120. A full list of Crampton's many articles on this subject can be found in Shock's *Classified Bibliography of Gerontology and Geriatrics*, 3 vols. (to 1961); Klumpp biography in

Survey 88 (May 1952): 228; "More Doctors Devote Full Time to the Aged," *Wall Street Journal* (January 12, 1961), 1:4.

6. Warren and Fremont-Smith comments in *Conference on Problems of Aging, September 7–8, 1951*, pp. 36–37; Shock, *Trends in Geronotology*, pp. 38–41; FSA, *Aging . . . A Community Problem* (Washington, D.C.: 1952).

7. Frank Hinman, M.D., "The Story of Old Age," *Journal of Geronotology*, 2 (1947): pp. 103–109; C. Fleming, "Needed—A Social Philosophy for Aging," *Geriatrics* 10 (1955): 549–551. A good, if technical summary of advances and objectives in geriatric medicine is Stieglitz' "The Relation of Gerontology to Clinical Medicine" in Macy Foundation, *Conference on Problems of Aging, February 6–7, 1950* (New York: 1950), pp. 113–139.

8. Stieglitz and Lawton quoted in Cowdry, *Problems of Aging*, 2nd ed.; Frank, "Gerontology," *Journal of Gerontology* 1 (1946): 1–11; on the growing importance of social science research, see the analysis of papers published between 1946 and 1948 in the *Journal*—18 biological, 9 clinical, 16 general, and 10 socioeconomic—see "Can Research on Aging Flourish?" ibid. 3 (1948): 141–142; Havighurst, "Our Aging Population—What does it Mean?" *Hygeia* 25 (1947): 799.

9. *12th Conference on the Problems of Aging, Feb. 6–7, 1950* (New York: 1950), pp. 11, 37, 42. Another interdisciplinary effort that has been treated in an earlier context was the 1950 FSA-sponsored National Conference on Aging, where representatives from numerous disciplines met to discuss new approaches to the problems of the aged.

10. Simmons, *The Role of the Aged . . .* (New Haven: 1947). The importance of Simmons' contribution to social gerontology may be gauged by the frequency with which his volume was cited in the monographs and articles on aging appearing during the 1950s and 1960s, and his lengthy contribution to the AAAPSS collection of 1952, vol. 279; and the 1960 *Handbook of Gerontology*, edited by Clark Tibbitts. Mead, "Cultural Context of Aging," in N.Y. Joint State Legislative Committee, *No Time to Grow Old* (Albany: 1951), pp. 49–51.

11. Riesman, "Some Clinical Aspects of Aging," *American Journal of Sociology* 59 (1953–1954): 379–383.

12. Ginzburg, "The Negative Attitude Toward the Elderly," *Geriatrics* 7 (1952): 297–302; Barron, "Minority Group Characteristics of the Aged in American Society," *Journal of Gerontology* 8 (1953): 477–482.

13. A good summary of gerontological reservations about Barron's model is Nathan Kogan, "Attitudes toward Old People," *Journal of Abnormal and Social Psychology* 62 (1961): 44–54.

14. Havighurst's comments from *14th Annual Conference on Aging, 1951* (New York: 1952), pp. 65–66, 70. Other attempts to relate social science concepts to gerontological theory include, L. F. Greenleigh, *Psychological Problems of our Aging Population* (NIMH; 1952); R. I. Watson, "The Personality of the Aged: A Review," and E. P. Mason, "Some Correlates of Self-Judgements of the Aged," in *Journal of Gerontology* 9 (1954): 309–315, 324–337, respectively; Tuckman and Lavell, "Self-Classification as Old or Not Old," *Geriatrics* 12 (1957): 666–671; R. W. Davis, "The Relationship of Social Preferability to Self-Concept in the Aged Population," *Journal of Gerontology* 17 (1962): 431–436; Leonard D. Egerman, "The Self-Image of the Aging Person," *Lutheran Social Welfare Quarterly* 3 (March 1963): 13–19; Rosalie H. Rosenfelt, "The Elderly Mystique," *Journal of Social Issues* 21 (October 1965): 37–43.

15. "Attitudes Toward Old People," *Journal of Social Psychology* 37 (1953): 249–260.

16. "The Best Years of Life: A Study in Ranking," *Journal of Psychology* 34 (1952): 137–149.

17. "Attitudes Toward Older Workers," *Journal of Applied Psychology,* 56 (1952), 149–153; "The Influence of Course on the Psychology of the Adult on Attitudes toward Older People and Older Workers," *Journal of Educational Psychology* 43 (1952): 400–407.

18. "Attitudes of Junior and Senior High School Students Toward Aging," in N.Y. State Legislative Committee, *Growing with the Years* (Albany: 1952), pp. 59–61; "The Effect of Family Environment on Attitudes Toward Old People and Older Workers," *Journal of Social Psychology* 38 (1953): 207–218.

19. Tuckman and Lorge, "Experts Biases Toward Older Workers," *Science* 115 (1952): 685–687; "Attitudes Toward Aging of Individuals with Experience with Aging," *Journal of Genetic Psychology* 92 (1958): 199–204; Arnhoff and Lorge, "Stereotypes about Aging and the Aged," *School and Society* 88 (1960): 70–71. Confirming, through personal experiences, the theory that exposure to the most hopeless cases among the aging tends to harden the disposition to see aging as irreversible loss are: Hugh Mullan, M.D., "The Personality of Those Who Care for the Aging," *The Gerontologist* 1 (1960): 42–50; Robert M. Butler, M.D., "The Healthy Aged versus the Cherished Stereotypes," *Geriatric Institutions* (January–February 1963) 8–10; Robert Kastenbaum, "The Reluctant Therapist," *Geriatrics* 18 (April 1963): 296–301.

20. See the articles of Drs. E. L. Bortz and Frank J. Sladen (medicine), E. W. Burgess (sociology), and Nathan W. Shock (biology) on the need for health maintenance centers in *Health in the Later Years: Third Annual Southern Conference on Gerontology* (Tallahassee: 1951); Breslow, "Aging and Community Health Programs," *Journal of Gerontology* 9 (1954): 224–227; see as well M. E. Linden, M.D., "Effects of Social Attitudes on the Mental Health of the Aging," *Geriatrics* 12 (1957): 109–114; and "Relationship between Social Attitudes Toward Aging and the Delinquencies of Youth," *American Journal of Psychiatry* 114 (July–December 1957): 444–448; all of these stress connection between social attitudes toward the health of the aging and the social/psychological situation of the aged.

21. Tuckman and Lorge, "Best Years of Life," *Journal of Psychology* 34: 137–149; "Attitudes toward Old People," *Journal of Social Psychology* 37: 249–260; "The Effect of Institutionalization on Attitudes Toward Old People," *Journal of Abnormal Psychology* 47 (1952): 337–344; with George Spooner, "The Effect of Family Environment . . . ," *Journal of Social Psychology* 38:207–218; "Attitudes . . . of Individuals with Experience with the Aged," *Journal of Genetic Psychology* 92:199–204.

22. Woodrow W. Hunter and Helen Maurice, *Older People Tell Their Story* (Ann Arbor: 1953); Bernard Kutner et al., *Five Hundred Over 60* (New York: 1956); Ethel Shanas et al., *The Health of Older People: A Social Survey* (Cambridge, Mass.: 1961); confirmatory, but less well-documented treatments of the issue include E. A. Confrey and M. S. Goldstein, "The Health Status of Older People," in Tibbitts (ed.), *Handbook of Social Gerontology* (1960); James W. Wiggins and Helmut Shoek, "A Profile of the Aging: USA," *Geriatrics* 16 (July 1961): 336–342.

4

Social Scientists and Images of the Aged: Providing the Basis for Action

We can, for ease of analysis, view the evolution of psychosocial theories of aging as a series of overlapping stages. In the first stage, spanning the years from 1945 to 1955, gerontology developed into a distinct discipline. During this time, its main concerns, beyond those associated with self-organization, included the promotion of interest in the subject, the publication of the problems and needs of the nation's elderly population, and the evolution of an initial set of concepts by which the social and psychological dislocations suffered by many older persons could be understood. A basically paternalistic philosophy characterized this early stage, probably necessarily so, given the early gerontologists' tendency to emphasize the "need" aspect of aging, especially in the realm of social services. There was little disagreement on policy among the prime movers within the movement. The theory and practice of gerontology changed very little during this time. The second period, roughly from 1955 into the early 60s, witnessed the first challenges to the dominance of the original generation of social gerontologists. During this period, some (mostly younger) practitioners, more oriented toward empirical observation and analysis of data and less given to *ex cathedra* pronouncement, placed more stress on the developmental capacities of the aged and showed more flexibility in their approach to the problems of aging. During this period of activity, they prepared the way for the upheaval that was to characterize the last of the three periods, which began in the early 60s and continues to this day. The publication of Cumming and Henry's *Growing Old: The Process of Disengagement* in 1961 released the creative internal tensions which only a heated debate over theory and practice could stimulate. The so-called "disengagement theory" proposed that the social withdrawal of the elderly, so much decried by gerontologists, was natural. Disengagement, Cumming, and Henry argued, facilitated the process of adjustment by conserving, through reduced social participation, the dwindling energies of the aging individual. In response, gerontological traditionalists charged that such a view merely rationalized a youth-worshipping society's inhumane rejection of the elderly and reiterated their contention that the best path to adjustment was one of continuing social participation. Out of this clash emerged one of the most hopeful developments in the evolution of social gerontology—the beginnings of the search for a positive and flexible model for explaining the process of aging. The "developmental field" gerontologists were in the forefront of this search. Relying upon Erik Erikson's description of the life cycle as a series of developmental stages, beginning with infancy and the establishment of "trust"—terminating in old age and the achievement of "integrity," the "developmental field" theorists sought to balance the conflicting claims of the "activity" (traditional) with "disengagement" schools and to synthesize the "truths" (the need for social roles versus the fact of biological loss) expressed so inflexibly by each. The undertaking of this search heralded, as we shall see, not only a new gerontological theory, but the development of a frame of mind among gerontologists which fostered closer ties between them and the action people in the fields of education, social work, labor, management, and so forth.

The most important source of funding and inspiration for gerontology in the pioneering (1945–1955) period was the Social Science Research Council, an umbrella group for representatives from the social sciences of history, economics, sociology, psychology, etc. According to its presidential report for 1946–1947, the Council had as its primary objective the investigation of social problems and the creation of proposals for their resolution. Indeed, SSRC leaders regarded the development of policy suggestions as the Council's sole legitimate concern. Yet, Council members complained, they increasingly found themselves in the business of applying as well as making policy, "because the positive results of social science research have not been adequately translated for immediate applications by administrators, social workers, and others who may be properly termed 'social engineers'." To aid in this "translation" and thus keep theoreticians out of the implementation effort, the Council sought the establishment of "channels of communication between scientists and practitioners sponsored . . . in universities and by such organizations as the Council, research institutions, and government agencies." In the field of gerontology, the Committee on Social Adjustment's subcommittee on Adjustment in Old Age provided such a channel of communication. The subcommittee was founded in 1943 to prepare an annotated bibliography of research contributions to the field of gerontology, develop new research methods and tools for use in the study of later maturity, and issue research planning reports on the subject. The first of these reports, Otto Pollak's interim statement on aging and social adjustment, was issued in 1946. The heavy demand for copies of this report "served to emphasize the need for intensifying and enlarging the scope of the Council's activity in this area." In response, the organization upgraded the Adjustment in Old Age subcommittee to full committee status in 1947.[1]

Pollak's *Social Adjustment in Old Age* (1948), along with Ruth S. Cavan, et al., *Personal Adjustment in Old Age* (1949), constituted the Council's main contributions toward establishing "conditions conducive to effective planning of research" in the field of aging.

Pollak's concern was an examination of the barriers to successful adjustment to aging erected by society, while Cavan and her associates studied the stresses which the later years imposed upon the individual. Together, these two volumes provided perhaps the best collection and evaluation of data available to pioneer gerontologists. They also made important conceptual contributions to the infant science of gerontology. Considering first Pollak's contribution, one of his major themes was the need to substitute functional for existing chronological definitions of old age. He argued that while age-based definitions of oldness lumped all people over a certain age into the same category, in fact, the various forms of social participation and the persistence of subgroup identifications made such monolithic groupings useless from an analytical point of view. Defining age as a series of changes, Pollak urged social scientists to discriminate among these social, physical, and psychological alterations and observe the ways in which older people responded to them, with special attention to the difficulties of adjustment that these problems posed. He called their attention as well to the usefulness of such social science concepts as social roles, social expectations, and status in helping to explain the variety of ways in which an individual might experience the process of aging. The adjustment of the older individual, Pollak declared, depended upon the number, type, acceptability, and mutual compatibility of the different social roles available to him. But society, not the individual, determined the range of social roles—and contemporary society systematically displaced the elderly from their homes and work places without providing replacement roles.[2]

An important institution from which society more and more tended to exclude the elderly, he pointed out, was the family. The family structure provided the basic social roles of mate, parent, and provider or helpmeet. The aging individual's eventual loss of these roles owing to changes wrought by time in his immediate environment and his person would be traumatic under the best of circumstances. They were doubly disruptive, he continued, given society's failure to provide replacement roles.

This failure was brought into sharp relief by the loosening up of traditional family ties, a phenomenon reflective of the decreasing number of children per family, the replacement of the extended nuclear family by the conjugal family unit, and the heightened geographic mobility of offspring. Researchers, Pollak felt, ought to concentrate upon investigating the origins of filial responsibility and describing the degree of change in its influence, and the effect of changes upon the self-image of the older person.

Besides the family, of nearly equal importance in modern industrial cultures, Pollak examined the institution of work. Beyond earning income, occupations provided men and increasing numbers of women with senses of social identity, meaningful ways of passing time, and feelings of personal satisfaction as contributing members of society. Depriving the individual of access to such vital sources of self-esteem posed serious social and emotional problems. Here again, modern society not only deprived the older person of the occupational role, but did so by channelling him into an essentially roleless state called "retirement." The most immediate solution to this situation, Pollak felt, involved an expansion of employment opportunities for older workers. The emergence of retirement as a fact of the life cycle, however, indicated that, in the long run, researchers would need to explore the factors influencing adjustment to the workless state, how to predict an individual's reaction to the loss of an occupational role, and what interventions—financial and psychological—might help to ease the adjustment process.

Finally, in addition to the institutions of family and work, Pollak noted, aging affected the participation of individuals in a number of lesser areas, like recreational opportunities, education, politics, and religion. In these spheres, stereotypical notions of older people as sedentary, unteachable, conservative, and prone to orthodoxy operated against easy or comfortable adjustments to advancing age. Obviously, the elimination of such stereotypes would have to be made a priority matter. He thus urged social scientists, in partnership with biological researchers, to begin working on the development of reliable indices of age-related human capacity. With such indices available, a realistic appraisal of the adaptive capabilities of the aging person would at last be possible, and the popular inclination to base expectations of older people upon stereotype and negative bias could be ended. The consequent raising of social expectations would permit expansion in the number of meaningful social roles available to those outside the traditional family setting and/or in retirement. Through the act of providing such roles, he concluded, society could best ensure each person the opportunity to adjust successfully to later years.

Personal Adjustment in Old Age by Ruth S. Cavan, E. W. Burgess, R. J. Havighurst, and H. Goldhammer, served as the companion to Pollak's "research planning report," in that it designed and tested tools to assist in the kind of investigations that his volume suggested. In the preface, Cavan and her collaborators addressed the volume to four different groups: social researchers; those "engaged in services to the aged;" educators and students in disciplines with gerontological aspects; and members of the general public (especially older persons) concerned with the problems of aging and interested in the ways new research methods could help solve them. The key concept of the book, as the title indicated, was "personal adjustment," which the authors defined as "the reorientation of the attitudes and behavior of the person to meet the requirements of a changed situation." The key assumption was that, because of the association of aging with loss, the "reorientation" process demanded by the onset of old age was peculiarly difficult. To illuminate this difficulty and to determine its origin, they proposed the use of such socio-psychological concepts as "adjustment," "mobility," "aspiration," "frustration," and "expectation." Society at large and the peer group formulated expectations governing the behavior of the elderly according to a view of aging that tended to stress its degenerative aspects. Like Pollak, Cavan and her colleagues argued that research and action in the field should be geared to an appreciation of this relationship between social expectation and stereotype, fueled by a recognition that such a relationship ill-served the cause of personal adjustment.[3]

Unlike Pollak, who restricted himself to theorizing and suggesting empirical testing of his ideas, the authors of *Personal Adjustment in Old Age* rested their case heavily on observation and recording of the adjustment process exhibited within a sample of older people—499 men, median age 73.5 and 759 women, median age 71.4. Cavan and associates started from the premise that any judgment of the capacity for personal adjustment in the later years would have to be based on a knowledge of each individual's lifelong capacity for adjustment; the changes in roles and status which aging provoked and the nature of personal reactions to them; the breakdown of "habit systems" and the difficulty or ease of constructing new ones; the tendency toward the liberation of suppressed desires, increased in later life by the lapsing of the restraints formerly imposed by familial, social, or occupational position; and the degree to which loss of physical mobility contracted one's social world. Using this approach in their study of the sample population, the research team posited four basic "adjustment cycles" as characteristic of the aged. The first was good adjustment in adult life continuing into old age without a break; the second was a readjustment after a minimum of maladjustment (the duration of the maladjustment period depended upon the gradualness of change and the care with which it was prepared for); the third involved a longer, more difficult period of maladjustment, with readjustment gradually achieved; and the fourth offered only continuing isolation and maladjustment. The obvious next questions were what determined the adjustment pattern that an aging person exhibited, how could such patterns be predicted, and what could be done beforehand to promote good adjustment—forestall maladjustment.

Cavan and her colleagues could not answer these questions, but they did develop two potentially useful tools for measuring and predicting individual adaptive capacities—the "Attitude" and "Activity" inventories. Having come to the study lacking any "valid and reliable measure of adjustment," and with the full knowledge that previous inquiries had typically used vague terms like "happiness" or "adjustment," their aim from the outset was to put the measurement of personal adjustment upon a more precise and scientific footing. The two inventories represented the partial fulfillment of this aim. The "Attitude Inventory" consisted of a battery of 100 statements, ten each under the headings; Health, Family, Friends, Leisure, Organizations, Work, Security, Religion, Usefulness, and Happiness, evaluated by a panel of psychologists and weighted on a scale from most negative to most positive. The objective criteria for formulating these statements were (1) satisfaction with activities and status (2) general happiness and (3) feelings of usefulness. The "Activity Inventory" was a battery of 19 questions dealing with various areas of social involvement and offering choices as to the degree of involvement available under each. The uses for these two inventories, according to their developers, were fourfold. First, they would be valuable in gaining insight into the social aspects of aging (i.e., the degrees and kinds of social participation desired by the statuses, roles available to persons over sixty, and their attitudes toward these roles) and into what factors influence them. Second, they could provide a realistic, objective assessment of the efficaciousness of programs and policies designed to improve the situation of the elderly. Third, the completion of these inventories provided a basis for diagnosis of individual adjustment chances, and if necessary, for the preparation of an appropriate counseling program designed to improve those chances. Fourth as model instruments for measuring personal adjustments, these inventories laid the foundation for continuing attempts to revise and perfect such vitally needed instruments.

Though first, in point of time, the SSRC was not the only such organized effort investigating the problems of the aged nor the only agency attempting to bring to bear on these problems the varying but complementary skills of the social sciences. The University of Michigan's Institute for Human Adjustment under the joint direction of Wilma Donahue and Clark Tibbitts was another important contributor to the growing institutional interest in social gerontology. The Institute's basic concern—adult education services administered through the University's extension program—led it quite naturally into the field of aging. Between 1949 and 1951, the Institute published three volumes on aging, attesting to its interest in the problems of older Americans and in promulgating proposals for their solution to practitioners in gerontological specialties. The appearance of this series was an expression of the convictions of Tibbitts, Donahue, and their Institutional associates: (1) that the negative concept of old age held by society at large had resulted in the exclusion of the elderly from many significant social roles and activities; (2) that this unwarranted exclusion of the elderly, in turn, caused maladjustment by denying to them any opportunity to fulfill their basic needs and drives; (3) that the aged, as a group, were more alert and capable than society believed; and (4) that progress toward the goal of facilitating personal and social adjustment to aging depended upon awakening everyone to the nature and extent of the problems so that individual and community could take the necessary actions to solve them.[4]

The University of Michigan trilogy was less technical and much more accessible to the lay reader than the SSRC adjustment volumes. Thus, while Pollak and Cavan, as representatives of the SSRC, addressed themselves chiefly to fellow social scientists, The University of Michigan Institute, as part of the school's extension program, had a somewhat more general aim, and a less specific view of its mission. The University of Michigan's contributions employed the essay format, including contributions by doctors, psychiatrists, educators, and social scientists of both the theoretical and practical stripe. By concentrating on social rather than personal origins of adjustment problems in old age, the various writers emphasized their belief in the reversibility of many of the conditions which led to difficulty of adjustment. As E. W. Burgess, a University of Chicago sociologist and collaborator with Cavan on her SSRC volume, flatly put it in a 1949 contribution, society was maladjusted to its older population, rather than vice versa. The social origins of maladjustment, all agreed, rested chiefly upon the general lack of understanding of the aging process as a biological and psychological phenomenon. The replacement of myth and stereotype by fact based on solid research data constituted the (sometimes unjustified, in view of the paucity of empirical observation) *raison d'etre* for each of the three publications. Contributors from both the biomedical and social science field, for example, attacked all chronological definitions of age as unrealistic in view of the broad range of biological, psychological, and social changes which such a unitary criterion had to encompass. Some chose to emphasize the cultural, economic, and social bases of adjustment difficulty and variously offered plans to attack these sources within the political and social sphere—improved housing design, anti-discrimination legislation, increased OASDI benefits, or educational activities. Others discussed ways in which working with the individual—through casework services, counseling rehabilitation, recreational programs, psychotherapy—could help facilitate adjustment. Whether concentrating on external or internal factors, the overall message of the University's Institute for Human Adjustment was clear—the problems of adjustment could be dealt with; they did not, in most cases, originate in the pathology of aging; and once these views were accepted, social expectations (the foundations of personal adjustment toward old age) could be altered, and the elderly reintegrate into society.[5]

At about the same time, the Industrial Relations Research Association, an interdisciplinary organization of social and medical scientists, sponsored a "research symposium" entitled *The Aged and Society*. Following The University of Michigan format of collecting papers of interest, the editorial board of J. Douglas Brown, Clark Kerr, and Edwin Witte compiled a volume of essays generally treating the issue of employment and aging. Organized into sections focusing on (1) the new age distribution in the modern industrial society (2) the position of the older worker in that society and (3) the kinds of research and research tools needed to change the employment status of the elderly, the published symposium reviewed the rolelessness of the aged in industrial society and their weak position in the labor market, with the aid of social science data and techniques. The various contributors treated the economics of aging in terms of the personal and social adjustment process (E. W. Burgess), the need for methodological tools (N. W. Shock), the mental health angle (O. Kaplan), and medical-social aspects of aging (J. H. Sheldon) and related them all to the problem of unemployment.[6]

The American Academy of Political and Social Sciences, which devoted its January 1952 edition of the *Annals* to *Social Contributions by the Aging,* provided another example of a social science research institute venturing into the field of aging. As the volume's editor, Clark Tibbitts, declared, its purpose was "to present an inventory of the characteristics of aging people, to assess their potentialities for further integration in community life, and to examine the conditions essential to maintain such integration." All the contributors, Tibbitts observed, accepted the "underlying philosophy . . . (a) that there are positive roles for aging and aged people through which they can make valuable contributions to American society, and (b) that these roles offer opportunity for continued, if not increased, individual satisfaction in later years." What was needed, and what this volume of essays hoped to foster, he continued, was "a new concept of aging . . . that gives recognition to the positive as well as the negative aspects of maturation." Noting that much of the biomedical pessimism about conditions associated with aging had been eliminated by research findings, he asserted that "social attitudes that define aging are clearly susceptible of change" as well. The composition of the AAPSS effort followed the basic pattern for such compilations, including contributions on the sociopsychological needs of older people and its effect upon his personal adjustment (Havighurst), the physiobiological changes of aging (Drs. A. J. Carlson and E. J. Stieglitz), the psychological alterations (O. Kaplan), and the cultural origins of the modern situation (L. W. Simmons). Other essayists talked about aging from the points of view of labor and labor relations, education, and social welfare. Society's capacity, as well as its responsibility to facilitate personal adjustment to old age, provided the familiar organizational theme for the collection. As Havighurst stated in his essay on the sociopsychological needs of the elderly: "In modern America, the community must carry the responsibility for creating conditions that make it possible for the great majority of older people to lead the independent and emotionally satisfying lives of which they are capable."[7]

Besides these autonomous or quasi-autonomous research centers, the academy, as a research institution, exhibited increasing interest in research on the social implications of an aging population. In 1950, for example, the Rockefeller Foundation awarded a grant to Cornell University for a study of social adjustment of a New York City sample of over-sixties, noting that "research on the problems of old age has generally been concerned with the medical and economic aspects; an equally important aspect of the aging process is the adjustment of human relations when family, friends, community and work are all subject to more or less drastic change." The foundation looked forward to the production of a report which it expected would provide "a realistic picture of how old people living in social groups, meet the problems of old age and how the community seeks to meet these same problems." A year later, the foundation awarded two more grants in the field of aging, one to The University of Chicago for an investigation of the meaning of work in the lives of a sample of retired persons and the development of new retirement practices; the other, to the University of California–Berkeley for a study of the political and economic aspects of aging, with a special interest in finding usable physical and psychological measurements of age to replace the usual reliance on chronological measurement. Additionally, the University of Florida's newly founded Institute of Gerontology sponsored the First Annual Southern Conference on Gerontology in March 1951, and published the proceedings thereof as *The Problems of America's Aging Population*. This conference discussed at length the need for more data on the process of successful adjustment to old age and for an alternative to chronology as the measure of age. All told, according to Shock's *Trends in Gerontology* (1957 ed.), between the late 1940s and mid-1950s, similar institutes were established by five universities (not counting The University of Michigan), either as interdisciplinary entities or within their medical schools or social science divisions. The aim of these academic undertakings was probably best put by the directors of one Russell Sage foundation-funded study carried out by the Sociology, Anthropology, and Public Health Departments of Cornell: "Social research as a tool in the hands of practitioners can lend great weight to decisions concerning proper courses of action in the development, modification and evaluation of services and programs in the field of aging."[8]

In addition to the research centers and universities, certain professional organizations and government agencies carried out and disseminated the results of their researches in the field of aging. The Gerontological Society, founded in 1945, and the medically-oriented American Geriatrics Society, founded shortly thereafter, are the two most obvious examples of professionally organized interest in research on aging. Through their journals, the *Journal of Gerontology* and *Journal of the American Geriatrics Society,* these organizations indicated a growing awareness that many of the problems of old age were rooted as much in socio-cultural as in biological conditions. The increasing numbers of articles based on social research in both periodicals were suggestive of this emergent sensitivity. The American Psychological Association organized a Division on Maturity and Old Age in 1946 through which it channeled research in gerontological psychology and informed members of the profession of advances and findings in the field. An indication of the variety of research sponsored by the APA is provided by the symposium held in 1956 on the psychological aspects of aging. This meeting reviewed the literature accumulated in the field over the previous few years, with special reference to findings in the areas of personal and social adjustment, and the assessment of age based upon such indices as perceptive/intellective capacities, learning motivation and educability, functional efficiency and skills, and employability. In 1951, the federal government moved formally into gerontological research as well by establishing a section on aging under the aegis of the National Institutes of Mental Health.

Shortly thereafter, the institutes published, under the authorship of Dr. L. J. Greenleigh, a volume on the problems of aging which argued that social attitudes reflected a consistent underestimation of the capacities of older people and pointed up the negative influence upon aging of such remediable, nonbiological conditions as existing social and self-concepts, contraction of social world, loss of occupational function, and the failure of society to provide alternative roles for the elderly.[9]

Such, briefly, were the institutional sources of social research in gerontology. But institutions are often little more than collections of individuals seeking to accomplish as a group something beyond the capacity of disjointed and isolated efforts. The increasing recognition of the interrelatedness of the biological, medical, and sociopsychological aspects of aging in the postwar era quite naturally governed the shape taken by the institutions. But it was the people associated with these institutions that gave them their convictions and inclinations—and the people consistently mentioned in connection with such institutions were actually few in number. The backbone of this social gerontology group included Nathan W. Shock, Clark Tibbitts, Lawrence K. Frank, R. J. Havighurst, E. W. Burgess, Ruth Cavan, and Wilma J. Donahue. There is a remarkable similarity of background among these seven immediate postwar leaders which may account for their generally monolithic agreement and approach to the problems of aging. In 1950, their ages ranged from forty-four to sixty-four, with 4 of them clustered around the fifty-year mark, 1, fourty-seven, 2, fifty and 1, fifty-four. All save 1, were midwestern-born, with Illinois (2), Indiana (1), Ohio (2), and Iowa (1) represented. And despite varying professional specialties—physiology, sociology, education, and public administration—5 of this group were affiliated at one time or another, either as student or teacher, with The University of Chicago. The two exceptions—Donahue and Frank—were associated with the others by virtue of their positions with The University of Michigan Institute for Human Adjustment and the Macy Foundation, respectively. Of the group, 6 belonged to the Gerontological Society from its inception in 1945, with 4—Frank, Burgess,

Havighurst, and Shock—having served one year terms as president of that organization at one time or another. Of them, five participated during this period in the Macy Foundation conferences, while 4 each claimed membership in the American Sociological Association and 3 more belonged to the Maturity and Old Age Division of the American Psychological Association. In addition, 4 of them had been elected fellows of The American Academy of Arts and Sciences. There can be little doubt that contact between these pioneer architects of gerontological policy was frequent and of long duration. The constancy of this contact—especially that centered in The University of Chicago— lent the sort of continuity of thought necessary to the emergence of gerontology as a distinct discipline.[10]

From the outset, these theoreticians subscribed to certain notions about the old, which came to be known as "activity theory." In the long run, they may have become overly committed to this theory and allowed it to degenerate into dogma. But in the early stages of the movement, this uniformity of opinion was vital to the awakening of interest in gerontology. Proponents of "activity" theory felt that an individual's age depended upon how society allowed him to act, as well as upon the calendar. The role deprivations which accompanied advancing years and the constriction of the older person's sphere of social action that these deprivations brought about, they argued, tended to "age" an individual. As The University of Chicago sociologist E. W. Burgess put it: "There are two conceptions held both by older people and by society. The traditional notion is that people should accept the inevitable and grow old gracefully. The modern conception, however, is that old age is not chronological. It is rather psychological in that a person is as young as he feels. It is also sociological in that a person is as young as he acts." In most cases, Burgess was saying, senescence could be put off by providing people with an environment in which they could act and feel "young", well into chronological "old age." "Activity" school adherents proposed that the ideal social environment for them include housing that did not segregate them from younger population groups, equal employment opportunities, and ready

111

access to cultural, educational, and recreational institutions and services.[11]

Such views dominated the 1950 National Conference on Aging, sponsored by the Federal Security Administration. For example, a view of work as an emotional necessity dictated the Conference's opposition to retirement, rather than acceptance of it as a social fact and commitment to facilitation of the retirement adjustment process. Wilbur Cohen, of the Federal Security Administration's staff, exemplified this attitude within the government. As a participant in the September 1951 Annual Conference on Aging, sponsored by the Macy Foundation, Cohen traced the exclusionary treatment of older workers by the labor market to the $15 monthly wage ceiling imposed on those over sixty-five by the Social Security Act. He named this restriction as responsible for the idea that the most positive economic contribution an older person could make was to give up his job to a younger man and declared that the recent elevation of the ceiling to $50 per month evidenced a new governmental "emphasis on the contribution which the aged may make to the national economy by work, and the contribution which work may make to the welfare of the aged." The Committee on Aging and Geriatrics of the FSA seconded Cohen's remarks in a 1952 pamphlet, calling increased employment opportunities the "most crying need" of older people and attacking fixed retirement as a "severe hardship" both economically and emotionally. "For the vast majority," the Committee asserted, "the chance to work—to have useful and gainful employment so long as health and strength permit—is the key to a happy, unfrustrated old age." This kind of pleading, while promoting the idea, based on biochemical evidence that most older workers were physically and mentally capable of working well past the common retirement age seemed, at least by implication, to deny them a similar capacity for adjustment to life in retirement. In subsequent chapters, we shall look at the various means by which the latent capacity for adjustment of the retired was cultivated; for the present we shall concentrate on how the basic uniformity of opinion among social gerontologists tended to prevent consideration, except among a few, of this potential among the aged and retired.[12]

The "activity" school of gerontology was also very insistent upon the need for mixed-age housing environments in which the aged could "see perambulators as well as hearses." Isolation of the elderly in age-segregated housing projects, according to the Housing Committee of the American Public Health Association, had an emotionally destructive effect upon them. As Lewis Mumford explained it in an architectural journal, such an effect was produced when the elderly were separated "from the presence of their families, their neighbors, and their friends . . . from their normal interests and responsibilities, to live in desolate idleness, relieved only by the presence of others in a similar plight." The use of such value-laden words as "desolate idleness" and "plight," and the assumptions that older people had a defined set of "interests and responsibilities," and assured places in the family and community, were used to argue against the creation of senior communities. As we shall see in greater detail in a later chapter, such gerontological arguments justified the reluctance of the construction industry to move into the old age housing market. Private developers tended to regard the elderly as a group with poor economic prospects and to shy away from treating them as a market. Not even the comparative cheapness of standardized old age housing complexes, when measured against the costs of building more complicated mixed-age environments favored by gerontologists, seemed attractive to profit-oriented private builders. The ascendency of "activity" theory made it easy for them to ignore the aged as a potential housing market by rejecting the first alternative as unprofitable and the second as unwise.[13]

The financial community abetted the reluctance of private builders by adopting a discriminatory loan policy against older persons. Lenders asked larger down payments of older buyers, placed greater emphasis on amount of annual income, often demanded pledges of assets to ensure full repayment if the debtor died before his repayment schedule was completed and, in some cases the cosignature of children. Adding yet another dimension to lender indisposition, a spokesman for the National Saving and Loan League evoked the gerontological distaste for age-segregated housing by making public the League's refusal to consider loan applications for the purchase of such housing. The public sector (state and federal governments) had not as yet become involved on a large scale in underwriting public housing and was probably sensitive to charges of "socialism" leveled against such proposed interventions in the housing market by organizations like the National Association of Home Builders. Thus, official agencies in Washington and in the various state capitals tended to echo sentiments about the social undesirability of age-segregated housing and to accept the refusal of private builders to undertake mixed-age complexes on the grounds of unprofitability. The net result of this collective reluctance was that, with the exception of a few, apparently successful (according at least to their sponsors) age-specific projects created by private agencies, municipalities, and a few adventurous private builders (i.e., the Upholsterers' Union complex in Florida, a public housing project in Waltham, Massachusetts and "Youngtown," a private builder's senior village in Arizona), no construction efforts aimed at providing housing for the elderly were being undertaken. One of the chief barriers to this much needed construction program continued to be gerontological arguments against the most economically feasible and (according to a Florida survey of the older citizens by the State Improvement Commission) and increasingly desirable (45%) housing alternative—the "senior citizen" development.[14]

The thinking of gerontologists on these two key sample issues—retirement and housing—provides examples of how consensus limited innovative policy making. The lack of internal disagreement, while it lent authority to their pronouncements, blinded them to certain alternative interpretations of the mounting sociological and psychological data on older people and their abilities, desires, and needs. Such policy making could come only with the evolution of new schools of social gerontology, and the challenges they posed to classical gerontological thought on these and other issues. Out of such a conflict would come compromise, experimentation, and modification of social policy and, in general, a more flexible and fruitful approach. Conflict would force contending parties into the field to do more research by way of supporting their theoretical speculations. The result would be not only more considered assessment of policy but increasingly greater amounts of empirical data upon which to generalize.

Social gerontology had arisen initially to challenge society's neglectful attitudes toward, and stereotypical concepts of, the older person. Now, nearly ten years after the founding of the Gerontological Society, sociologist C. Fleming voiced disappointment with the contributions of the social sciences, particularly sociology, to progress in the field. This unimpressive showing, he asserted, derived from the lack of a "critical, synthesizing, and interpretive . . . social philosophy" to guide the evolution of theory. That no such "interpretive social philosophy" was developed, one could argue, stemmed from the absence of debate among gerontologists about different ways of approaching what Fleming called a "major social change." Yet, as we shall see in subsequent chapters on marketing and retirement planning, even as Fleming expressed these sentiments, younger members of the profession were beginning to raise questions about some of the more enduring pieties of gerontological dogma. The idea that retirement was bad for the average individual, for example, came under attack, as did the notion that older people were only happy when residing in age-mixed environments. And the emergence of these young turks had a modifying influence on existing theory.[15]

The best gauge of the effects of this *arriviste* school of criticism can be found in the *Handbook of Gerontology,* edited by Clark Tibbitts, which appeared in 1960. In it certain attitudes were quietly dropped, even by those long associated with them, and new interpretations were set forth by those younger gerontologists invited to contribute essays to the volume. A comparison of the *Handbook* with the earlier cited University of Michigan trilogy issued during 1949–1951, offers a good indication of the change. One of the founding figures of social gerontology, Wilma Donahue, long an opponent of involuntary retirement, showed in her contribution to the *Handbook* that she had been influenced by the work of the younger thinkers and researchers on the meanings of retirement. From a somewhat negative assessment of the capacity of the healthy, active older person to adjust to life in retirement, Donahue had come to the conclusion that the provision of alternate social roles for the elderly, so long as they were "meaningful," could make departure from the working world relatively painless. Gordon Streib and Wayne Thompson, more recent entrants into the field of aging, attempted to assess the place of the aged within the family structure. They suggested that older people were not, as frequently supposed, dissatisfied with their intrafamilial position and that family situation was not that important a source of maladjustment in old age. Numerous attitude surveys, they argued, showed that older people, in fact, accepted the modern "conjugal family" as norm. Older people did not make claims upon the family based upon outmoded notions about its structure. However, many gerontological professionals still used the extended family as a reference point and assumed that the elderly did so as well. This warped their conclusions, although certain aspects of "activity" theory persisted unchallenged. Thus, E. A. Friedmann, an associate of Havighurst at The University of Chicago, attacked the tendency toward residential segregation of the elderly as expensive if done right and discriminatory if done improperly. He insisted that segregation robbed society of valuable physical and economic resources—though he did not follow this assertion through by examining society's willingness to make use of such "resources." University of Minnesota Professor of Architecture, Water K. Vivrett, writing on housing and community settings, continued the traditional gerontological insistence upon the need for heterogeneous communities—that is, age-mixed environments—even though he expressed familiarity with recent studies which suggested "that homogeneity (aims, objectives, and common interests) of the social structure fosters good adjustment of the group and its members." These assertions stemmed from the "activity" school's conviction that older people were not appreciatively different in needs and capacities from younger people, and to treat them differently was to do both them and society a grave disservice. It was an idea that died hard.[16]

Obviously, if these pet theories and durable pieties were ever to be challenged, someone would have to introduce an element of controversy into the field. Elaine Cumming and William Henry provided this source of contention in 1961 with the publication of *Growing Old: The Process of Disengagement.* The idea of "disengagement," as propounded by these two gerontologists, directly countered the "activity" school's central assumptions about the process of aging. Basically, Cumming and Henry proposed that much of the social withdrawal associated with aging was not, as gerontologists had traditionally insisted, imposed upon them by a hostile society. It might well be, they suggested, that observed decreases in social interaction as a function of age were as much the result of internal (individual) inclination as of external (societal) pressures. Their alternative hypothesis as to the origins of social withdrawal in later life proceeded from what they considered some serious omissions and misconceptions fostered by the adherents of "activity" theory. For one thing, they felt that current theory tended to ignore the fact of approaching death. It was unreasonable to avoid this subject, Cumming and Henry argued, because of its undoubtedly profound influence upon the way an individual responded to his social environment. Similarly, they challenged the professionally popular notion that older people wanted to meet the "usefulness" criteria appropriate to earlier stages of life (i.e., producer, parent, friend, member of the community, etc.) and disputed the traditional gerontological representation of the later years as lonely, fearful, and replete with unfulfilled needs for social contact and involve-

117

ment. They did not deny that society sanctioned this with-drawal—the adoption of the institution of retirement, for example, was such a sanction. They felt, however, that this fact did not preclude the possibility that the aging individual also approved the withdrawal process; that he or she might even initiate it at certain levels.[17]

To investigate the potential of the "disengagement" thesis, Cumming and Henry assembled a sample of white, middle, and working class residents of Kansas City, aged fifty to seventy (with a small additional number of subjects over eighty), all of whom were in good health. Probing this sample by means of questionnaires and direct interview techniques over a period of several years, Cumming, Henry, and their associates concen-trated upon observing the degree of social interaction, including the number of social contacts, the amounts of time they con-sumed, and their purposes. Specifically, this involved counting the number of roles actively filled by the subject—householder, kinsman, friend, neighbor, worker, etc.—and noting any changes which appeared to relate to advancing years. To determine whether age brought with it personality changes designed to encourage an individual to participate voluntarily in the with-drawal/exclusion process, Cumming and Henry tested their sub-jects against the "authoritarianism" scale developed by T. W. Adorno et al. in *The Authoritarian Personality*. Finally. they em-ployed Thematic Apperception Tests (captioned pictures about which the subject was asked to tell a story) to gain insight into the ego structure of the aged, for the orientation of the aged individual's ego was crucial to their theory. If they could show a turning inward as characteristic of later life, they could claim strong support for "disengagement" theory.

The results of Cumming and Henry's role-count among their sample came as no surprise. Role loss was associated with ad-vancing years. Survey data from questionnaires and interviews showed that between fifty and sixty-four, role involvement re-mained constant in number and intensity; but after sixty-five—the socially defined beginning of old age—such involvement lessened precipitously. They also found that, in terms of impact made upon the aging individual, the intensity of social interaction decreased and that, on a monthly basis, the number of "significant social encounters" (that is, the most intense ones) dropped off sharply. Of themselves, these findings tended to support what gerontologists had always assumed to be the case. Further findings, and Cumming and Henry's interpretation of them, provided the fundamental challenges to "activity" theory. Thus, after sixty-five, the people in their sample increasingly tended to define friendship as a "helping" rather than a "social" relation. This, Cumming and Henry suggested, constituted a self-imposed limitation upon the number and quality of such relationships. Nor did the behavior of subjects over sixty-five appear to be impelled by the same motives—social approval, love, and so forth—which had governed it in earlier life. Indeed, there was every indication that with advancing years behavior became increasingly inner-directed. To document this alleged inner-directedness, Cumming and Henry measured their subjects against the "authoritarianism" scale. Results indicated that older people (those over sixty-five) tended to exhibit narrowness, rigidity of outlook, and egocentricity. Besides being facets of the very stereotype which the gerontological profession had been assailing for years, these qualities were the foundations of the inner-directed personality. To buttress this argument, the two researchers took advantage of earlier studies utilizing Thematic Apperception Tests which gave insight into the ego structure of the aging. The TAT results for men aged sixty to seventy-one clustered in the analytical categories of "passive coping" and "inner retreat," thus adding support to the Cumming and Henry contention that the elderly were more inclined to accommodate themselves to a given environment than younger people, whom, tests showed, were more likely to seek alterations in the environment. TAT results of older female subjects, the surveyors conceded, showed stronger nonaccommodative urges than those for men, but they offered no explanation for this datum.

Basically, all the data compiled by the various survey techniques enabled Cumming and Henry to build upon the "disengagement" concept. Older people, their evidence suggested, tended to be more responsive to inner than to outer stimulation; to withdraw from emotional involvement; to renounce assertive involvement; and to avoid challenges. Cumming and Henry's simultaneous assessments of morale—which gerontologists of all camps agreed was the key to successful aging—drawn from questionnaire and interview material, found it highest among the fully "engaged" (married, working, usually under sixty-five) and the fully "disengaged" (single, nonworking, over sixty-five) portions of their sample, and lower among those in the two intermediate levels of partial disengagement. Thus, they argued, poor adjustment in old age was, in the average case, a temporary and unavoidable consequence of the disengagement process, rather than a response to the fact of aging itself. After discussing the differences in the disengagement process as a function of the sex role (i.e., homemaker versus provider), they focused on their very old (over eighty) sample. The chief characteristics of this fully disengaged group, Cumming and Henry reported, were contentment, tranquillity, stability of status, acceptance of the nearness of death, pride in their agedness, and high morale. From this, they generalized that as life satisfaction depended upon high morale, so among the aging, high morale depended upon the degree of disengagement achieved. Hence, satisfaction (or "good adjustment" in gerontological terminology) was the product of fully completed disengagement.

Disengagement theory, though well argued and not unsupported by substantive data, was hardly conclusive as a repudiation of the "activity" school of thought. Moreover, it labored under the handicap of seeming often, if unintentionally, reactionary in the support it provided for the exclusionist tendencies of modern industrial society. But it was an alternative theory nonetheless. As psychologist Robert Kastenbaum put it in a 1965 article: "Disengagement enjoys the advantage of having started its own tradition, and the further advantage of being the first conceptual framework developed especially for application to psychosocial aspects of aging." He noted that the theory's appearance immediately plunged the gerontological community into what he called the "disengagement years," during which its concepts "were hastily embraced by some, as hastily condemned by others, talked about by virtually everyone, [and] seriously explored by few." The emergence of an alternative view of the aging process—regardless of its validity—contributed an element heretofore lacking within the small, ingrown group of social scientists. If at times the debate became polemical, it also motivated a certain amount of solid empirical research and some deep rethinking of once unassailable positions.[18]

Overall, disengagement theory never found many uncritical defenders within the profession. Most empirical tests succeeding its publication reported finding little, if any, support for the Cumming and Henry formulation. Mark Zborowski of the Age Center of New England, for example, in a pair of articles in the *Journal of Gerontology* during 1962, reported that his surveys of the recreational habits and preferences, and of general social participation, (with Lorraine Eyde) of a sample of 204 men and women (aged fifty-one to ninety-two, median age, sixty-nine) drawn from the Center's members, showed no disposition among older people to disengage. Zborowski summed up his research with a quote from one of his subjects, a seventy-year-old woman: "I am holding onto life with both hands, but I feel that as life goes on, society pries loose one finger after another." George L. Maddox of Duke University Medical School's Department of Psychiatry, also rejected disengagement. On the basis of a three-year inventory of activities and attitudes of a sample of 250 North Carolina residents aged sixty to ninety-four, with a median age of seventy, Maddox found no evidence to convince him of the validity of disengagement theory. In fact, the working hypothesis of his study—that activity bore positively on morale in old age—offered perhaps the best indication of his own attitude toward the new theory. Although allowing that there was more—good health, for example—to the maintenance of high morale in the later years than simply keeping up social contacts or staying busy, he nonetheless staunchly contended: "Reported activity is a positive correlate of morale among the aging." Psychologist Paul Cameron, in a 1967 investigation of "happiness" (defined as "a preponderance of moods of happiness over moods of sadness") as a function of age among a 320 subject sample, one-half of them aged and other half young, explicitly challenged the Cumming and Henry formulation. His critique focused on methodology (the Kansas study was of too short a duration and did not include a control group of under-fiftys, thus making implied comparisons between young and old misleading); and emphasized his own findings that: (1) morale (or "ego strength") of the aged is systematically lower than it is among younger people; (2) the normal aged are as happy as the young, but there is no evidence that happiness increases with aging; and (3) "sadness" and "happiness" are similarly defined by younger and older subjects.[19]

As ubiquitous and frequently strident as these attacks on disengagement theory were, a more significant by-product of the debate was the emergence, during the early 1960s, of a compromise position. This school of thought, called "developmental field theory," reached into each of the two extreme camps, and attempted, by sifting through the claims of each, to forge a new model to explain the process of aging; a model that would be less involved with ideological considerations and thus more effective as an analytical tool. Flexible in approach, unhampered by overly rigid views of the aged, and well-suited to an "action" philosophy (that is, through improved liaison with field practitioners), the developmental field gerontologists constructed a theory which could help bridge the gap between the "golden years" and "sociobiological disaster" interpretations of aging. As Tibbitts' *Handbook* (1960) provided a good compendium of "activity" school philosophy and Cumming and Henry (1961) constituted the bible of the disengagement group, the manifesto of the Developmental Field theorists appeared in the October 1965 *Journal of Social Issues*. Edited by psychologist Robert Kastenbaum, this collection consisted of but six articles, covering not quite 100 pages. Yet, it served as an indicator of the pragmatic mix of theory and empirical insight which featured this approach to social gerontology. It included an inquiry into the history of social gerontology in America by a French philosopher, Michel Philibert; an article on the "interplay of social science research and administrative decision making" by sociologist and former official in the Office of Aging, Donald Kent; and psychologist Rosalie Rosenfelt's provocative utilization of Freidan's "mystique" concept as a means of explaining the gestalt of aging in modern industrial cultures.[20]

Kastenbaum's essay, however, provided the real heart of this collection. His piece, "Theories of Aging: the Search for a Conceptual Framework," treated the potential of general developmental field theory as an organizing principle for gerontological knowledge, both biological and sociopsychological. The biggest obstacle to general theories on gerontology, Kastenbaum argued, was that "at each level of description [of various biological and psychological indices of aging] there are such distinct sets of facts and concepts that it is exceeedingly difficult to interrelate levels, whatever one's preferred mode of interrelation." The most coherent attempt to date to synthesize such a framework, he observed, had resulted in Cumming and Henry's disengagement theory. Although this theory did not reflect the true "psychological thinking" which the task demanded, Kastenbaum thought "one might accept the notion of aging as a facet of normal human development—the provision being that the notion prove heuristic in theory and research and not deteriorate into a comfortable slogan." Disengagment theory had two valuable influences on gerontology. First, in contradicting many of the assumptions about aging held by the activity school, it encouraged, on both sides of the debate, "theoretical statements of utmost clarity, the construction of intervening steps between general and specific application, and the pursuit of relevant, critical investigation." Secondly, it did not "shy away from the most fundamental human problems. . . .the concepts of time and death." Although Cumming and Henry could not claim to have adduced convincing proof that death's approach leads to "introspective reflections on the meaning of life," they had at least liberated the question of its role in aging from the comfortable neglect to which gerontology had assigned it.[21]

Kastenbaum's own answer to the question raised by his article's title was "developmental field" theory, which he described as "a consolidation of concepts, experimental procedures, and research findings" for sorting out the "variety of perspectives from which to view the personal time–death relationship." This construct viewed change with aging as occurring on numerous psychobiological fronts at varying rates of speed. The overall process of aging and how the individual responded to it, depended upon what systems were affected at what rates of speed. Major and rapid change in a subsystem would not necessarily have great impact upon personality if the overall system of which it was a part maintained a relative equilibrium. Putting it in more common terms, gray hair and wrinkles are not severe discontinuities of themselves—but multiply such structural or functional discontinuities throughout the various psychological and biological systems and the result is increasing and major alterations in the organism.

Two important additional concepts introduced by this new theory were "engrossment" and "perspective." The first was described as total immersion in one's situation; the second as the ability to look at one's situation from a variety of different, external vantage points. Kastenbaum felt that the mature adult needed to possess both of these abilities in order to maintain adaptive potential. The engrossment—perspective concepts permitted formulation of a set of hypotheses about aging which suggested that the maturing individual had a choice of adjustment possibilities based on his previous patterns of engrossment–perspective. These were: (1) to maintain his general perspective or integration at the highest possible level, regardless of cost; (2) to reorganize life on a simpler level and become engrossed with one small part of the former whole; or (3) to vacillate between higher and lower central organizations (perspectives) or between engrossment in one or another of the differentiated systems. This formulation in turn permitted speculation about the probable effects of aging on the individual, given previous patterns of engrossment–perspective. The availability of Developmental Field Theory as a point of reference, Kastenbaum concluded, permitted gerontologists to at least think about diagnosing the individual's chances for successful aging and perhaps intervening selectively to enhance those chances. As he put it: "Those who do not develop or socially inherit adequate modes for shaping their experience will tend to experience aging as an increasingly purposeless marking of time, while losses and impairments appear to strike randomly from both outside and inside. How much distance needs to be travelled between this broad conceptualization and the present state of knowledge is all too evident, but there is the illusion of progress being made."

N O T E S

1. President's Report, *SSRC Annual Report,* 1946–1947, p. 18, and *Annual Reports* for 1943, p. 33; and 1945–1946, p. 54, for information on the founding and initial activities of the aging project.
2. *SSRC Annual Report, 1947–1948;* Pollak, *Social Adjustment in Old Age* (New York: 1948) SSRC Bulletin No. 59.
3. Cavan *et al., Personal Adjustment in Old Age* (New York: SSRC, 1949).
4. The volumes in question are Tibbitts (ed.), *Living Through the Later Years* (Ann Arbor: 1949); Donahue and Tibbitts (eds.) *Planning the Older Years* (Ann Arbor: 1950) and *Growing in the Older Years* (Ann Arbor: 1951).
5. Particularly good for the treatment of the problems of old age and the prospects for relief of them are Burgess "The Growing Problem of Aging"; Dr. E. J. Stieglitz, "The Personal Challenge of Aging: Biological and Maintenance of Health"; Donahue, "Changes in Psychological Processes with Aging," and Dr. Moses Frohlich, "Mental Hygiene in Old Age, in *Living Through the Later Years;* O. M. Randall, "Living Arrangements to Meet the Needs of Older People," and R. J. Havighurst, "Public Attitudes Toward Various Activities of Older People" in *Planning the Older Years;* Dr. J. Weinberg, "Psychiatric Techniques in the Treatment of Older People," Dr. M. Dacso, "Physical Restoration of the Older Person," and E. Soop, "Proposed Programs in Education for an Aging Population" in *Growing in the Older Years.*
6. Brown, Kerr, and Witte, *The Aged and Society* (1960).
7. Tibbitts (ed.), "Social Contributions by the Aging," *Annals of the AAPSS* 279 (January 1952).
8. *Rockefeller Foundation Annual Reports,* 1950, 1951, pp. 199–200 and 70–72. The Uni-

versity of Chicago study produced: E. A. Friedmann and R. J. Havighurst, *The Meaning of Work and Retirement* (Chicago: 1954); Ruth Albrecht and Havighurst, *Older People* (New York: 1953); T. L. Smith (ed.), *America's Aging Population* (Gainesville, Florida: 1951); B. Kutner et al., *Five Hundred over 60* (New York: 1956).

9. Information on the establishment of these special research units within professional associations and governmental agencies can be found in Shock, *Trends in Gerontology* (1957 ed.), especially his chapters on "Education" and "Research Potentials." The APA symposium provided a good summary of psychological research and its implications. See J. E. Anderson (ed.), *The Psychological Aspects of Aging* (APA: 1956); Greenleigh, *Psychological Problems of Our Aging Population* (NIMH: 1956).

10. Biographical information on Shock, Tibbitts, Havighurst, Burgess, and Donahue from *Who's Who, 1960;* on Frank, *Who's Who, 1965;* and on Cavan in *Who's Who of American Women, 1965.* The importance of The University of Chicago as a social gerontological center confirmed by the dedication of an entire issue of the *American Journal of Sociology* (a university-based publication) to the subject of aging and retirement, edited by E. W. Burgess, in 1954.

11. Definitive statements of the activity theory can be found in the earlier cited Tibbitts and Donahue volumes published by the University of Michigan Institute for Human Adjustment, the *AAPSS Annals* for 1952, and Havighurst and Albrecht, *Older People* (New York: 1953); Burgess, "The Role of Sociology," in *Health in the Later Years: Third Annual Southern Conference on Gerontology* (Tallahassee: 1953), pp. 37.

12. FSA, *Man and His Years,* pp. 42–43 76–78; Cohen, "Economics, Employment and Welfare," *14th Annual Conference on Aging, September 1951;* Committee on Aging and Geriatrics, *Aging . . . A Community Problem* (Washington, D.C.: 1952).

13. The chapter on Marketing will treat the approaches to the housing problem through the 1950s and 1960s as they reflected, first the consensus and later the conflict over optimum living arrangements; "Emotional Problems of the Aged," *American Journal of Public Health* 40 (September 1950): 1140–42; and APHA, *Housing an Aging Population* (New York: 1953); Mumford, "For Older People—Not Segregation but Integration," *Architectural Record* 119 (May 1956): 191–194; see comments of architect Henry Churchill on private disinterest in old age housing construction and his proposals for governmental underwriting in *2nd Annual Southern Conference on Gerontology* (January pp. 28–29. 1952).

14. "Lenders Oppose Segregation of Housing for the Aged," *Architectural Record* 112 (November 1952): 310; statements of private builders in Wilma Donahue (ed.), *Housing the Aged* (Ann Arbor: 1954), pp. 49, 70; the National Savings and Loan League position presented in FSA, *Man and His Years* (1951), pp. 159–180; Florida State Improvement Commission, *The Sponsored Neighborhood Village Idea in Florida* (Tallahassee: 1951).

15. Fleming, "Needed—A Social Philosophy for the Problems of Aging," *Geriatrics* 10 (1955): pp. 549–551.

16. Donahue, H. L. Orbach, and O. Pollak, "Retirement—The Emerging Social Pattern"—in this essay the concept of "meaningfulness" is an elevated one which rejects "busy work" or "hedonistic pursuits" as adequate roles; Streib and Thompson, "The Older Person in a Family Context," Friedmann, "The Impact of Aging on the Social Structure," and Vivrett, "Housing and Community Settings for Older People" in Tibbitts (ed.), *Handbook of Social Gerontology* (1960).

17. Cumming and Henry, *Growing Old* (New York: 1961).

18. Kastenbaum, "Theories of Aging: The Search for a Conceptual Framework," *Journal of Social Issues* 21 (October 1965): 27.

126

19. Zborowski, "Aging and Recreation," and Zborowski and Eyde, "Aging and Social Participation" in *Journal of Gerontology* 17 (1962): 302–309 and 424–430, respectively; Maddox, "Activity and Morale: A Longitudinal Study of Elderly Subjects," *Social Forces* 42 (1963–1964): 195–204; see also his assault on the disengagers for failure to assess the implications of their own findings in "Disengagement Theory: A Critical Evaluation," *Gerontologist* 4 (1964): pp. 80–83, and "Fact and Artifact: Evidence Bearing Disengagement Theory from the Duke Geriatrics Project," *Human Development* 8 (1965): 117–130; Cameron, "Ego Strength and Happiness of the Aged," *Journal of Gerontology* 22 (1967): 199–202; other attacks include D. E. Tanenbaum, "Loneliness in the Aged," *Mental Hygiene* 51 (1967): 91–99; "Why the Elderly are Depressed," *Transaction* 5 June 1968: 4; E. G. Youmans, "Orientations to Old Age," *Gerontologist* 8 (1968): 1954–1958; P. L. Klapnick et al., "Political Behavior in the Aged: Some New Data," *Journal of Gerontology* 23 (1968): 305–310; E. Palmore, "Effects of Aging on Activities and Attitudes," *Gerontologist* 8 (1968): 259–263; S. L. Harsanyi, "Social Attitudes Regarding Aging as a Disability," *Journal of Rehabilitation* 36 (November–December 1970): 24–27.

20. Kastenbaum (ed.), "Old Age as a Social Issue," *Journal of Social Issues* 21 (October 1965).

21. For a record of Kastenbaum's evolutionary work in this area, see his pieces in *New Thoughts on Old Age* (New York: 1967) and *Contributions to the Psychobiology of Aging* (New York: 1965), both edited by him and "Multiple Personality in Later Life," *Gerontology* 4 (1964): 16–20.

5

Education and the Image of the Aging: The Formal Institutions

With increasing public education concerning the nature of the aged and of aging as a process of change rather than merely a state of being, it is likely that greater acceptance of older people will become possible, with concomitant reversal of social judgments and, hence, self-conceptions. This sort of change may eventually lead to the integration of aging individuals into the social fabric.

Leonard Breen, "The Aging Individual" in C. Tibbitts (ed.), *The Handbook of Social Gerontology* (Chicago, 1960).

Americans have traditionally placed great faith in the educational system as a means of promoting and ensuring social order. The Massachusetts School Acts of the seventeenth century provide the earliest examples of the use of education to gain a social end—in these cases religious orthodoxy. Horace Mann, in his mid-nineteenth century reports, as the Massachusetts State Superintendent of Education, argued that universal public education constituted the best means of maintaining a healthy democratic tradition. The turn of the century found Lester Ward assigning to public education the major responsibility for social progress. "The problem of education," he wrote in 1897, ". . . is, in short, whether the social system shall always be left to nature . . . allowed to drift aimlessly on, intrusted to the by no means always progressive influences which have developed it and brought it to its present condition, or whether it shall be regarded as a proper subject of art, treated as other natural products have been treated by human intelligence and made . . . superior to nature. . . ."[1]

Although Ward, as part of the Progressive vanguard, helped to lay the theoretical basis for later political and social activists, it remained for the American philosopher, John Dewey, to illuminate fully the potential of education as an agent of social change. Social organization and social continuity, Dewey argued in his 1915 volume, *Democracy and Education,* depended on the "communication of ideals, hopes, expectations, standards, opinions," from one generation to another. Such communications processes took place not only in the formal school system; indeed, he remarked, compared to other agencies, the school was actually "a relatively superficial means" of transmitting values. Still, the formal school setting did have an important role in overseeing the transmission process. The school-as-institution alone possessed the power "to eliminate, so far as possible, the unworthy features of the existing environment." By selective transmission, the school "aims not only at simplifying, but at weeding out what is undesirable. . . ." To the school, Dewey charged the task "of omitting such things from the environment which it supplies and thereby doing what it can to counteract their influence in the ordinary social environment." He could not in 1915 have foreseen the tremendous impact which the rise of the mass media would have in the realms of noninstitutional education.[2]

Dewey's view of the role of education was at the root of the educational system's efforts to bring about change in society's conception of the aging process and the aged themselves. Thus, advancing to midcentury, we find the State University system of New York issuing a pamphlet on adult education in which it is noted: "The problem [of aging] . . . needs specialized concern on the part of the school. . . . Society with the help of the public schools can build into all people a new concept of old age as a period of continued usefulness; a period of activity rather than idleness." Adult education expert Arthur Carstens was more specific in calling for a reorganization of the school curriculum, including the introduction of material designed to stimulate thinking about the fact of aging in the earliest grades and a program of continuing education into adult life. Such a reformed system would help the individual to prepare himself or herself to face his or her own old age with greater equanimity. In a similar vein, Nathan Shock, chief of the National Heart Institute, declared in his 1951 edition of *Trends in Gerontology:* "Education is our most effective device for altering attitudes. If we are ever to eliminate the idea that aging means uselessness, an accumulated disease, we must begin at the elementary and high school level to teach the children something about the aging process." Shock, perhaps, restricted too narrowly the focus, and forecast, too optimistically the role of the school as an instrument of social change. The school system, consisting of the various public and private institutions of learning, constituted only one part of the total educational apparatus. Increasingly, the mass media played a large role in the communication of knowledge to the public. Even with the assistance of these new educational tools working outside of the classroom, Shock, like many other educators, doubted that the conceptions of aging and the aged could be very rapidly altered. An educator, writing in the journal of the National Education Association, advised his colleagues not to expect overnight success in gaining their objectives. The tasks of introducing suitable material into the curriculum and of extending the influence of education into the adult years would be long-term assignments. If educators, however, accepted their responsibility to educate for "dynamic maturity" (successful, active old age), the progress, if slow, would be steady. Nor should they expect revolutionary changes in attitude: "We may not yet reach the height of Browning's lie 'Grow old along with me!/The best is yet to be' but we may yet get as far as Tennyson's 'Old age hath yet his honor and his toil.' "[3]

One of the earliest efforts within the educational establishment to address the problems of aging occurred in 1949, when the Department of Adult Education of the National Education Association created the Committee on Education for an Aging Population. The charter members of this body—including such vanguard gerontological professionals as Wilma Donahue, Clark Tibbits, Robert Havighurst, and Ollie Randall—viewed education as serving two functions. First, it could help the aging to adjust to the physical and psychological change which passing time caused; second, it could help American society as a whole adjust to, and appreciate, its increasing numbers of older people. Admitting that education for aging constituted a "new frontier," the Committee urged immediate action in view of the "acute and widespread" need for a positive educational policy. As set down by the Committee, these immediate actions included: (1) "revision of the attitudes of all community groups in order to achieve recognition of the usefulness, the dignity, and the needs of older people"; (2) "creation of educational activities that will prepare all people for the second half of life and that will meet their needs as alert functioning members of society"; (3) "retraining of older workers for employment in occupations suited to their changing capacities"; and (4) "the training of professionals in all fields involving extensive contact with the aged." As a priority list, this set of proposals reflected accurately the preoccupations of gerontology and set the pattern for subsequent stirrings within the field of education.[4]

Following the lead of this pioneering statement by the NEA group, a field work organization, the Welfare Council of metropolitan Chicago, offered a three-part view of education's role in the gerontological movement. Each of these aspects of education's overall responsibility called for a different emphasis. The first was "community education"; that is, broad, general education of the public both about and for aging; the second was the creation of adult education programs aimed specifically at older persons, with the goal of providing satisfactory and healthful means of spending the lesisure of retirement years; and the third was educating those destined to work in gerontological–geriatric specialties, in both the biomedical and social disciplines. The most immediate of these three, the one upon which all gerontological progress depended, was the first. As Shock put it, speaking before the First Annual Southern Gerontological Conference in 1951, education's primary responsibility in the field of aging was that of alerting the broader public to the problems and needs of older people, and in so doing, create popular support for the kinds of research and social policies aimed at meeting these problems and assuaging these needs. Moreover, this general education would also help to prepare the younger citizen for his own later years by giving him a sense of the pitfalls ahead. When the representatives of various state commissions on aging met in Washington, D.C., in September 1952, they concentrated upon education for aging; the physical, psychological, and social preparation of the individual for his eventual senescence. This effort, they agreed, should involve not merely the formal public institutions of learning (school, colleges, universities, and libraries), but private agencies (churches, labor unions, and professional civic and fraternal bodies) and the media (print and audiovisual). To carry out this task, gerontologists would require access to each of these means, since the education and reeducation problems were complex and interrelated.[5]

In a paper on education for the aging published in the American Academy of Polticial and Social Sciences *Annals* in 1952, Wilma Donahue chided the public school system for not having taken its share of responsibility to educate the population about, and for, aging; especially in altering the negative attitudes about aging which American culture encouraged outside the classroom. The creation of attitudes favorable to the elderly, she observed, could ease the process of society's adjustment to its older population, while serving to open up opportunities heretofore limited by chronological age. Beyond this, the improvement of the abstract image of old age was presumed to have a self-fulfilling quality. Educational theorists argued that human behavior tended to reflect social expectations; thus, more positive expectations vis à vis the elderly would result in more positive behavior patterns. The school offers a logical, if not the only, place to begin testing this theory. The September 1952 Conference of State Commissions on Aging observed that methodological tools developed by psychologists and data amassed by biologists and anthropologists now enabled them to understand the role of social expectation in defining "old age." These tools and information also made possible a "scientific approach" to the goal of altering social expectations. Already, the conference reported, the Federal Security Administration's Office of Education, the American Teachers' Association, and National Education Association were busy compiling lists of pertinent educational materials aimed at redefining old age by introducing a higher level of expectation. The first important step toward achieving this, the conference noted, would involve the use of these materials to establish in the younger generation a respect for age that is, at present, notably lacking.[6]

By the mid-1950s, a number of concerned organizations had rallied to the cause and were attempting to pursue the various educational tasks confronting them. Under the auspices of the Department of Adult Education of the NEA, the State University of New York, the AAPSS, the Southern Conference on Gerontology, and the New York State Governor's Conference on the Problems of Aging, meetings and handbooks probed and discussed the issues involved. The targets of the proposed programs included society in general, and in particular, youths, employers, educators, school administrators, various professionals whose work brought them into frequent contact with the elderly, and older persons themselves. Those involved in this activity considered education the preserver of a "democratic social order" through the promulgation of desirable social change, as well as a worthwhile, postretirement activity for older people, a means of preparing everyone for aging and retirement, and a vehicle for eliminating stereotypes of the aged. As Jacob Tuckman of Columbia University Teachers' College observed in an NEA handbook, the elimination of "prejudices and erroneous notions about old age held by the young and by the old themselves" would create a "cultural climate . . . conducive to feelings of adequacy, usefulness, security and good adjustment in later years." Increasingly, social researchers were uncovering data which suggested that, contrary to popular belief, the elderly were no less able to learn and retain new material than younger people. It was the duty of educators, Tuckman argued, to assimilate these findings and to give correspondingly greater attention to the creation of adult education programs specifically directed at the elderly. In Tuckman's view, more and more older people would participate in such programs, and their presence and enthusiasm would be a continuing promotion of the idea of adult education and of the image of the active, alert older American. The reluctance of many educators and school administrators to accept the value of such programs would thus melt away before this demonstration, and ultimately the social image of aging would be altered for the good by just such innovations as these. The New York State Governor's Conference also viewed education as a means of correcting "the many misconceptions that exist with respect to aging," and stressed the use of the schools and the mass media as a means of getting the new image across to the public.[7]

Education "about" aging in the institutional setting offered not only a means of closing the existing breach in the social order between young and old, but it was, in fact, the first step in the process of formal education "for" aging. On the most basic level, education about aging meant alerting students to the facts about older persons in the United States by making clear their increasing numbers, life expectancy, retirement probability, and economic condition—while implanting a realization of old age as a personal problem, a situation with which they themselves would have to deal someday. Studies had shown, noted three members of the Columbia University Teachers' College faculty, that old age and retirement carried negative social connotations among virtually all age and occupational groups surveyed. "There is a strong suggestion in our case studies," the trio reported, "that adjustment in later maturity and retirement is an accentuation of the kind of adjustment the individual has made as a youth, a young adult, or a middle-aged adult." Given this view of development, they observed, "it is essential to help the younger adult develop patterns of adjustment which will aid him in preparing for the stresses of later maturity." The negative stereotypes of aging that contributed so much to the disadvantaged status of older people in our society constituted learned responses, which could, conversely, be eliminated through the process of education, especially among the young. "Emphasis should be on the positive aspects of aging," they advised, "rather than on the negative . . . ability rather than disability, on variability rather than on uniformity of the individual. . . ." At the public school level, they called for the introduction of adequate instructional materials (including films) to help young people recognize and adjust to aging parents and to develop interests and skills designed to keep them active and involved throughout their own lives. Colleges required a curriculum on aging similar to those already developed in the areas of childhood and adolescence.[8]

As an adult education specialist, Thomas Van Sant, director of that activity for the Baltimore Department of Education, accepted a responsibility for improving the status of the elderly. His chief interest was the development of educational programs for the aged. By way of apologizing for his profession's tardiness in this regard, he pointed to the sudden increase in the number of older persons and the change from the 'bare ruin'd choirs' concept of old age to the reality of "vigorous, active, demanding men and women," which so recently began to disturb the social environment. Thus far, he conceded, his profession's response has been unsatisfactory, offering only golden age clubs and mindless recreational diversions—"second and third class entertainment"—but he detected an increasing recognition among forward-looking educators that in education, as in life, the child was father to the man. "Education for the later years," Van Sant asserted, "must become part of the entire fabric of education." If senior citizens were to enjoy "richer and happier lives," this continuing educational program required constant cultivation. Key problems of the later years, noted another writer, were the abundance of leisure provided by earlier retirement and longer life spans, and the question of how to use it constructively and in personally satisfying ways. Not only were the present beneficiaries of all this leisure unable to deal with it successfully, but current educational policies seemed to ensure that future generations would remain similarly "illiterate." The public schools, he argued, had not only the ability, but the obligation, to make constructive use of leisure part of the curriculum. Parents could not, after all, communicate to offspring talents they themselves lacked. As Robert Havighurst noted, modern culture did not prepare people for the extensive leisure of retirement years. As things now stood, there existed no precedent for unlimited free time, either in the formative (school) or adult (work) years. Satisfactory use of this free time was an area in which educators could make a vital contribution. The school years, busy as they were, could be filled with calculated intimations of lesiure to come. The 1951 California State Conference on the Problems of Aging concluded that the combined efforts of all sectors of the educational system—public schools, colleges, extension services, and public and private agencies—could be of great significance "in developing the interests, habit and attitudes that would prepare individuals the more effectively to deal with the leisure to come later." A continuing program of broad, liberal arts education, the conference suggested, provided the best medium for advancement to this end. A key role in the success or failure of these efforts would be played by the public schoool system, for the early grades would lay the bases not only for future attitudes toward leisure, but for an enduring receptivity toward the experience of learning as well.[9]

During the 1960s, the dynamic view of education—the school as a tool for social change rather than merely a communicator of information—more and more caught the imagination of those involved with the teaching professions. The problems of the aged offered an area in which such educational theories could be tested. Speaking before a 1962 state conference on the problems of aging, the president of the University of Maryland evoked this concept of education. Helping people to prepare for old age in modern society, he contended, "will take much more than just a higher level of formal education. . . . It will require some fundatmental changes in our value system and a whole new approach to the problem of retirement." One specific task upon which educators could concentrate, he suggested, was the elimination of the notion that only remunerative work was worthwhile. He warned that this would not be an easy task. Teachers would have to combat such otherwise well-meaning institutions as the 1961 White House Conference on Aging, with its emphasis upon job retraining and expanded employment opportunities for older workers, and the American Medical Association, which attacked retirement systems for taking from the older individual that "which gave his whole life meaning" prior to age 65 in a 1958 pamphlet on aging. Gerontologists, he further stated, were themselves guilty of working against the best interests of the elderly by adopting an essentially paternalistic approach toward them. Here, too, education could provide the needed antidote by concentrating at all levels—grade school through adult education programs—upon the development of the "resources of mind and spirit that make the individual primarily dependent on himself."[10]

By the early 1960s, then, the educational establishment had developed a sense of responsibility with respect to the needs and problems faced by older people. This sense communicated itself not only through the efforts of the school to educate society to the latest findings about the aged, but in a determination to foster a more positive social attitude toward aging by empasizing the positive aspects and eliminating stereotypes. A social scientist and former administrator in the Federal Office of Aging, Donald P. Kent, told the American Home Economics Association's 1962 Workshop on Aging that many of the stereotypes that were applied to aging could be traced to the youth bias in the fields of fashion, entertainment, and advertising—all areas of high impact on popular opinion. His own experience in Washington, he wrote, suggested that government could help by coordinating and evaluating programs aimed at improving the older person's social situation. Real progress in this regard, however, remained largely dependent upon social approval of, and belief in, the goals of such programs. Here, Kent argued, educational institutions could make their greatest contributions to change society's attitudes toward the elderly by beginning in elementary school, to continue on every level thereafter to present an optimistic view of aging, and to promote the idea that older persons had valuable social roles to play. In another forum, the same writer further illuminated the role of education. Ideally the school should present its student with a balanced picture of life by ensuring that the positive aspects of each stage of life—daring and energy in youth; wisdom and detachment in later years—receive equal treatment. Success in this undertaking, he concluded, would not only brighten the general concept of old age but, by making aging individuals less apprehensive about the process, would improve their chances for rapid and successful adjustment to it as well.[11]

Members of the educational establishment were clearly aware of the criticism that they had not taken an active role in helping the older population achieve a more favored social position. According to one educator, the problem of educating for, and about, aging had been a preoccupation of professional conferences for a number of years; interest and motivation existed, and some progress had been made. He conceded that educators need a new approach. The time has come, he argued, to stop emphasizing facts about "aging" and to begin teaching about "maturity," to define it as active and stimulating, "in effect, *dynamic*." Traditionally, the schools have treated the subject of aging as a series of economic, medical, and social problems requiring the intervention of various welfare agencies. His "dynamic maturity" concept, however, assigned to education a major role in preparing people for the approach of old age by creating in them the ability to evaluate the later years in positive terms. An article in *Adult Leadership* echoed this view: "To the extent that the educational agencies of our society can increase the educational attainments of the aged, there will be a lessening of the [economic, social, and medical] problems created by a growing older population." A better educated person was less likely to be dependent, more likely to find satisfying and useful ways of passing the leisure of the postworking years. He would not be 'old' or 'aged' in the sense that society tended to use these terms. Yet another writer referred to the role of semantics in shaping the conduct of the elderly, declaring: "There should be no such words as 'aged' or 'old' in the vocabulary of a dynamic society or a dynamic human being. We are not 'aged' or 'old'— we are just a little further along the tortuous trail that leads to the spiritual and intellectual immortality of the human species."[12]

Besides educating the general public, the school system most importantly in its postgraduate and professional branches, bore responsibility for training the people—educators, social workers, clergy, doctors, other health professionals, and social and biological researchers—whose particular metiers involved work with the aged and whose attitudes were both reflective of, and influential upon, the larger society. Thus, a participant in the Higher Education Conference of December 1965 observed a "growing interest on the part of progressive universities in the problems of older people in our society," and an increasing acceptance of gerontology–geriatrics as valid parts of the curriculum. Despite such encouraging signs, however, the Senate Labor Committee observed in a 1957 report that "the shortage of persons to work with older people in the health, welfare, recreation and unemployment areas constitutes the most serious deficiency in the field since it prevents the effective application of knowledge already developed." The dimensions of the shortage, as shown by a 1960 Gerontological Society inquiry, indicated especially acute situations in the fields of psychological and social research, medicine, and asocial work, though the creation of "gerontological institutions" by fifteen universities was an encouraging trend. In 1955, these schools constituted themselves into a consortium through which they could better meet the needs of the discipline. Called the Inter University Training Institute in Social Gerontology, this organization explored and published the research and personnel needs of social gerontology and offered a training network using the facilities and faculties of interested universities. The IUTI's first two summer institutes—in 1958 at the University of Connecticut and in 1959 at the University of California–Berkeley—trained 75 faculty members from the various member schools as an "intial cadre of instructors in social gerontology . . . the nuclei from which further development of the field will emanate." Although still woefully undermanned and undertrained, a growing awareness of these needs was beginning to stimulate action. Offering evidence that such awareness was becoming influential at the student level, Dr. Joseph Freedman found in a 1961 survey of 470 medical students and interns that interest in increased training in geriatrics was widespread.[13]

Increaingly, the Federal government took an interest in encouraging professional training—generically designated "social gerontology"—in the areas of the social sciences, psychology, social work, and education. In 1965, the Department of Health, Education and Welfare proposed and published a two-year social gerontology curriculum which, it was hoped, would spur more universities and professional schools into offering such training. The program included basic courses in biology, psychology, the social and economic aspects of aging, and gerontology field experience designed to link theory to practice in the various areas of need—health, income security, housing, and recreation. Designed to attract students with broad liberal arts backgrounds, this program would lead to a master's degree in social gerontology and would provide trained personnel to fill the increasing numbers of positions available in public and private sectors. More concrete was a work-study program administered by the University of Denver under a grant from HEW's Administered on Aging. This program aimed to attract bright young undergraduates to the field by providing them an opportunity to specialize in work with older people during their third and fourth years of college. Directed by a sociolgist, the program offered a mix of academic work and field experience spread over three academic quarters (about 30 weeks). Initial evaluations indicated that students behaved positively in both attitude and response. But the Denver program was only a small pilot project of rather limited duration. Ultimately, given the number and complexity of the problems associated with aging and the precise skills needed to deal with them, the graduate professional schools—of medicine, social work, education, etc.—provided the best sources of gerontologically sophisticated manpower.[14]

A key institution, in any overview of professional training for work in the field of gerontology, is the school of social work; for here is where society trains a good part of the manpower needed to wage the constant struggle in behalf of the dependent. The educational failings of this institution, in fact, were the failings of professional education in aging in general. Social work schools, argued social work educator William Posner in 1957, could not change professional attitudes toward the aging, simply because they had "done little to interest students in the field of aging." Indeed, he felt that the profession, like the society it served, was youth-oriented. A product of the larger culture, the typical caseworker brought to his work many acquired attitudes and values. Among these was a set of generally negative expectations toward the aging. For this reason, Posner, a pioneer in casework with the older person, felt that the tasks of changing social attitudes and changing professional attitudes were one and the same. "We want a reorganization of attitudes and feelings on the part of society as a whole," he wrote, as well as in professional disciplines like social work. As in the larger social setting, attitudes toward an older client were too often influenced by these expectations and stereotypes. Social workers could least of all afford to entertain such negative values, argued another advocate of geriatric casework training. As society's chief contact point with the dependent and needy older person, they had to attempt to convey to the elderly client a sense of social concern for his problems. If the caseworker failed in this, he ran the risk of harming the client by convincing him that he was unworthy and therefore deserving of neglect. As Posner put it, once the profession accepted "the belief that older persons, through acceptance, can continue to grow and to change," geriatric casework services and in-school training for them, would not only be rapidly established, but be successful as well. Such was the overweening importance of attitude.[15]

In a seminar held in September 1958 at Aspen, Colorado, the Council on Social Work Education explored the role of the school of social work in the preparation of its graduates to serve the elderly. One participant, Joseph Meisels, suggested that the social service sequence within the general curriculum provided the logical place for inclusion of special material on aging. He agreed that most entering students brought to school a set of attitudes about youth and old age derived from their contacts and associations within the larger society. He also felt that such attitudes, if left unchanged, would hamper graduate social workers in their abilities to work with the aged. This, Meisels proposed, constituted the chief argument for the reform of this course sequence. The optimum goals of such a reform included a comprehensive definition of "need" as regarded the aging, the investigation of social attitudes and their importance, and the introduction of social science concepts like "role" and "social change" to help the students better understand the aging process. Speaking for the administrators of schools of social work, Arlien Johnson, dean of Stanford's Social Work School, acknowledged that the educational process should give more consideration to the problems of aging but insisted as well upon the need for in-service training. "We need both short-range measures and long-range planning to incorporate new knowledge into education and practice." Dean Johnson wrote: "We need the cooperative endeavor of school and field to put knowledge into action for service to all and, of course, that includes the aging."[16]

Despite these encouragements to the advocates of special geriatric training, the "generic" principle remained firmly embedded in the educational traditions of social work. In a background paper for the planners of the 1961 White House Conference on Aging, Professor A. W. Kadushin of the University of Wisconsin

School of Social Work, a member of the Council on Social Work Education, discouraged the idea of geriatric specialization: "In view of the trend in social work education, it would appear unlikely that a specialized sequence of courses for social work with the aging will be adopted in the curriculum for the master's degree." Similarly, A. E. Fink of the Central Bureau for the Jewish Aged, emphasized the centrality of the generic principle in social work education. While conceding that effective teaching could help students to value the aged and to reject common stereotypes about them, he felt that ceasing to link the words "aging" and "problems" would go a long way toward deemphasizing the negative connotations of old age. The field, Fink insisted, was the best place to gain the skills peculiar to geriatric casework; that is, by learning in practice how to modify the basic casework principles taught in the classroom.[17]

The conflict between the "generic" and the "specific" schools of thought has not yet been settled, but the debate has served to underline the need for increased knowledge about the older client. As a result of the debate, the Ford Foundation awarded an $800,000 grant to be administered by the American Public Welfare Association, toward "the improvement of in-service and academic programs at selected schools of social work." Aging specialist Ollie Randall noted the increased interest in the area of geriatric casework, as apparent in the Foundation's action and gave credit for this to the 1958 seminar at Aspen, Colorado. This conference, argued Randall, began the process of reducing the traditional resistance of social work schools to "specialized attention" for the aged, and initiated an era of "increased awareness" of the particular needs of the elderly. Obviously, the future success of the movement to get aging more firmly rooted in the social work curriculum will depend upon the phasing out of negative attitudes about the aged amid those who administer social work schools and field agencies. Thus, the contribution of the social work schools to date—and in this respect it is prototypical of the professional school—has been more in the area of shaping its role than in assuming it.[18]

N O T E S

1. The New England educational system and its functions are discussed in Bernard Bailyn, *Education and the Forming of American Society* (New York: 1960), pp. 15–21; Mann reports from Lawrence Cremin (ed.), *The Republic and the School* (New York: 1957); and Ward, *Dynamic Sociology* II (New York: 1926), pp. 632–633.
2. Dewey, *Democracy and Education* (New York: 1937), pp. 3–4, 10, 24.
3. SUNY, *Adult Education in New York State* (mimeo, 1950); Carstens, "Community Attitudes and Older Citizens," *Adult Education* 1–2 (December 1950): 51–55; Shock, *Trends in Gerontology* (Baltimore: Conference on the Aging, 1951), pp. 132–133. For an early recognition of the role of the mass media in social change, see Franklin Fearing (ed.), *Mass Media: Content, Function and Measurement*, vol. III, no. 3, of the *Journal of Social Issues* (Summer 1947); McIntyre, "Wanting is . . . What? in Education," *Education* 71 (June 1951): 616.
4. First report of the Committee on Education for an Aging Population is "Education for an Aging Population," *Adult Education Bulletin* 14 (December 1949): 60–62; similar priorities set by Tibbitts and Donahue "Developments in Education for Later Maturity," *Review of Educational Research* 23 (June 1953): 202–217; and later by G. B. Davis, "Education for Aging," *Adult Leadership* 8–9 (May 1960): 2–25.
5. Welfare Council of Metropolitan Chicago, *Community Service for Older People* (Chicago: 1952), p. 160; Shock quoted in *Problems of America's Aging Population: First Annual Southern Conference on Geronotology, March 19–20, 1951* (Gainesville: 1951); *Man and His Years*, 135–142; Conference of State Commissions on Aging, *Official State Groups on Aging: Elements of Organization and Programs* (Washington, D.C.: 1954), pp. 56–57.
6. Donahue contribution to *AAPSS Annals: Social Contributions by the Aging* (C. Tibbitts, ed.), p. 270 (January 1952), pp. 115–125; theories of education for aging discussed in Tibbitts and Donahue "Developments in Education for Later Maturity," loc. cit.; link between expectations and behavior noted in Senate Labor Committe, *Surveys of State and Local Projects* (Washington: 1957), p. 19; a good example of a project aimed at using the accomplishments of old people to elevate expectations of the public with a mutually reinforcing effect on the elderly reported by Wilma Donahue. "Grand Rapids Learns about Aging," *Adult Leadership* 3 (May 1954): 22–24; *Official State Groups on Aging*, p. 29.
7. Early attention to adult education as good therapy for roleless older folk given in SUNY, *Adult Education in New York State* (mimeo, 1960); and "What's the Next Move for Our Aged?" *Occupations* 30 (October 1951): 59–60; see contributions of Donahue and H. Wheeler to the *AAPSS Annals* (1952), pp. 92, 115–125; NEA collection compiled between 1952 and 1955 is Donahue (ed.) *Education for Later Maturity* (New York: 1955), pp. 1–8, (Frank), 95 (Tuckman); *Aging and Retirement: Fifth Annual Southern Conference on Gerontology, December 28–30, 1954* (Gainesville, Fla., 1955), pp. 112–116 (Irving Webber); and New York Governor's Conference, *Charter for the Aging* (Albany, 1955), pp. 81–84.
8. Such facts on aging contained in the articles "America Grows Older" and "Does the U.S. Treat Its Senior Citizens Fairly?" both in the high school study guide periodical *Senior Scholastic*, vols. 60 (March 26, 1952) and 90 (May 12, 1967). P. L. Essert, Irving Lorge, and Jacob Tuckman, "Preparation for a Constructive Approach to Later Maturity," *Teachers' College Record* 53 (1951–1952): 70–75. One of the more ingenious devices aimed at manipulating the attitudes of the very young was a coloring book prepared by Sister Kathleen Gibbons and Rosemary G. Larson entitled *The Golden*

Years, which introduced itself to children as a book, not only to enjoy, but one which would teach them about older people, and promised "if and when you do get to know them, you will soon discover that they are the nicest people you will ever want to know." (1967).

9. Van Sant, "Responsibility of Education to the Older Adult," *Geriatrics* 6 (1951): 195–197; see also the comments of the NEA's Dr. William T. Van Orman in *Senate Labor Committee Hearings, August 4–6, 1959,* 36, 88th Congress, 1st Session (Washington, D.C.: 1959), and Henriette Rabe, "The Role of the Public School in Education for the Aging and Aged," *Adult Leadership* 8–9 (May 1960): 27; E. D. Partidge, "Adolescents Need Education for Leisure," *High School Journal* 34, no. 2 (February 1951): 42–45; Havighurst, "Employment, Retirement and Education in the Mature Years," in *Aging and Retirement: Fifth Annual Southern Conference on Gerontology,* pp. 57–62; California Governor's Conference proceedings from Senate Labor Committee, *Studies of the Aged and Aging,* V; similar sentiments as to the necessity of broad "education for life" programs from R. F. W. Smith (Dean of NYU's Division of General Education), "Education for a Lifetime," *Journal of Educational Sociology* 30, no. 5 (January 1957): 216–220, and Robert B. Meyner (Governor, New Jersey), "The Rights of Our Senior Citizens," *Vital Speeches,* 22, 585–587 (speech delivered before the National Conference on the Problems of Aging, June 5, 1956).

10. Horn's keynote address "The Role of Education in the Field of Aging," from HEW Office of Education's *State Leadership in Action for Education in Aging* (Washington, 1962), pp. 6–8. Horn's debt to Erikson's theories about continuing development, if not stated, is nonetheless implicit in his reference to the "resources of mind and spirit."

11. Kent, "Aging: A National Concern," *Journal of Home Economics,* 54, no. 8 (October 1962): 683–684, and "Current Developments in Educational Programming for Older People," *American School Board Journal* 149 (September 1964): 27, 30; on the same theme, see D. O. Moberg, "Life Enrichment and Educational Needs of Older People," ibid. 11 (December 1962): 164, 185.

12. H. L. Dunn, "A Positive View of Aging Asks Much of Education," *School Life* 46 (January–February 1964): 30–34; Linton and Spence, "The Aged: A Challenge to Education," *Adult Leadership* 12 (March 1964): 270; A. P. Crabtee, "Education—The Key to Successful Aging," *Adult Education* 17 (Spring 1967): 157–165.

13. C. V. Newsome, "A Challenge to Higher Education," *Journal of Educational Sociology* 30, no. 5 (January 1957): 210–215; see similar positive sentiments in *Social Work Year Book, 1960* (New York: 1960), pp. 99–100; Senate Labor Committee, *Surveys of State and Local Projects* (Washington, D.C.: 1957), p. 1; Helen S. Wilson, "University Programs in the Field of Aging," *Geriatrics* 15 (September 1960): 665–669; W. Donahue and H. L. Orbach, "Training in Social Gerontology," *Adult Leadership,* 8–9 (May 1960): 3–5, 26; Freedman "Survey of Education in Geriatrics," *Gerontologist* 1 (1961): 120–126; an excellent overall view of the state of professional training in gerontology is offered by WHCoA *Background Paper on Role and Training of Professional Personnel* (May 1960).

14. HEW, *Training in Social Gerontology* (Washington, D.C.: 1965): E. R. Sherman and M. R. Brittan, *A Plan to Span: Work-Study in Social Gerontology* (HEW Patterns for Progress Series, 1970); a table on programs in gerontology at major universities during 1960–1970 offered in *Aging* (March–April 1969): 5, lists 15, with only one (Southern Florida University) offering a "Social Gerontology" degree (M.A.). The earliest of these programs was begun in 1966. See also R. A. Kalish, "Manpower Requirements in Social Gerontology," *Gerontologist* 8 no. 3 (1968): 215–220 and J. L.

145

Moore and J. E. Bireen, "Doctoral Training in Gerontology . . . 1934–1969," *Journal of Gerontology* 26, no. 2 (1971): 249–257, for quantitiative analyses.

15. Posner, "Adapting and Sharpening Casework Knowledge and Skills in Serving the Aging," *Social Work* 13 (1957): 37–42; see also his contribution to "Changing Concepts in the Care of the Aged: A Symposium," *American Journal of Orthopsychiatry* 28 (1958): 322–342; his articles "Casework with the Aged: Developments and Trends" in Council on Social Work Education, *Social Work Education for Better Services to the Aging* (1959), 1–9, and "Basic Issues in Casework with Older People," *Social Casework* (May–June 1961): 234–240 (special issue on aging); R. L. Levine, "Casework and Counseling Services for the Aged," *Public Welfare* 15 (1957): 17–20; similar thoughts on social workers as cultural conduits and the significance of attitude in M. C. Cairns and M. R. Friend, "The Psychiatric Social Worker and the Problems of Aging," *Mental Hospitals* 10 (September 1959): 28–30.

16. Meisels, "Learning About Aging in the Social Services Curriculum," in CSWE, *Social Work Education . . .*, pp. 58–66; Johnson, "The Social Work Curriculum in New Fields of Practice," ibid., pp. 73–82. For confirmation of Meisels' view on the vital role of social work education in helping students to orient attitude, see Marcella Farrar and Martin Bloom, "Social Work Education and the Reduction of Stereotypes about the Aged," a paper read before the Gerontological Society, November 9, 1967. Their survey of first and second year students found that field work experiences actually tended to harden negative stereotypes in a large number of cases, and they suggested that one answer to this was the inclusion of more coursework material aimed at altering these attitudes.

17. Kadushin from WHCoA, *Background Paper on Role and Training of Professional Personnel*, pp. 60–61; Fink, "Professional and Undergraduate Education" in *Dynamic Factors in the Role of Casework with the Aged* (New York: 1962), pp. 33–34.

18. *Ford Foundation Annual Report, 1962*, p. 46; Randall quoted in Ford Foundation, *Golden Years?* (New York: 1963), p. 13.

146

6

Education and the Image of the Aging: The Informal Institutions

Having reviewed the role of education on public attitudes toward the aging through the medium of the school—called for the purposes of topical organization "formal institutions"—let us now consider the educational process that is constantly in session outside the classroom. This process takes place in what we will call "the informal institutions," by which we mean the various modes of communication—the electronic and print media—and personal experience. Gerontologists recognized early on the significance of these devices in the field of aging. John E. Anderson, a leading figure in the American Psychological Association's Section on Old Age and Maturity, observed in a 1954 article: "The mass media . . . are of much importance . . . especially for older people. . . . Radio and television have unusual advantages because they bring the world directly . . . millions of older people . . . who for much of the time have little or no contact with other people." But the media were also important influences on millions of younger Americans, both in and out of school, as well. "No student of education," Anderson urged, "can afford to ignore the mass media nor their effects upon all, whether old, middle-aged or young."[1]

That the media influence the popular mind; that people learn from radio, television, newspapers, books, and movies, is a truism that scarcely bears repeating. That the media can be used, premeditatedly, to shape social thought on an issue by weaning the public mind away from one set of values to be replaced with new values, however feasible in theory, is something that must be demonstrated. A gerontological intent to use the media in this way is easily established. Thus, in 1958, the U.S. Department of Health, Education and Welfare's Office of Education was urged by the Federal Council on Aging (an umbrella group in which both governmental and private sectors were represented) to enlist the mass media in efforts "to promote improved social attitudes toward the aging," Woodrow W. Hunter, of The University of Michigan's Institute for Human Adjustment, was also a proponent to involve these extra-mural facilities in the task to educate the public for, and about, aging. "The use of all forms of mass media," he wrote in the journal *Geriatrics*, "of community-wide forums and conferences and of demonstrations and exhibitions can be stimulated within the framework of education *for* the aging in order to change entrenched attitudes *toward* the aging" [emphasis added].[2]

Various individual organizations appeared to accept unreservedly their educational role. Thomas Desmond, chairman of the New York State Legislative Committee on aging, called "the monumental task of altering attitudes toward old age" the committee's major priority and declared that a similar result "should rank as the number one objective of all groups and individuals who are working with and for aging." The Kansas Legislative Council, discussing its public educational responsibility expressed the same sentiment. "Public information operations most commonly consist in publishing a report of the committee's findings. In addition, however, certain fact-finding operations may also serve to direct public attention to and stimulate interest in the needs of older people." The Kansas council noted that public hearings and fact finding panels could "direct the attention of the public to these facts [about older persons] through news coverage of the commission's work." Federal

Welfare Commissioner Ellen Winston, reporting to the U.S. Senate's Special Committee on Aging in January 1964 on the efforts of those agencies concerned with the aging in thirty-seven states, emphasized the duty of these organizations to foster "public awareness and understanding of the needs and potentials of older persons," and she pointed to the communications media as the best means of carrying out this responsibility.[3]

Nor are examples of the uses of these means of communication by groups involved with gerontological concerns difficult to find. Early on, such organizations expressed strong interest in the establishment of relations with the media, not only for the purpose of advertising their work, but for the purpose of informing the public of the latest findings on the subject of aging, as well. A 1952 conference of official state agencies on aging examining the roles of participant bodies in "education and guidance," agreed that the collection and dissemination to the public of all available information upon the life situations and capacities of the aged were a primary responsibility of the agency. The best means of getting this data to the general population, the conferees decided, besides the issuance of full, periodic reports which few would bother to read, was in the use of the press, radio, television, and specially produced films. The Welfare Council of Metropolitan Chicago, a privately funded (Wieboldt Foundation) organization, reported after a two-year (1947-1949) inquiry into the determination, planning, and promotion of services for the elderly, that the chief methods for getting information into the public domain have been exploitation of contacts within the media community, especially the press, and working through special groups, like churches and clubs. Yet another aggressive state agency, the Minnesota Governor's Council, called public education a sine qua non for any improvement in the social and economic status of the elderly. This group reported constant efforts to ensure good publicity for its activities, particularly in the press. The wide public impact which the media gave Council undertakings was more educational than dozens of "official" reports.[4]

The kinds of events and programs which best lent themselves

to the media approach included various "senior citizen" activities such as "senior citizen weeks," special crafts, and social programs. The most effective of these always coupled their programs with an active promotional apparatus. Of such efforts, the first was the "Senior Citizen's Month" proclaimed in New York City in May 1952 "to focus public attention on our senior citizens, on their contributions—mental, spiritual, material—to our society, and our obligation to them for their contributions." Beneath this upbeat rhetoric, the objective, as cited by the events' planning guide, was elementary: "Constructive social action can be accelerated by social pressure. The culture pattern [of discrimination against the aged] can be changed, if leadership influences the public to speed up change." This guide also supplied suggestions for orchestrating publicity in the print and audiovisual media to gain maximum exposure for these "influences." The Department of Health, Education and Welfare's Office of Aging looked approvingly upon such efforts. Reporting on a "Senior Citizen's Week" celebration in St. Petersburgh, Florida, in its monthly newletter *Aging,* the office declared: "Through [such] continued appropriate programming, the stigma of 'senior citizen,' which seems to exist in some quarters, may be removed, and the older men and women of the community can recognize the honor that is theirs." The President's Council on the Aging, in preparing a guide for the national observance of Senior Citizen's Month (May 1965), stated the aims of such celebrations. First, they informed people about the needs and problems of the elderly; second, they brought home to the younger generation the fact that they would themselves be old one day; and third, they gained public support for continuing efforts, public and private, to solve the problems of the aged. In each of these evocations of the educational potential of such events, the crucial role of the media was emphasized.[5]

High visibility community action programs, properly publicized, offered yet another means of educating society. "Senior City," the government's exhibit in the 1958 New York State Fair provided a novel and effective public information device.

The project, wrote its director, Selma Brody, simulated a model community designed to help the public in gaining "an awareness and understanding of what still remained to be done to provide older people with good health and housing, the outlets needed for a full and useful life at any age, and freedom from want." Besides "literally hundreds of thousands" of visitors, events at Senior City "were recorded for radio, taped for TV, and written about in newspapers, rotogravure sections, and magazines." Her own sense of the project's overall contribution was "that it contributed significantly to the recognition of older people and their needs, that it afforded the State Government and its departments a unique opportunity to demonstrate their concern and services for senior citizens, that it provided information and new concepts to visitors of all ages, and that it offered scores of older people the opporunity to demonstrate skills and artistic abilities." Another project, "Little House," a senior citizen activity center founded at Menlo Park, California, in 1949, provided not only an action program for the elderly, but created an effective instrument for public education as well. From the program's outset, the sponsoring agency, Peninsula Volunteers, "submitted weekly news releases . . . , wangled feature articles in local and San Francisco metropolitan press and appropriate magazines . . . , circularized TV and radio stations with 'spot' announcements and arranged for reprints of articles or editorials [for] groups requesting printed descriptive leaflets and brochures."[6]

A more direct use of the radio and television media involved special programming sponsored as a public service or by a voluntary agency, a commercial interest, or the broadcaster. Surveying 155 different communities of over 75,000 residents in 1952, Philip Swartz reported: "Educational and interpretational activities were weak and some of the new media like television and radio did not receive as much use as more routine methods." In evidence, he submitted the following figures: 12.3 percent of the respondent communities (19) had radio programs devoted to the subject of aging; 2.6 percent (4) had television shows; and 43.9 percent made regular use of newspaper publicity. Nonetheless, these underutilized modes of education gained rapidly in popularity once their effectiveness had been established. An analysis of fifteen weekly television and radio shows between 1951 and 1969 indicates that the average program ran fifteen minutes, though there were occasional half-hour presentations. Most of these programs were directed at two separate audiences: the aged, in order to give them information, encouragement, the sense that someone is taking an interest in them; and the general community, to alert it to the needs and the capacities of its older population. Nearly all of these shows organized themselves along discussion or lecture lines dealing with topics of general concern to the aged—income, housing, health, employment—and producers often attempted to open up channels of communication between the broadcasters and the audience by soliciting mail and phone calls and making available to viewers/listeners transcripts of shows or printed materials dealing with various aspects of aging. Although a few adopted entertainment formats—"What's with My Line?" a "senior citizen quiz program" (WJTM-TV, Lansing, Michigan), for example—most were quite serious in approach and content. Several of these (the network entries) featured well-known personalities as moderators: H. V. Kaltenborn chaired an NBC series based on the Twentieth Century Fund study, *The Economic Needs of Older People;* Walter Able presided over ABC's weekly "Years of Happier Living"; Edward R. Murrow narrated a prime-time CBS half-hour documentary "The Face of Retirement "; and Leon Pearson of NBC served as master of cermonies for "The Living End," a program "about the joys and problems of old age." Most of the programs, however, were regional in origin and depended greatly upon the active participation of the local community's older population.[7]

When the Cleveland Women's City Club Foundation originated the series, "The Best Years", for airing over local station WEWS–TV in January and February of 1953, it cited, as a "primary objective", the need "to interpret and dramatize for the family and the community the problems and needs of the older person." The producers also sought to stimulate senior citizens into assuming a more positive life style and to inform them of available community services and resources. Wilma Donahue, a University of Michigan psychologist upon whose ideas "The Best Years" was modeled, originally envisioned the series as a means of communicating factual data to the public. Upon evaluation of its impact, however, She found that "almost unknowingly ... we were demonstrating the use of television as a medium for interpretation of social welfare." A similar series, "Unfinished Business," sponsored over WNDU–TV (Notre Dame University) in South Bend, Indiana, during the winter of 1956–1957 by the local Junior League, stated a like purpose: "To present the aspects of gerontology and its full meanings in today's pattern of community living. . . . Educating the public was the basic theme in our discussion of the aged and aging problem". A 1960 NBC Public Affairs Department production— "The Living End"—was a network attempt to counter "stereotypes ... being pounded into our culture by the youth mania that possesses Hollywood" through an orchestrated "testimony to the creativity and potential among our aged."[8]

What audiences were the chief targets of such programming? M. E. Collins, Jr., program director of radio station WOI in Ames, Iowa, and a man with some experience in this area, argued against aiming solely at the homebound and lonely aged, on the assumption that they were most in need of diversion, of "company." This view ignored the immense educational potential of radio and television. Collins felt these media should aim as well at the "active, mature elderly and the interested younger person who, by combining energies can aid in solving problems of the aged on a community, state and national level." One attempt to reach such an audience was the joint effort of the Minnesota Governor's Council on the aging and the Twin Cities Area Educational Television Corporation, entitled "seminars for seniors." The goal of the "seminars" series was "to learn . . . what issues they [older people] feel are pertinent, which ones need public discussion . . . and where resource people can be obtained to lead the discussion so that the information that the state agency wants disseminated can be spread as quickly and efficiently as possible." To facilitate the achievement of such a goal, the format of the program encouraged audience participation. In support of this project, the federal Administration on Aging awarded the State agency a grant of $81,530 to help underwrite production and administrative costs. Indeed, from its creation in 1965 (Title II of the Older Americans Act), the Administration on Aging showed a continuing interest in the use of the media as a means of carrying out its educational responsibilites. With the power to fund worthwhile field work, research, and demonstration projects through direct grants to state (Title III) or public and non-profit private (Title IV) agencies, the Administration also supported similar media projects in Hawaii and in Hershey, Pennsylvania.[9]

Besides these documentary and public service programs, commercial programs also played a part in focusing attention on America's aged. Television was most important in this respect. Although radio of the 1940s spread the image of garrulous and musty old age through its weekly series "Life Begins at Eighty," in which dirty old men and ladies with ridiculous opinions and loud voices too often held center stage; television, on the whole, behaved more responsibly. Coming of age during the period of initial heavy involvement in the field of gerontology, the visual medium achieved a more balanced entertainment-informational policy. While it could not resist airing "Life Begins at 80" (by adding the visual component, making the end result even more insulting to senior citizenhood), a consistent feature of television's prime-time programming in the 1950s was the production of live one-hour or ninety minute plays. The Lux Video Theatre, Studio One, Playhouse 90, and the Philco Television Playhouse all provided exposure for the work of some of the best young playwrights—Paddy Chayefsky, Horton Foote, Robert A. Arthur, Tad Mosel—of the period. Indeed, serious playwrights made for serious plays; theatre not only entertained but strove for educational impact by dealing with matters of topical concern.[10]

Several examples of this kind of dramatic craftsmanship dealt seriously with the subject of aging and the problems associated with it. "The Mother," a one-hour play appearing on the Philco Television Playhouse on April 4, 1954, was such a play. The story was that of an unemployed, recently widowed woman living alone in a two-and-one-half room apartment in a "lower middle class" Bronx neighborhood. Her desire to return to work, against the strenuous objections of an overzealous daughter, provided the main theme. Her son-in-law analyzed her motives—"She wants to support herself. She doesn't want to be a burden on her children."—while her daughter appraised her chances of finding work—"If you get a job, you get fired before the day is over. You're too old, Ma, and they don't want to hire old people. . . . They don't want to hire white-haired old ladies." A move into her daughter's apartment failed after only one night. She left the next morning to return to her search for work and declared: "I'm a woman of respect. I can take care of myself. I always have. . . . Work is the meaning of my life. It's all I know what to do. I can't change my ways at this late time." Another play, "Fear Begins at Forty," first shown on CBS in 1947 also dealt with the twin problems of aging and unemployment. Basically, according to the CBS brochure announcing the production, it concerned "those who are 'too old'—'too old' to be employed, 'too old' to maintain themselves with dignity, 'too old' to make the economic and cultural contributions of which they are still capable." A dramatic presentation based on field research by the CBS Documentary Unit, its stated goal was to "bring home to Americans the necessity for thoughtful action on a problem that concerns us all."[11]

Another dramatic variation upon the theme of retirement and old age was "Such a Busy Day Tomorrow," a Robert Montgomery Presents offering during the summer of 1954. According to a review of this play in *Aging,* it was "a highly moving story of an elderly widower, retired from work and more or less out of contact with his family." His successful escape from this, all too typical, situation comes about as a result of joining a senior citizen's club. "Taken against the background of the Hodson Center in New York City," the review continued, "it is in all ways an authentic study of a situation of this sort." In addition to its telecast, Johnson's Wax, the Robert Montgomery program sponsor, made the kinescope available to interested groups free of charge. (One of the groups to take advantage of this offer was the 1954 Annual University of Michigan Conference on Gerontology. The tape was used, according to conference organizers, "to underscore the value of plays and movies as techniques in the organization of group meetings and other gatherings.") The March 1960 CBS–TV documentary "Woman! The Lonely Years," starring Helen Hayes, provided the television audience with a look at aging from the distaff side. Miss Hayes took the role of an old woman "Alone, Unwanted, Forgotten," explaining to her audience that the play was "about old age. About you and me. About the fact that—alone among all women who have ever lived—we can *expect* to grow old." Describing the crises of aging, she ended her prologue with the promise: "During the next hour we are going to see how one woman began to face this crisis in her life."[12]

Radio and television thus made good use of dramatic presentations for purposes of both entertainment and instruction. As The University of Michigan Conference on Gerontology noted in showing the Robert Montgomery Presents tape at its 1954 meeting, drama could have an educational role without media participation. Although of minor importance in numbers reached, proponents of the use of live drama emphasized its impact and its capacity for presenting the facts about aging in a memorable way. Relations between aging parents and adult children provided the subject material for dramatic exposition in Nora's Stirling's "The Room Upstairs" (1953) and "A Choice to Make" (1963), and Isobel McFadden's "Five in a Living Room" (1962). In each of these plays, the older person is initially introduced in stereotypical terms—grouchy, forgetful, oversensitive, backward looking—and then the reasons for such behavior—feelings of dependence, loss of useful employment, acceptance of culturally conditioned negative expectations toward old age—is raised and discussed. In each case a denouement, whether it involves finding a part-time job, having a good, honest discussion of differences, or obtaining professional counseling, releases the older subjects from their stereotypical personas, after which they fit quite normally into the family unit. Two other pieces, "The People vs. Henry Johnson" (1958) and "Ever Since April" (1960), treated the phenomenon of compulsory retirement and its emotionally debilitating effect on the older person. Both plays built upon the theory that work is a necessity, either as a means of economic maintenance or as a social role which confers a sense of usefulness. In "Ever Since April," the adoption of a postretirement activity revivified a man who had been in decline physically and mentally because of the disappearance of the work role.[13]

The record of the American movie industry with respect to the image of the aged has not been a good one. Among those who blame America's youth fixation for society's devaluation of the elderly, Hollywood has long been a favorite, and not unfairly chosen, target. The most popular themes—romantic love, physical conquest—traditionally require displays of beauty, daring, strength, and endurance, which are all qualities generally associated with youth. Thus, younger actors and actresses are "stars," while older ones (with certain familiar exceptions—Cary Grant, John Wayne, Katherine Hepburn, etc.) are usually identified as "character actors" and awarded supporting roles. Often these supporting roles have involved an exaggerated focus on age. Especially in westerns, which were most popular among the young Saturday matinee set, the disservices done the elderly have been legion, among them Gabby Hayes, Fuzzy Knight, Raymond Hatton, and Wallace Beery. Speaking before a 1958 Social Work Education Symposium, an educator spoke of the "vibrant older character . . . in *South Pacific* and . . . *Love in the Afternoon,* but he could just as easily have noted that for every Ezio Pinza, Gary Cooper, and Maurice Chevalier, there existed a dozen comic relief characters—familiar of face if not of name—whose chief attribute was a crotchety or senile old age. The most recent cinematic trends are mixed, with perhaps a decline in the tendency of scriptwriters to include peripheral older characters as comic asides. This derives, in all probability, from the disappearance of the action-western and the swashbuckler as major cinematic forms and the consequent reduction in the need for "sidekicks." Still, the treatment of the aged in today's films shows no particular deference to gerontological theories and can as easily devalue as exalt the later years. Thus, Ruth Gordon is at once triumphant in the role of Maud in *Harold and Maud* (the story of a love affair between a boy of twenty and a woman of eighty) and laughably pathetic as the senile mother in *Where's Poppa?* (the cruelly funny saga of a son trying to put his mother in an old age home over the objections posed by an obsessive sense of filial responsibility), to cite only two recent examples, each having enjoyed box office success. To date, there seems to be no disposition, similar to that shown by television, to use the cinema in a calculated attempt to alter popular images of the aged. However, the tendency to make use, for comic purposes, of the stereotypical frailties of age seems to have diminished in recent years. Given the cinema's emphasis upon box office receipts, perhaps this is the most gerontologists can hope for.[14]

The medium of print probably had less effect in changing public opinion than the livelier audiovisual media, because it reached a smaller and more selective audience. Defined for present purposes, the print medium includes the kinds of things people read outside of their professional and work situations. This definition encompasses newspapers, news magazines, popular periodicals, books (factual and fictional), and graphics. In earlier chapters, we have cited enough newspaper and magazine articles to justify their inclusion as important sources of information on aging. One representative example of this medium's attempt to place highly factual information in a popular format was the four-part series "Old Age: Personal Crisis, U.S. problem," which appeared in *Life* Magazine during July and August 1959. Passionate and imaginative volumes such as de Beauvoir's *The*

Coming of Age and Harrington's *The Other America,* among others, while not significant with regard to numbers reached, have had substantial impact on certain influential groups. Speaking of the potential of the printed word, Germaine Krettek, director of the Washington Office of the American Library Association, urged public librarians to make children, young adults, and teachers aware of "books and periodicals which deal constructively with the problems of the older population." Such contact, she felt, could help prepare them not only to deal with older people encountered in day-to-day living, but for their own aging as well.[15]

Turning to fiction, we can note, with *New York Times* reviewer Anatole Broyard, the emergence of a "new breed in elderly people, one that has turned the traditional image upside down or inside out. Whimsical, unpredictable, radical, ironical, devil-may-care, they are the very opposite of the 'typical' older person." In his review of the Josh Greenfield–Paul Mazursky book *Harry and Tonto,* Broyard pointed to Bellow's *Mr. Sammler's Planet,* Wright Morris' *A Life,* Patrick White's *The Eye of the Storm,* and Barry Unworth's *Mooncranker's Gift* as works which demonstrated his thesis. "These [fictional older] people," he argued, "have realized that, having no future, as some sociologists put it, they might as well make the most of the present, kick up their heels on the rim of the grave." Iris Murdoch's 1962 novel, *An Unofficial Rose* and Graham Greene's *Travels with My Aunt,* a 1969 publication, are further examples of the kind of book Broyard has referred to. In her work, Murdoch thoughtfully examines the roles of love, desire, and sex in the lives of the elderly through the device of a geriatric triangle—a seventyish widower, his past-sixty former mistress and a sixty-year-old woman friend who has always loved the hero and now intends "to have him" sexually. Treating the topic seriously, with her peculiarly elegant technique, Murdoch manages to craft a novel that can only be termed "sexy." Greene's Aunt Augusta cannot be described briefly, but she is a woman whose drives, biological and emotional, have seemingly been augmented by the process of aging; a woman who quite simply puts the mid-dleaged narrator to shame in almost every aspect of living. The appearance of such novels, inconceivable a generation earlier, depended to a large extent upon the proper climate of opinion—that is, a positive view of the older person. (E. M. Forster's novel *Maurice,* written in 1909 but published only recently, offers a parallel case with respect to the fictional treatment of homosex-uality without guilt.) In the act of accepting a view and building a literary work upon it, however, the author provides at once an indicator and a reinforcement of social approval.[16]

Within the newspaper industry, interest in the phenomenon of aging increased rapidly and steadily during the decade of the 1950s. Noting the growing popularity of this topic with the working press in 1957, William Posner, a social work adminis-trator and teacher, remarked: "This is a heartening advance, since only a few short years ago it was hard to get so much as notice in the local press informing the public of the existence of the welfare council's hobby show for older persons." Newspaper awareness of the aged as a segment of the reading public came quite early. One of the pioneers in this recognition of the elderly was Tom Collins, a feature editor for the *Chicago Daily News.* In 1950, he and the paper's managing editor decided to include more material addressed specifically to older people. The result-ing regular column, "The Golden Years," focused on the prob-lems, solutions, and achievements of the elderly and solicited their participation via letter. In an article in 1956 on Collins' success, *Time Magazine* reported that the column was not only syndicated to 94 United States newpapers, but had been collected into a book which his publisher had designated "a potential best-seller." This was certainly a tribute to the column's popularity. R. O. Beckman wrote a similar feature, "The Vintage Years," which appeared on a weekly basis in a number of Florida news-papers beginning in May 1954. According to an article in *Florida Living,* Beckman's column provided "answers to your questions on how to keep happy, healthy, busy—and maybe even pros-perous—in the years to come." Sample columns reveal him to be a kind of Abigail Van Buren for the senior set. Other successful syndicated columnists included Robert L. Peterson ("Your Best Years," King Features) and Ray Henry ("Security for You," AP Newsservice), both of whom launched their columns in the mid-1950s amidst great optimism on the part of the sponsoring syndicates.[17]

On the level of graphic art, such as that used in cartoons or to simplify complex notions, the case is fairly straightforward. A cartoon feature such as "The Lively Ones," with its frolicsome elderly subjects, provides an example of the use of an entertaining popular art form to promote an optimistic image of old age. The older lady at the bar who orders "anything but an old-fashioned," or the elderly gentleman paying court to two bikini-clad girls on the beach provide well-meant caricatures of the kinds of models of aging proposed in more complex terms by gerontologists. Similarly, the cartoon reports prepared by the Mississippi State Welfare Department and the Connecticut Commission on the Potential of Aging demonstrated the use of illustrative art to place otherwise dry and technical reports in the public domain. Of themselves, such efforts might seem relatively insignificant; but against a backdrop of movement on a number of other educational fronts, both formal and informal, these seemingly negligible contributions might play a role in reinforcing desired changes in attitude.[18]

In a 1962 symposium on aging and education, John R. Voris commended the pioneering activities of the mass media upon behalf of the older American. "Through much publicizing by the communications media," he declared, "the country has become increasingly conscious of the 'Problem of Aging,' 'The Care of the Aged,' 'Our Elderly Population,' 'America's Senior Citizens,' etc. . . , or by whatever term may be used." This consciousness did not, to be sure, mean that the "problems of the aging" had been solved, that the "care of the aged" had been improved, that the "elderly" or the "senior citizens" were being perceived only in benign terms. However, this consciousness was certainly a prerequisite to such material and social advances as gerontologists sought for the older citizen. In laying the groundwork; in creating a heightened degree of public recognition for subsequent concrete efforts to elevate the status of the aged in American culture, education (within and without the school room) was an early and willing partner in the social gerontology coalition.

N O T E S

1. Anderson, "Teaching and Learning," in Donahue (ed.), *Education for Later Maturity*, 85–86.
2. Federal Council on Aging, *Aiding Older Persons* (Washington, D.C., 1956); Hunter, "Pre-Retirement Education," *Geriatrics* 15 part 2 (November 1960): 793–800.
3. Desmond quoted in *Growing With the Years* (Albany, 1954), 1; Kansas Legislative Council, *Problems Pertaining to Aging* (1955), 1; Winston testimony before the full committee's subcommittee on State and Local Services in *Hearings*, 149, 88th Congress, 2nd Session. The relative obscurity in which most "official" reports remained after publication is highlighted by the comments of a Mississippi delegate to a conference of state agencies that none of his state's legislators had read a recent report by the State Commission on Aging; see Senate Labor Committee, *Studies of the Aged and Aging*, I, 38.
4. Conference of State Commissions, *Official State Groups on Aging* (1954), 71–86; Welfare Council of Metropolitan Chicago, *Community Services for Older People* (Chicago, 1952), 6–12; activities of Minnesota's Council reported in *Aging* (January 1960): 1–3.
5. "Senior Citizens' Month," *Science Newsletter*, 63: May 23, 1953, p. 324; New York City, *New York City Observes Senior-Citizens' Month* (May 1956), pp. 3, 7; et passim; *Aging*, September 1959; President's Council, *Projects and Promotion Guide for Senior Citizens' Month* (Washington, D.C., 1965); National Council on Aging Library has HEW promotional material on Senior Citizens' Month celebrations across the country which emphasize the public relations rather than the concrete program aspects of such events in most areas; see HEW, "How Communities Observed Senior Citizens' Month, 1967" (clippings), and *Meeting the Challenge of Later Years* (an HEW public relations packet).
6. Brody, "Senior City at the New York State Fair," Case Study No. 11 in *Patterns of Progress for Aging* (Washington, D.C.), July 1961; J. M. Cutter, E. B. Russell, and E. A. Stettler, "An Activity Center for Senior Citizens," Case Study No. 3, ibid. (June 1961). See also President's Council on Aging, *The Senior Center: Its Goals, Functions and Programs* (Washington, D.C., 1964) for a general discussion of the public relations potential inherent in such programs and White House Conference on Aging (hereafter WHCoA), *Background Paper on Local Community Organizations* (March 1960), for specific examples of educational senior center projects operating in Ohio and Oregon and the success they have enjoyed.
7. Swartz, "Organized Planning for Old Age," *Geriatrics* 7 (1952): 63–69. References to these radio and television shows compiled from the volumes of *Aging* and from

the vertical files on Broadcasting at the NCoA Library in Washington, D.C. Only those for which some descriptive data was available were noted. The list is hardly exhaustive.

8. 'The Best Years'—Sponsored by the Cleveland Women's City Club Foundation (Washington, D.C.: NCoA Library); Association of Junior Leagues of America, Health and Welfare (Geriatrics) Project on Television (September 1956–January 1957) (NCoA Library); George Lefferts, "The Living End" program note at NCoA Library.

9. Collins, "Reaching the Elderly Population Through Broadcasting." April 1, 1960 (Mimeo, NCoA Library); Twin City Area Television Corp., "Seminars for Seniors, 1969" (NCoA Library); description of Older Americans Act and AoA responsibilities from Aging (August 1965): 1–4; the Hawaiian and Pennsylvania programs mentioned in "TV Tunes in on Later Years," ibid. (August–September 1969): 17.

10. See "Bright Galaxy of Playwrights," Life 37 (October 25, 1954): 77–81, for sketches of Chayefsky (a "family problems expert"); Arthur ("mainly concerned with relationships between parents and children"); and Foote ("writes with great craft and knowledge of the problems of youth and old age.").

11. Paddy Chayefsky, "The Mother," in Gore Vidal (ed.), Best Television Plays (New York: 1956), pp. 1–31, and "Fear Begins at Forty" (undated CBS Brochure, NCoA Library). Note how each of these plays reflected the classic gerontological thinking of the period—i.e., that work was the panacea, both economic and emotional, for the problems of older people.

12. Play review from Aging (July 1954); note on conference's use of kinescope, ibid. (September 1954); Fred Freed, "Woman! The Lonely Years" NCoA Library, (March 1960).

13. Nora Stirling, "The Room Upstairs" (American Theater Wing Community Plays, New York, 1953), "Ever Since April" (Plays for Living, Family Service Associations of America, 1960), "A Choice to Make" (FSAA, Project on Aging, 1963); Roy Flynn, "The People vs. Henry Johnson" (Florida Governor's Conference on Aging, October 16, 1958—mimeo, NCoA Library); Isobel McFadden, "Five in a Living Room" (New York: Friendship Press, 1962).

14. While there is no need to treat educational films in any detail, a huge list of dramatic/documentary filmstrips is available from the NCoA with rental sale or loan information included. In numbers alone, this is an important phenomenon. Quote from J. M. Maxwell, "Implications for Social Work Practice," in Council on Social Work Education. Social Work Education for Better Services to the Aging (New York: 1959), p. 56.

15. Krettek quoted in testimony before the Senate Labor Committee, "National Organizations in the Field of Aging," S.L.C. Hearings, 1959, p. 52.

16. Broyard, "A Medicare Existentialist," New York Times [Books], June 6, 1974; one perhaps less artful, but wider reaching effort to use literature to renovate the image of the older person was the kind of short stories featured in the popular monthly pulp magazines. One example of this I found particularly worthy of note was Barbara Robinson, "Honor Thy Father-in-Law," McCall's, 90 (May 1963): 93–97+.

17. Posner, "Adapting and Sharpening Social Work Knowledge and Skills in Serving the Aged." Social Work 13 (October 1957): 37–42; "Life Can Be Golden," Time 67 (May 14, 1956): 87–88.

18. "The Lively Ones," a syndicate portfolio on file at NCoA Library; the success of the Mississippi effort noted by a delegate to the Conference of State Commissions on Aging in 1952—see Senate Labor Committee, Studies of the Aged and Aging, I, p. 38; Connecticut's cartoon summary of official state report entitled Golden Years in the Silver City, described in Aging (March 1955).

163

7

Images of the Aging:
Contributions of the
Social Work Profession

The problem of proper care for the aged has been
neglected for years, though it is increasingly
acute. We have an imposing edifice of social work
in this country. . . .But by some subtle process
beginning in the professional schools and going
on in their work, the consciences of social workers are dulled and, in the end, they do not even
perceive when their work is ineffective or
undone. . . .

Letter to the Editor, *Survey*, 86 (1950), 50

Preeminent among technicians of social action, the welfare fields,
both public and private, have played major roles in our modern
"discovery" of the aged. In applying and modifying the gerontological theories of social and biomedical scientists, in promoting professional self-education and, through numerous
demonstration projects, heightening public consciousness, social
workers and social agencies have done much to alter the popular
image of the aging in the postwar era. One might, in fact, consider the profession the cutting edge of the altruistic movement
(as opposed to more self-interested or ideological efforts) to rev-
olutionize the depressed status of the older person in American
culture. Unbound by the frequently rigid preconceptions of academic gerontologists and trained as field workers, social work
technicians were freer to test the findings of theorists and to
adopt, modify, or reject them based on their success in practical

situations. In so doing, they could also collect primary data useful for the establishment of in-service, field education programs, and through these, help to educate the public to a new vision of old age.

The emphasis on practices that increasingly thrust the social work profession into the forefront of the gerontological crusade originated in the Progressive Era. The charity organization movement of the late nineteenth century which defined and pro-fessionalized the concept of welfare, and the emergence of the settlement house in the early twentieth century which introduced the principle of service as an adjunct or alternative to bare ma-terial assistance, not only created the modern social work profes-sion, but supplied it as well with a philosophical framework that would be useful in approaching the problems of aging. With an action orientation and a tradition of sensitivity to the problems of dependency and deviancy, social welfare agencies would, in time, play important roles in the field of gerontology.

The Social Security Act of 1935 provided a convenient, if arbitrary, milestone in the history of the welfare profession's assumption of responsibility for the elderly. The administration of simple money grants, while far from the modern concepts of geriatric casework and services, nonetheless created within the public welfare establishment an awareness of the nation's in-creasing older population and their needs. As one commentator on the role of social work in the field of aging observed; the emerging concept of public assistance for the elderly, as a right, constituted "the greatest philosophical contribution of the public assistance program." With this right established, further modes of nonmaterial assistance were made possible. Out of this situ-ation new attitudes and methods of social agency involvement would gradually emerge within welfare's public and private spheres.[1]

Despite a helping tradition and statistical proof that the num-ber of older people in need of assistance was growing, the wel-fare establishment did not move with any great alacrity into the field of geriatrics. As the organizers of one community action project in Chicago put it: "The last section of our population to receive the serious attention of students and practitioners in the field of human behavior was the older age group." Even in the largest cities, they noted, "one must often search to find the agency or the organization which gives the problems of older people the same degree of attention and quality of service offered to children and younger adults." This fact is easily understood when it is recognized that, as a profession, social work reflected the composition and attitudes of the society it served more accurately than any of the other groups or elements with which we will deal in the course of the study. Thus, the slowness of the transition is not surprising. To begin with, the already cited conservative attitude of schools of social work towards specialization within the formal curriculum continually stifled efforts to attract students and give them the special skills needed to work in this area. Then, opportunities for in-service training in work with the aging were not only few, but such programs as did exist had difficulty recruiting from a pool of social work graduates imbued with the child-centered theories of Freud and Piaget, and oriented toward work with youth, adolescents, and young adults. (As late as 1957, one observer noted that fully one-third of all caseworkers serving the aging had no formal gerontological training.) Finally, the "goal-direction" that had traditionally provided much of the motivation to the social work career was found lacking in work with the aged. Older people, the thinking went, were less amenable to the casework process, and results took longer to achieve and were less dramatically observable. To the achievement-oriented social worker, geriatric casework offered few attractions. For these reasons, lacks within the profession—the needs for new definitions of aging, for greater interest in the elderly clientele within the school setting, and for a more realistic assessment of the capacity of the older person—mirrored those applicable to society in general. Only by altering their own attitudes and reconstituting their own value systems would social workers ultimately recognize their responsibility to extend this process to the larger society.[2]

Suggestions designed to promote a changing view of the elderly among welfare workers—from one stressing dependency to one emphasizing developmental capacity—first arose toward the end of World War II. One pioneering social worker, writing in *The Family* in late 1944, chided her colleagues for continuing to associate old age with physical and mental deterioration, slovenliness, and unsociability. "As caseworkers" she urged, "we need to recognize the rich field of opportunity for casework that the aged offer. . . . Casework has much to give old people in helping them make their adjustment to one of the most difficult periods of life." Such advice took on added significance when the census data for 1940 was analyzed. John Griffen, director of the Bureau of Old Age Assistance in Somerville, Massachusetts, pointed to this statistical material and analyzed it with regard to its "vast implications" for the field of social work. Given the traditional negative view of old age as a period of unalterable decline, social workers tended to shy away from work with older people in favor of what seemed a more rewarding investment of time with children and young adults. Yet the figures on age distribution indicated that the welfare establishment could not afford much longer to be so exclusive. Citing the stirrings within the medical profession, Griffen insisted that social work had an obligation to assimilate and promulgate all scientific developments in geriatrics through its professional schools, journals, and seminars and to develop both a "science" and an "integrated philosophy" of geriatric casework. "The suffering aged," he concluded, "await our action."[3]

Those within the profession who were advocating and experimenting with programs designed to tap the alleged capabilities of the elderly, at this early date, were largely involved in trial and error processes. When such a program as the pioneering senior citizen settlement house of the Hodson Community Center of Bronx, New York, showed results, the Center's founders were quick to publish them. Thus, Center co-directors Dora Fuchs and Harry Levine, writing for the *Journal of Gerontology* in its first issue in 1946, declared: "Millions are spent yearly on health and public assistance programs for the older person. He remains an unproductive, disgruntled being. . . . How much wiser the spending would be if we planned with perspective, if we worked toward developing the strengths of the older person, enabling him to participate as an emotionally healthy, creative member of the community." The Hodson Center, observed psychologist George Lawton at a conference on recreation for older people in April 1946, provided the prototype for a whole system of "facilities for promoting the development of the older person" by making available to him "a combination of psychological rehabilitation, education, creative expression and group recreational and diversional activities." Hertha Kraus, director of a pathmark study of the aged of Allegheny County, Pennsylvania in the 1930s, lauded such shifts from data collection to program implementation. She asserted that the field required improved physical facilities, changes in attitude and policies, and widespread public cooperation. "It will not be easy, or a quick accomplishment," she warned, "it will challenge some favorite traditions, some vested interests, some deep-seated loyalties, and even more deep-seated indifference. . . ."[4]

The *Social Work Year Book,* which appears at regular two year intervals, did not include a section on "Aging" before 1945, and even this recognition comprised little more than a summary of the problems and needs faced by the elderly. It was not until the 1951 issue that the *Year Book* actually made policy recommendations designed to relieve the conditions it had heretofore catalogued. With regard to the financial condition of the elderly, the article, written by Margaret Wagner, proposed an end to compulsory retirement based on age and expansion of OASDI coverage and continued strengthening of the private pension system. In the realm of housing, shortages of suitable facilities for independent living as well as high rents offered examples of problems which required the attention of social welfare agencies and religious groups. Health care for the aged had been too long burdened by an ameliorative philosophy, when evidence increasingly suggested the efficacy of a rehabilitative approach. In addition, she encouraged such positive programs as housekeeping/

168

homemaker services, preventive health care facilities, adult education programs, and day activity centers as the best means of maximizing the potential of the older person for independent living. Similarly, Chester Bowles, the governor of Connecticut, stressed the need to help older people to help themselves. "[A]lthough we have made important gains from the point of view of meeting the financial needs of our older citizens, we have not yet done very much to help them within their social setting . . . by and large we have not met the overall challenge of providing them with facilities for individual and group activities." And E. V. Andrews, a social work professional, joined Bowles in emphasizing the need for noneconomic services. "Our social workers in their regular contacts can help recipients grow old gracefully, accept and understand physical limitations, participate in activities and hobbies which interest them . . . ."[5]

Except for these few, however; the idea that nonfinancial services like casework, groupwork, family counseling, or psychotherapy had a role to play in assisting the elderly did not find widespread acceptance among social work theorists in the immediate postwar period. Here again, the Freudian bias intruded. The tradition within the welfare professions was either to define the aged in terms of indigency and dependence or to ignore them altogether. Low income provided the only criterion of need applicable to the older person. Their limited capacities and foreshortened futures, argued the majority of these theorists, typed the older person as a waste of professional energy and skill. A Freudian analyst, Dr. Marc Hollender provided an example of this mode of thought when he denied the applicability of the psychoanalytic process to people over fifty. According to him, "there is not enough to hope for in the future to provide the motivation needed to endure the tensions mobilized by analysis." Indeed, charged a critic of this view, psychoanalysis was so dominated by the Freudian theory of neurosis that analysts refused to treat older people simply to avoid a rethinking of the whole theory.[6]

Despite the Freudian *mortemain,* conditions were changing. As social and biological scientists continued to amass theoretical and empirical information about the physical and psychosocial processes of aging, the more sophisticated members of the social work profession increasingly called for reformed practices in the field. One of the earliest calls was made in a paper delivered to the National Conference of Social Workers in 1945. "New developments in psychology and sociology are concerned with the aged," the contributor noted. "The mental and emotional effects of aging and the ways in which mental and physical alertness can be preserved in advancing years are subjects of study. Casework with aged individuals is changing in content and scope, because of our growing understanding of human behavior. . . . Improved understanding of the process of aging and new methods of treatment are making it possible for many persons to live more comfortably and actively." And social worker Joseph P. Anderson, testifying before the New York State Legislative Committee on the Aging, made much the same point when he declared: "Social workers must have knowledge from related disciplines . . . knowledge about our social institutions . . . communities and the groups that make up these communities, . . . of agencies and programs [and] of the laws on which these programs are based."[7]

Margery J. Smith, a public welfare theorist, gave a good example of the kind of sociological-psychological data which social workers could put to use in their practices. She noted the findings of social psychologists who had traced the roots of dependency to idleness. In the younger person, illness or unemployment for an extended period of time often gave rise to feelings of dependency. Now among the aged, idleness in retirement, regardless of state of health, could release similar urges. This suggested that dependency found among the aged was not necessarily pathological; that it was potentially as reversible as in the case of the younger adult recovering from illness or finding new employment. If this sense of dependency in the aged were not reversed by therapeutic measure or by a return to the work force, Smith suggested, they became self-reinforcing phenomena. Since work for the elderly was becoming increasingly difficult to find, the emphasis upon therapy would have to increase. Applying this hypothesis and providing social services to restore or perpetuate a measure of independence for the aged individual rested squarely with the welfare profession. "I believe we could prevent a large share of the problems arising out of premature senility breakdowns which are filling our mental institutions," she insisted, "if we had a program for older people offering something more than financial aid."[8]

From the realm of sociology, C. V. Willie, writing in *Social Casework,* suggested that "role theory" had great potential as an analytical tool for geriatric caseworkers. The average older person, excluded from employment, family, and most areas of social involvement provided a classic example of the "roleless" state. This "rolelessness" caused the older person not only to acquiesce but to sink more deeply into a state of social isolation with all the grave psychological and emotional problems which that condition implied. By adopting a role theory framework, Willie declared, the social worker could better define his relationship to the older client, and within the bounds of that relationship, help the client to meet and overcome his situation with minimal personal or social disturbance. The caseworker, he continued, could approach his task from three different directions. First, he could attempt to modify or alter the social institutions which encouraged role loss among the elderly. Second he could work to provide alternative roles for older clients within a special supportive social environment. And third, he could attempt to evolve new defintions of the aging process which recognized both its limitations and potentials and was neither unrealistically optimistic or inhibitively pessimistic. Role theory, then, offered a basis for concrete action, whether it was fighting against compulsory retirement or discriminatory age barriers, organizing golden age clubs, senior centers, or simply making well-advertised public use of the talents and capacities of older people.[9]

Social group worker Jerome Kaplan of Minneapolis adopted

such theories early on in his work with the aged of Hennepin County, Minnesota and wrote enthusiastically of his success in providing an age-specific, normative environment within which socially isolated oldsters interacted happily and smoothly with their peers. Although he accepted the "activity" school's contention that the best solution for the long run involved changing society's attitudes toward the elderly and reintegrating them in the larger social context, until this was done supportive social groupings of age peers provided the ideal means to guard against the indignities of rolessness and isolation. Another group worker, Georgene Bowen, director of Philadelphia's innovative recreation program for the aged, agreed with Kaplan's analysis of the problem as well as with his proposed solution. She went a step further, however, in asserting that the example of the older person, contentedly acting within the peer group setting, would ultimately help to change popular expectations vis à vis the aged individual, by providing a demonstration of his capacities for adjustment and for normal social interaction. Older people in such milieux, she wrote, "are quietly and forcefully pressing the point home that age can be something to look forward to." In both these cases, the client group included both public assistance and nonpublic assistance elderly, a point that gave support to those few within the welfare establishment who argued that the needs of the elderly were not solely economic; that their social, emotional, and psychological problems were as real as those of the child, the adolescent, and the young adult. In this light, social agencies had an ongoing obligation to minister to these problems and, according to Ollie Randall, the responsibility as well to stay abreast of all the data and theories compiled by social, biological, and medical science, with an eye to adopting it, where appropriate, to field practice.[10]

The importance of Erikson (a Freudian) and the neo-Freudians in emphasizing the continuing developmental capacities of the human being, cannot be overstressed for their revolutionary contributions to social work theory. Although one of the more important figures in the adaptation of their theories to social work practice, Berta Fantl never specifically dealt with the problems of aging. Yet her insights appear, in retrospect, to have had particular relevance to the field of geriatric casework. Writing in the late 1950s, Fantl explicated Heinz Hartmann's "secondary ego autonomy" theory (i.e., ego has the internal capacity for growth irrespective of past environmental experiences) and stressed its "implications for assertive casework." The special significance of her contribution tested with the assertion that the resourcefulness of the ego need have no age boundaries—that it was, by nature, a consistent quality throughout life. She drew, as well, on Erikson's view that the human psyche is plastic throughout the life cycle—a view that supported a growing feeling within the social work profession that older people could respond to casework methods once thought to apply only to the young.[11]

It was, of course, one thing to proclaim the need for extensive casework services for the elderly and even to provide compelling reasons and analytical tools for such action. It was quite another to get such views and programs accepted by the social work establishment. Given the profession's absorption with the theories of Freud and Piaget and a shortage of geriatric casework training programs, the acceptance of such new responsibilities entailed the changing of attitudes and values within the academy and the agency. Elizabeth Breckinridge of the American Public Welfare Association's Project on Aging, sought to underline this when she wrote: " . . . in no other field of social service has there been so great a lack of specialized, professional training." Helen Francis of the Community Service Society, a private New York City agency, agreed with Breckinridge and traced this situation to the dominance of stereotypical notions about the aged among social work educators and administrators. She also urged caseworkers to confront their own anxieties in working with the aged and to accept the reality that such work was simply not a short-term, high-return endeavor. With the removal of these intellectual and emotional barriers, the profession could begin to consider how it could be of use to older people, both in the classroom and in the field.[12]

As time passed, social workers increasingly agreed that improvement of social services to the aged depended very much upon changing professional attitudes and destroying the stereotypes about old age, which too often marred the casework process. At the Arden House Seminar on Casework with the Aging, sponsored by the National Council on the Aging in 1961, the issue of professional attitude received close scrutiny. One participant stressed the need for a good attitude at the top of the agency staff,—that negative attitudes and stereotypes among supervisory personnel often influenced the efforts of field workers; while another viewed the whole seminar exercise as one in which "we are all engaged in changing some of our customary assumptions, not only about persons we refer to as aging and aged, but also about older people as clients as well as about ourselves as professional helping persons." In a set of papers on casework with the aging, prepared as a memorial to the late William Posner, one of the contributors stated flatly that professional attitude was the base upon which practice rested. "It is incumbent upon the caseworker . . . to subject his attitude and feelings to close examination and to become fully aware of those prejudices and distortions that may adversely affect the giving of sensitive, professional help to the aging client."

In a practical illustration of the interrelation of attitude and diligence in the field, a survey of 80 randomly selected OAA and ADC cases in two different agencies, involving a total of 26 caseworkers, revealed that those caseworkers who liked working with the aged spent more time and effort on them than did those who preferred ADC cases. The special relevance of attitude to the geriatric caseworkers, moreover, was emphasized by the fact that case workers who preferred OAA cases did not neglect their ADC cases to the same extent that those with ADC preferences neglected the OAA clients in their case loads. Attitudinal change, more and more appeared the sine qua non of effective casework with, and service to, the aged; how to achieve it remained the single biggest unanswered question.[13]

Unlike the formal social work school setting which, as we have seen, is usually organized along generalist lines and thus not particularly adaptable to the need for more gerontological specialization, the field has always been the source of practical experience in new areas of casework. Thus, within the area of geriatric casework, we find the earliest awareness of the aging as a particular client group among field workers. For example, the Hodson Day Center, in Bronx, New York, was established in 1943 under City Department of Welfare auspices to serve as "a mental health and adult education program which promotes social and emotional adjustment of the older person" by recognizing and emphasizing his strengths and capacities. Indeed, as a founder of the center later wrote, one of the express purposes of the project was the altering of the community's stereotyped views of the aging and to attempt to generate public support for programs designed to assist them. Since there were no blueprints for such an endeavor, the center evolved out of trial and error field procedure. Similarly, the Hartford (Connecticut) Family Service Society adopted, as early as 1947, a small demonstration project which sent case workers out into the field to minister to the needs of the older person. The goals of this program included, not only getting services to older clients, but altering negative attitudes about aging often held by both the caseworker and his client, mediating the hostilities existing within the family structure, and transmitting information about the situation of the aged to the community at large. The tools used included housekeeping services, an institutional visiting program, golden age clubs and centers, and a good working relation with the local press, through which project efforts were advertised. Many of these pioneering efforts, even when basically recreational in nature—like the summer camp program of the Cleveland Welfare Foundation (1949) or the various senior citizens' clubs which grew up in places like Iron City, Michigan, Minneapolis, or Findlay, Ohio—served as important sources of data about the needs and capacities of older people. Project directors consistently reported that the elderly involved in such programs seemed to prefer activity and sociability and appeared much more flexible, capable, and good humored as a result of their participation.[14]

These early efforts, while neither extensive nor significant in terms of concrete accomplishment, had their quiet impact none-theless. As early as January–April 1951, a survey on organized planning for older people in 215 communities of over 75,000 population, revealed that concern for the needs of the aged was, an as yet unmarked, but a growing phenomenon. Of 155 replies received, survey analyst Philip Swartz observed that 57 had active planning organizations concerned with the problems of aging, 29 more planned to launch such an organization in the near future, while 69 had no such organization nor any plans for one. With respect to services provided by the community, recreation led the field (115 instances), followed by custodial programs such as old age homes (93), and hospital services (41). Communities displayed somewhat less interest in supportive services, including counseling (38), outpatient clinics (26), foster homes (22), and homemaker services (16). In this survey, however, the questions asked were actually more important than the answers received. Such queries implied a growing interest, on the policy making level, in the importance of supportive programs for the elderly and suggested that perhaps the enduring association of old age with the institution, or the dole, was beginning to weaken.[15]

Another indication of changing attitudes toward the problems and potentials of the aged on the social policy level was the increased tendency of the private philanthropic foundations to invest in action programs aimed at the elderly. Foundations, in fact, had long been involved in the field of aging but had generally concentrated in such areas as the role of custodial and protective institutions (Deutsch Foundation, *The Care of Older People,* 1931) and biomedical research (Macy Foundation, from 1937 on). In the postwar era, however, these charitable institutions began to absorb the social and biological evidence which suggested new interpretation of the aging process. Thus, private foundations increasingly concerned themselves with social welfare projects aimed at elevating the socioeconomic condition of the aged, educating the public to the necessity of such projects, and training professionals to carry them out. In Chicago, for example, the Wieboldt Family Foundation funded a project on aging, administered by the city's Metropolitan Welfare Council. Beginning in 1947, the project's directors announced their goals as: (1) the determination of the kinds of problems facing the city's older population; (2) the education of the community to these problems; (3) the operation of demonstration programs aimed at solving these problems; and (4) the development of policy to guide continuing future efforts by the community. Indeed, the final report of this project (1952) provided an example of the kind of data collection and promulgation effort which promised to legitimatize the idea of expanded service programs for the aged. The evaluation of its impact stressed "encouraging expansions in the amount of care provided for older people" by both public and private agencies, and a spreading "general awareness of the problems facing older age groups and the necessity of extending more services to them."[16]

In an American Public Welfare Association project, begun in 1952, the Doris Duke Foundation exemplified the emerging tendency to invest funds in practical geriatric social service programs. The Association's rationale for the problem, obviously shared by the grantor institution, cited "a growing awareness that neither our ideas nor our social arrangements are currently well-adapted to making these added years the social and personal asset they should be." The project report cited the barriers to a reformed approach toward the problems of the elderly—the decline of the family institution, economics, stereotypes about the aging process—and declared: "It is the job of all concerned with social planning to try to remedy these shortcomings in such a way that the later period of life need not be subject to social handicap, but may become . . . the final flowering and fruition of the process of growth." A necessary alteration in welfare policy, the APWA argued, would involve a shift from an ameliorative public assistance approach to a preventive and rehabilitative philosophy. Social services administered by social workers were the key tools in the implementation of this new philosophy. These included information, advice, referral, aid in securing

177

particular benefits or services "and other catalytic functions that lubricate an elaborate social machinery but carry with them no implication of inadequacy or failure on the part of those who receive them." Looking ahead to a time when society would no longer define old age in terms of economic dependency, the report asserted that the public welfare establishment would then be enabled to devote itself "to the other needs of people living in a condition of increasingly tight-knit interdependency." To date (1953), efforts in this direction "offer a good demonstration of the extent to which social work is becoming truly the democratic instrument of mutual aid for all the people."[17]

The APWA, again with Duke Foundation support, operated and evaluated a number of special projects for the aging during the early 1950s. The Association published the accounts and evaluations in a nine-pamphlet series under the title *How Public Welfare Serves Aging People*. According to the series director, Elizabeth Breckinridge, each of the pamphlets sought to help make up the "serious disparity between the broad concept of public welfare for the aging that we talk about in conferences and committee meetings, and the services we are in fact providing in our local offices." The topics addressed in the series included the general need for more social services to the aged (Maurice O. Hunt, August 1954), a social reintegration program for deinstitutionalized older mental patients to prevent future recommitments (A. M. Pemberton, September 1954), the development of social clubs for older people (E. B. Hoge, October 1954), the development and operation of day centers (H. L. McCarthy, December 1954), the use of high visibility social service programs to stimulate public interest in, and support for, all efforts to help older people in the community (J. Kaplan, February 1955), the provision of homemaker services to assist the partially disabled older person to stay independent (D. G. Kimmel, April 1955), the need for friendly visiting services to lonely and homebound aged (E. G. Watkins, May 1955), a referral service designed to help older people find the best institutional care available (V. L. Megowen, June 1955), and a general conclusion by editor Breckinridge (July 1955) that assessed where the APWA had been and, based on that knowledge, in what directions it had now to move.[18]

If the decade of the 50s saw an increase in the amount of foundation-supported social service field work, and professional and community education efforts by various welfare institutions, the decade of the 60s, not only adopted, but greatly expanded and improved upon such programs. The involvement of foundations in the area of social services to the aged, wrote the Syracuse University gerontologist Walter M. Beattie, Jr., in 1961, had changed the nature of the debate within the profession from why older people deserved attention, and whether they could profit from it, to how best to provide them with the necessary services. Thus, beyond providing assistance to the elderly in a variety of ways and suggesting different methods for doing this, these foundation-supported efforts helped bring home to the social work profession the value of such services—a growing awareness which in turn promoted the multiplication and expansion of such programs. In a background paper, dated March 1960, prepared to guide the deliberations of the social services section of the White House Conference on Aging (January 1961), this awareness was in evidence. "Independent living increasingly depends upon the community resources upon which individuals and their families can draw," the authors of the paper noted: "If these resources are inadequate, and they are for many, then personal and family difficulties, illness, loss of income and fear about the future take their toll in lost homes and premature disability." The provision of these services depended upon three elements— changed community attitudes, increased number of properly trained personnel to administer these programs, and adequate funding.[19]

Of these three elements, adequate funding was the initial requirement. Given proper financial support, one could underwrite programs, the operations of which would provide professional training, and the results of which would change community attitudes. Thomas H. Carroll, director of special grants for the

179

Ford Foundation, writing on the Foundation role vis à vis the aging for the White House Conference's final report, pointed to the Ford, Rockefeller, Russell Sage, and Lilly Foundations, among others, as organizations which had demonstrated a continuing interest in the aging. Without fanfare, foundation involvement had grown during the 1950s to the point that such organizations provided the largest share of the money invested in research and demonstration projects in the field of aging. Ford's concern, Carroll wrote, dated from a survey of the needs of the elderly, carried out in 1956–1957, which indicated that the critical areas were those of health, housing, and postretirement activity. The fund's first grant provided a half-million dollars to the National Welfare Assembly in 1958 for the purpose of creating the National Committee on Aging; an agency designed to act as a general clearing house for information about the aging. Over the next two years, Ford released 4.3 million more, including $782,000 for community organization and demonstration projects. "Because we in the Ford Foundation are convinced that the problems must be resolved primarily in the community where older persons live," he concluded, "our principal attention has been on the local level . . . the strengthening of community action and service." Conceding the importance of income maintenance, foundation officials, nonetheless, felt that "even if an older person has funds, the community must be concerned and organized to make it possible for him to use his funds most effectively."[20]

An early recipient of Ford Foundation money for community organization projects, the American Public Welfare Association noted in its 1958 report that association efforts on behalf of the elderly had reached a turning point with the recent announcement of a grant of $380,000. The proposed project, the association's planning committee announced, would concentrate on administration of public welfare programs for the aged, the strengthening of service offerings, improvement of community understanding and acceptance of the need for them, and research and demonstration of field techniques. The educational aspects of the undertaking, according to its initial report, encompassed the provision of "opportunities for improving understanding of the needs of older persons and the responsibilities public welfare must assume in helping them to a more satisfying life." The foundation's expectations for the project envisioned a shift in public welfare focus from economic relief of elderly dependents toward provision of services necessary to the maintenance of health and proper family relationships and a satisfactory degree of social involvement. An even more important objective of the project was the training of caseworkers, either through the sponsorship of institutes for welfare officials or through activities in the field "aimed directly at improving the competence of caseworkers in public agencies." To oversee and evaluate the APWA project, the foundation granted an additional $200,000 to the Brandeis University School of Social Work. Under the direction of Professor Robert W. Morris, the evaluating team was to determine, based upon field observation, how to plan most effectively for the mobilization of resources to meet the specialized needs of the elderly within a "generically" organized welfare system. Indeed, Morris and his investigators found that public welfare workers tended to accept many of the stereotypical images of the aged held by society in general. They felt, however, that the overall effects of working in the various local demonstrations into which the project was divided would teach workers that their chief functions with respect to the elderly involved keeping their clients out of institutions and providing them with opportunities to be socially useful, rather than removing them from relief roles, which constituted the more traditional public welfare goal.[21]

Reports from the field tended to bear out the original APWA and foundation estimates of the project's impact. Esther Twente, director of the Association's Marion County, Kansas, project, admittedly arrived on the scene with the usual predispositions of the public welfare worker—that is, oriented toward decrement and treatment, rather than increment and prevention. Yet, she reported, her experiences "proved . . . that despite popular and often professional opinion to the contrary, many older people have much potential but unused capacity and the desire to contribute." And Mel Spear, director of three county projects in California, reported that the field activities of his staff had resulted in "increasing sensitivity and understanding of the aged client and his needs," and thus improved service. Spear hoped, in fact, to develop a training syllabus for the education of future staff in the problems of aging based on the project's past experiences. Summarizing the accomplishments of the first Ford Foundation project (it granted the APWA an additional $800,000 in 1963), the Association's Annual Report for 1963 made reference to 15 training institutes, 5 seminars, 24 special publications, 18 issues of the project newsletter *Aging Highlights,* special sessions on aging at APWA conferences, and heightened participation of public welfare delegates in meetings and conferences on aging sponsored by other organizations. Under the new grant (Project II) educational plans were even more advanced. In Chicago, a project operated in cooperation with the University of Chicago and Drexel House, Inc., was to give geriatric training to 18 caseworkers under a field instructor. "It is believed," the annual report stated, "that such an emphasis on the aging will focus attention on its inclusion as part of the school curriculum, will provide a repository of current information for use by other faculty members, contribute to understanding of needs of older people, and increase the supply of knowledgeable personnel available to serve them."[22]

While the APWA sought to reeducate welfare professionals toward more progressive attitudes and modes of service respecting the elderly, it did not neglect its role as an educator of the public. Thus, a Project on Aging-sponsored seminar, held in May 1962, focused on public relations. Participants discussed ways of converting a basic public receptivity to assisting the elderly to positive action in the fields of income maintenance, housing, medical and nursing care, and casework and counseling services. "The job to be done outside the agency family," the final report of the Seminar declared, "obviously entails relationships with a wide variety of special publics. It also includes the provision of a continuous flow of information to the general public." The media—print and audiovisual—offered the best vehicles for this transmission process. When using the media, the report continued, the best public relations tactics involved addressing messages to key constituencies within the community, who were themselves capable of influencing public opinion. Similarly, the agencies had to keep the general public informed, via the same media, of their actions and programs in the field. Suggested directions for an agency public relations officer (an executive position which was itself a testimony to the growing importance of public education in the field of aging) included maximization of publicity for such positive and high impact programs as job retraining, adult education, and rehabilitation. Press coverage was important, and the HEW series, *Patterns for Progress in Aging,* received special APWA notice as a model for the kind of printed releases that would ultimately change the popular conception of public welfare activities from charity to deserved assistance: ". . . the image of *relief,* of the *hand-out* and the *chiseler* will unquestionably be supplanted by something a great deal more favorable."[23]

Another recipient of Ford money was the privately operated Family Service Association of America. In announcing this four-year, $300,000 project, the foundation called it "an effort to enable older persons to continue living in their own homes, thus avoiding the dislocations and costs of institutional care." Again, the grantor stressed the opportunities provided by the project for staff training in new concepts and techniques in geriatric casework. Theodore Isenstadt, the director of the FSAA program, regarded the upgrading of the "self-image of the aging" as the project's key objective. The association, he declared, "employing workers with small case loads can experiment with imaginative services to achieve this goal in the conviction that older people can respond to interest and care as well as the younger ones." Edna Wasser, in her 1966 volume, *Creative Approaches in Casework with the Aging,* summed up the results of the project. One of the given quantities recognized at the outset of the FSAA undertaking, she reported, involved the socially ubiquitous, negative attitudes about old age and older people that so many caseworkers brought into the profession with them. Such attitudes had the same effect within the field of welfare as it did with society at large—at worst, hostility to the older client; at best, lack of interest in him. As an antidote to such attitudes, Wasser explained, project staff "took the view that the caseworker could understand, appreciate, and become engaged in a relationship with the aging person both for what he is as an individual—physically, psychologically and socially—and for what he is in the context of his family relationships." The training component of the project encompassed five staff training institutes ("the major method used . . . to encourage member agencies to reorganize their counseling programs for the aged . . . and to train staff members in new concepts and new techniques.") and four interdisciplinary seminars, co-sponsored with the National Council on the Aging. These latter efforts dealt respectively with casework, community planning, state-level planning, and protective services (the proceedings of the first were published as a special issue of *Social Casework* and those of the last three as NCoA publications). The public relations aspect of this program aimed at promoting the image of the FSAA as a source of help for the older person and his family. To this end, the staff made "extensive use" of the mass media as a means of getting national and local "visibility" for their endeavors. In reviewing the project from outside the Association, the *Encyclopedia of Social Work* credited it with giving "both impetus to and understanding of" a whole new set of geriatric casework principles and causing a wholesale reevaluation of professional attitudes toward the elderly within the family agency."[24]

The efforts of foundations, working through various public and private welfare organizations, provided a strong impetus to expanded activities. In his *Annual Report for 1963,* the Ford Foundation's chief executive officer observed: "The surge of research on the problems of the older person which began in the mid-fifties, is now beginning to produce results. . . . " Among these results, United States Welfare commissioner Dr. Ellen Winston testified before a Senate subcommittee in January 1964 on the need to involve the 800 local planning and coordinating committees organized across the country in efforts to "assess the needs of older citizens, and stimulate public and voluntary agencies to provide community-wide programs of health, social services, employment, recreation, education, and housing." Perhaps too, increased federal government activities and money grants in the field of aging dispensed through such departments as the Office of Aging, the National Institute of Mental Health (within HEW), the Office of Economic Opportunity, and pursuant to the various titles of the Older Americans Act of 1965, could also be ultimately traced to the interest generated by the foundation-welfare agency tandem.[26]

Two examples of a new spirit of partnership between the government and the welfare agency included project FIND, administered by the NCoA on an OEO grant, and project SERVE, undertaken by the Community Service Society of New York and financed mainly by the Administration on Aging (although some private funds were involved). FIND (Friendless, Isolated, Needy, Disabled), the more extensive of the two, encompassed twelve separate demonstration projects across the country during 1967–1968; whereas SERVE (Serve and Enrich Retirement by Volunteer Experience) was restricted to a single pilot on Staten Island, New York. FIND was the more traditional approach and, as its acronym suggested, involved itself chiefly in locating those elderly in need of help and subsequently stimulating the appropriate responses on the part of the local community. SERVE's objective, on the other hand, was more limited—that is, helping to find outlets for useful activity while simultaneously providing the community with skilled and needed voluntary services. Both projects, however, emphasized in the evaluations of their efforts, the positive effects they had had upon the local community's orientation toward its older citizens. As the Community Service Society observed of its endeavors: "SERVE developed a new and clearly defined role and image of the older person as a community service volunteer. The assumption of this role both increased the self-esteem of the volunteer, and brought recognition and respect from the broader community." FIND, being the larger and better funded, put a high priority on the influence of the media—radio, television, and print—to inform the public of its efforts. The observable positive changes in attitudes, toward both welfare operations and their elderly clients, was attributed by FIND's evaluators, in large part, to the influence of the media.[27]

The crucial importance of field work projects rested primarily on the educational impact they made—upon the case worker, upon the older person himself and, ultimately, upon society at large. The Family Service Association project of the early 1960s assembled a case study book made up of the field experiences of the various programs within the project. The aim of this compilation was to provide "illustrations of how caseworkers and local agencies, as they become increasingly committed to serving older people and their families, find imaginative ways to do so, even when these ways seem at variance with their usual modes of working." Indeed, the emphasis of the field experience was as revolutionary as the school environment was conservative. Evidence from project evaluations indicates that such practical experience has had a positive impact on social work education. The *FSAA Case Book on Work With the Aging* noted in its introductory passages: "As caseworkers themselves accept the meaning of aging, they will see and feel with the older client for the person he is, counsel with him in his own frame of reference, and comprehend his struggle to meet the changes life requires of him." In the long run society as a whole would be led to accept the "meaning of aging" and the need for geriatric caseworkers abolished, in an environment which supported and sustained its elderly. For the moment, however, more, not fewer, enlightened caseworkers were needed. The field experience, continually expanded and strengthened, promised to supply them.

N O T E S

1. Some of the more comprehensive histories of the evolution of the social work profession include Robert Bremmer, *Out of the Depths* (1956); Roy Lubove, *The Professional Altruist* (1965); and C. A. Chambers, *Seedtime of Reform* (1967); Ellen Winston, "Social Problems of the Aged," *Social Forces* 26 (1947–1948): 57–61.

2. Welfare Council of Metropolitan Chicago, *Community Services for Older People* (Chicago, 1952), p. 170; for a treatment of the continuing debate between partisans of the generic and the specific in social work education, see chapter III; J. Duff, "Training for Leadership," *Journal of Educational Sociology* 30, no. 5 (January 1957): 221–225.

3. The first special entry for "Aged" in the authoritative *Social Work Year Book* occurred in 1945 (vol. 8, pp. 36–39); Margaret Wagner, "Mental Hazards of Old Age," *The Family* 24 no. 4 (1944), 132–137; Griffen, "The Growing Problem of the Aged," *Social Service Review*, 19 (1945), no. 4, pp. 506–515; and within the institutional setting, Julius Weil, "Changing Trends in the Care of the Aging," *Journal of Gerontology* 2, no. 2 (1947): 148–155, argued that 1940 can be considered the point in time when the view of administrators began to shift from one of old age as useless and outmoded toward one that placed greater stress on potential capacities.

4. Conference on recreation for the aged reported on by the *New York Times,* April 3, 1946, 27:3; see also Fuchs and Levine, "The Hodson Center: An Experiment in the Preservation of Personality,: *Journal of Gerontology* 1, no. 1 (1946): 55–59; and Kraus, "Community Planning for the Aged," ibid. 3, no. 2 (1948): 129–140.

5. "The Aged," *Social Work Year Book,* 1951, vol. 11, pp. 44–49; Bowles, "Cooperative Planning for Social Welfare by Government Organizations," in National Conference in National Conference of Social Workers, *The Social Welfare Forum, 1950* (New York: 1950), p. 177; Andrews, "Constructive Aspects of Public Assistance for the Aged," *The Social Welfare Forum, 1951* (New York, 1951), p. 240; an early list of services for the elderly in M. O. Hunt, *The Range of Public Welfare Services to Older People* (New York: 1954); see also "Serving Older Persons: A Multiple Approach by the Family Agency," *Social Casework,* 35 (1954): 299–308, for an early discussion of the importance of homemaker, casework, and family education services as means of facilitating adjustment to old age.

6. See E. V. Andrews, op. cit., for a general attack upon what he considers the prevailing view of the incapacity of older people; Hollender "Individualizing the Aged," in National Conference on Social Work, *Selected Papers on Aging* (1952), pp. 7–16; criticism of the Freudian establishment by Martin Gumpert from his "Profile" in the *New Yorker* (June 10, 1950): 35–36.

7. Rose McHugh, "A Constructive Program for the Aged," *Proceedings, National Conference of Social Workers, 1945* (New York: 1948), pp. 391–401; Anderson, "Social Workers' Action for the Aged," in NYSJLC, *No Time to Grow Old* (Albany: 1951), pp. 95–96.

8. Smith, "The Place of Services in the Public Assistance Program," *Public Welfare* 9 (1951): 161–163, 170; see also J. Kaplan, "The Role of the Public Welfare Agency in Meeting the Needs of Older People," ibid.: 2–8, 211.

9. Willie, "Group Relationships of the Elderly in Our Culture," *Social Casework* 35 (1954): 206–212; B. S. Philips, "A Role Theory Approach to Adjustment in Old Age," *American Sociological Review* 22 (1957): 212–221; loss of economic role has already been treated; on loss of family roles see B. B. Beard, "Are the Aged Ex-Family? *Social Forces* 27 (1949), 274–279; or E. G. Fried and K. Stern, "The Situation

of the Aged within the Family, *American Journal of Orthopsychiatry* 18 (1948): 31–54; support for Willie's concept of dynamic casework as a general principle within the profession of social work offered by G. H. Hamilton, "Role of Social Casework in Social Policy," in *Social Casework in the Fifties* (1952), p. 31; and as a specific principle in W. W. Boehm, "The Social Work Curriculum Study and Its Implications for Family Casework," ibid. (1959), p. 356.

10. Kaplan, "Helping the Older Adult to Keep Related to the Mainstream of Community Life," in NCSW, *Selected Papers on Aging,* pp. 17–22; Bowen, "Using the Unique Contributions of Later Maturity for the Well Being of the Community," ibid., pp. 23–29; see also G. Landau, "Restoration of Self-Esteem," *Geriatrics* 10 (1955): 141–143, for a similar account of the therapeutic benefits of the Hodson House program; Randall, "Adaptations of Social Agency Programs to the Needs of the Aging and Aged," in *Aging and Retirement: Fifth Annual Southern Conference on Gerontology,* December 28–30, 1954 (Gainesville, Florida: 1955), pp. 101–107.

11. Crucial to social work was the psychological data made possible by the work of Ruth S. Cavan, et al., *Personal Adjustment in Old Age;* specific practical links of data to practice made by Jerome Cohen (ed.), *The Work of Berta Fantl* (Smith College Series in Social Work, 1964), especially pp. 194–199, 204; see also M. E. Linden, "Some Sociopsychological Factors in Aging," in "Changing Concepts in Care of the Aged: A Workshop, 1957," *American Journal of Orthopsychiatry* 28 (1958): 322–328; R. Kastenbaum, "Theories of Human Aging," *Journal of Social Issues* 21 no. 4 (1965): 13–35; Erikson's *Identity and the Life Cycle* (1959) has already been mentioned in another context.

12. Lack of interest in aging within social work school curricula noted by I. Webber, "Current Research on Aging," *Aging and Retirement: Fifth Annual Southern Conference on Gerontology, December 28–30, 1954* (Gainesville, Florida, 1955), pp. 108–117; Breckenridge, *New Directions in Public Welfare Services for the Aged* (1955), pp. 10–11; Francis quoted from "Serving Older People: A Multiple Approach by a Family Agency," *Social Casework* 35 (1954): 209–308.

13. J. Regensburg, "The Implications of the Seminar for Staff Development," and Florence Stytz, "Implications of the Seminar for Casework Practice," in *Social Casework* (special issue), May–June 1961, pp. 284–286 and 281–284, respectively; Jewish Central Bureau for the Aging, *Dynamic Factors in the Role of the Caseworker,* p. 15; C. T. O'Reilly, "Caseworker Attitudes and Services to Older Clients," *Public Welfare* 21 (April 1963) pp. 29–31, 42–43.

14. H. L. McCarthy, *Day Centers for Older People* (APWS, 1954); Ruth Hall, "Focusing Attention on Older Persons' Needs," *Journal of Social Casework,* 30 (1949), pp. 405–411; W. E. Sinclair, "Summer Camp for Oldsters," *Public Welfare,* 8 (1950), pp. 78–80; B. B. Coggan, "A Review of Facilities Available for Older People," *Journal of Gerontology* 6, no. 4 (1951): 394–397; and J. Kaplan, *A Social Program for Older People* (Minneapolis, 1953).

15. Swartz, "Organized Planning for Old Age," *Geriatrics* 7 (1952): 63–69.

16. A compendium of the major foundations interested in aging, along with their areas of special concern found in the NCoA, *Resources for the Aging: An Action Handbook,* 2nd ed. (1969); specific information on grants 1960–1970 can be found in *Foundation News,* vols. I–XI. Welfare Council of Metropolitan Chicago, *Community Services for Older People* (1952), preface and pp. 175–176.

17. The most elaborate statement of the new social service orientation was Elizabeth Wickenden, *The Needs of Older People* (1953), pp. 1, 8, 63, 95–96, which was the final report of the Duke-funded study.

18. This series of nine pamphlets contained in *APWS Publications,* vol. 8, provides one of the earliest large scale efforts to get important information to the social welfare establishment, and by extension, to the public at large.
19. The emerging interest in geriatric field work is noted in the American Public Welfare Association's pamphlet, *Aging . . . Public Welfare's Role* (1960); Beattie, "Mobilizing Community Resources for Older Persons," *Public Welfare* 19 (1961): 97–102; WHCoA, *Background Paper on Social Services for the Aged* (March 1960), 6–7.
20. Carroll, "A National Foundation Expresses Its Interest in the Problems of Older People," in *Aging with a Future: Reports and Guidelines from the WHCoA,* series no. 1 (Washington, D.C., April 1961), 126–127, 131–134. By 1962 the Ford Foundation had distributed some 6.7 million, half for research and half for action and training programs—see Ford Foundation's *Golden Years?* (New York, 1963), pp. 7–8, and the foundation's *Annual Reports* for 1957 and 1958, respectively, 36–37 and 64–65, for the announcements of largest grants in the area of social welfare of the aging.
21. APWA, *Turning Points: Annual Report for 1958;* J. L. Roney, "Report to the Membership on the APWA Project on Aging," *Public Welfare* 19 (1961): 74–75; Ford Foundation, *Golden Years?* pp. 14–15; also the Foundation's *Annual Reports 1959,* pp. 60–61 and *1960,* pp. 45–46; Morris, "Community Planning for the Aged," in APWA, *Selected Biennial Papers, 1963,* pp. 98–103.
22. Twente, "Older People are to be Well Served," *Public Welfare,* 22 (1964), pp. 191–195; Spear, New Program Expectations in Serving the Aged," ibid., 24 (1966), pp. 211–216; Spear, *Developing Welfare Services for Older Persons* (APWA, 1967). His promised training syllabus was published by the association in 1970 under the title *Guide for In-Service Training for Developing Services for Older Persons.* APWA, *Changing Times: Annual Report for 1963.*
23. APWA, *Public Relations Focuses on Aging: Report of a Seminar held May, 1962* (New York, 1962).
24. Ford Foundation *Annual Report, 1961,* pp. 61–62; Isenstadt quoted in Ford Foundation, *Golden Years?* p. 14; Wasser, *Creative Approaches . . .* (New York, 1966). Basically, this FSAA project aimed at reeducating caseworkers in family agencies. If little effort was spent in seeking to educate the larger public, this was because its directors felt that the activities of enlightened caseworkers would ultimately constitute the best tool for improving popular images of the aged. *Encyclopedia of Social Work* 15 (1965): 74.
25. Winston testimony from "Services for Senior Citizens," Senate Special Committee on Aging, subcommittee on Federal, State and Local Services to the Elderly, *Hearings, January 16, 1964,* pp. 16–17.
26. NCoA, *The Golden Years . . . A Tarnished Myth: Project FIND* (1970), or J. Ossofsky, FIND's director, testimony before Senate *Special Committee, Long Range Programs and Research Needs in Aging, December 5–6, 1967* (Washington, D.C.: 1968), pp. 40–46; J. L. Sainer and M. O. Zander, *SERVE: Older Volunteers in Community Service* (1971).
27. FSAA, *Case Book on Work with the Aging* (New York: 1966).

8

Images of the Aged:
The Contributions of Marketers

> ... every time an advertisement or commercial
> appears, the objective is to have the reader or
> viewer *learn* something ... and it is the hope of
> the advertiser that the reader or viewer will *re-
> member* what he has learned and use this infor-
> mation at a later time.... An advertisement is a
> means of "teaching" a set of ideas to the public
> concerned, just as an instructor's lecture in the
> classroom "advertises" to his students the facts
> of his course.
>
> S. H. Britt, speech before the 13th annual Advertising
> Conference, quoted in *Advertising Age*
> (November 19, 1956): 14

Although its morality has frequently been questioned
and its methods deplored, advertising undoubtedly has
the power to shape public opinion. Gerontologists recognized
early on that this force could be used in the service of their
discipline, but they tended to be suspicious of its motivations.
Educator John Duff spoke for many a wary gerontologist when
he observed: "With full appreciation of the influence wielded by
the mass media, and with sorry recognition of the fact that this
influence is commercially controlled, we might be apprehensive
about what will happen in gerontology when it is discovered
that older adults are an important part of the mass market." On
the whole, however, marketers did not make this discovery any
more rapidly than society at large. The initial stirrings of recognition coincided with the first display of apprehension about

the growing number of elderly in American society. With this recognition came intimations of a future concern. Thus, as early as 1949, Harry W. Hepner, the author of a marketing text book, described the nation's older population as one that had "more leisure time to fish, travel, read, attend resorts." Far from regarding the elderly as economically disadvantaged and socially outcast, Hepner argued that their greater number meant more political power which would in turn mean "more money for leisure time pursuits" through increased social insurance benefits. Moreover, he predicted, "shifts in tastes, preferences, and nature of demand for many products" and an increasing demand for dentures, dry-skin creams, hearing aids and electric blankets. "Product development men," he counseled, "can reap a harvest by designing for old people . . . [who] will become an increasingly important part of the national market." Hepner was a premature advocate of advertising's involvement with the elderly consumer, but his view accurately forecast a trend.[1]

By the mid-50s, producers and sellers had begun to develop new attitudes toward the "mature" market. "Over the past few years," *Business Week* reported in June 1954, "new facts . . . about the needs, the numbers, the incomes and the spending tendencies [of the old] . . . have convinced businessmen that they have misjudged and underestimated the vigor and importance of the purchasing power of the 65-and-over market." Census figures and studies by the Brookings Institution and the Twentieth Century Fund revealed that this group was not only the fastest growing one in the nation, but that it possessed more purchasing power than heretofore supposed. With a higher proportion of disposable income than younger age groups and with fewer financial commitments, the over-sixty-fives emerged as a major consumer group. "It is quite possible," the article concluded, "that with an increasing 'maturing' population, some of the stress on youth that has preoccupied advertisers for so long will give way to advertising that appeals to a broader spectrum of age groups." *Tide,* the advertising and media journal, reviewed this growing market's potential and pronounced it already as large as the Negro market: "The potential is there. It may take only some ingenious product designing, some special advertising slant, even a public relations program to tap it."[2]

According to various trade organs, the areas into which marketers were looking included housing, travel, food, and drugs. Jergen's Lotion had begun to ask "Is a woman ever too old to hold a man's love?" Carrier Corporation exhibited an elderly couple enjoying their silver anniversary gift—an air conditioner. Panagra (Pan Am) Airways ads showed older people singing the praises of their recent South American vacations. The editor of the *American Druggist* advised pharamacists to set up geriatric departments in their retail outlets. A New York State Commerce Department study of markets in 1953 identified older people as a special need group and advised manufacturers to plan for demand shifts toward small scale, mult–purpose furniture, reduced-size food packages, dietetic foods, casual dress styled for mature wearers, smaller and more economical cars, garden supplies, and "new leisure" paraphernalia in general. While marketers did not yet widely consider older people a large market for durables, increasing amounts of research on their needs continued to suggest consumer areas worth exploiting, especially in the area of personal services. As *Business Week* pragmatically stated it: "Above all, old people fear being put on the shelf, the experts say. Any merchandiser who can bring them off the shelf should find a welcome."[3]

As the recognition grew that older people constituted a consumer group worthy of exploitation, marketers began seriously to consider methods in which they might best be approached. At the outset, two schools of thought debated this issue. One suggested that over sixty-fives would respond best to frank appeals to their age, while the other counseled that the subject of age be studiously avoided. Early experience, however, suggested that neither view was totally correct. Heinz Food's 1940s campaign to sell a geriatric diet line failed miserably because, company officials later admitted, their appeals were too blatantly based on the decrements of age. Cosmetic lines, on the other hand, successfully marketed the effectiveness of their products in hiding the evidences of aging. Builders represented both sides of the issue, with some, like Carl Mitnick of New Jersey, arguing that special design features actually offended the older buyer; others, like architect Rufus Nims, designer of the Upholsterer's International Union's retirement community, Salhaven, insisting upon the inclusion of features that unobtrusively took account of aging's toll on physical capacity. A coherent image of the older person had not yet emerged among marketers. But the dominant gerontological conviction that older people were not appreciably different in behavior or need from the general population was destined to influence market research. Vergil Reed of J. Walter Thompson Agency suggested this when he noted: "Older people are a market for special products it's true. But besides this, old people use practically everything everybody else uses." The dual nature of this consumer group, then, suggested that older people would best be approached by defining them in terms of youth to sell them the things everyone needed and by appealing to their desire to remain young to sell them special products.[4]

Marketer Pierre Martineau was among the earliest proponents of what would ultimately become a dynamic, activist, youthful senior citizen image. Although at the time he may not have been totally aware of it, his common sense observations on youth versus age in American society pointed out the direction the advertising industry would take. "Worlds and worlds of older people in our society," Martineau wrote, in a 1957 advertising primer, "want to look young, to be considered young beyond the reality of their years. But few young people want to be considered old." The cult of youth, which gerontologists held responsible for the all the social and economic discrimination practiced against the elderly provided the inspiration for advertising's proposed model of the modern older person. Admen, regarding it as a valuable marketing tool, consistently reinforced this youth fixation, rather than seeking to repress it, as social gerontologists argued must be done. Rather, they wished to blur the distinction between youth and age by eliminating, insofar as possible, the negative qualities associated with old age and to replace them with more youthful characteristics. This would make highly specialized and potentially counterproductive sales presentations unnecessary. Here, marketers approached the same problem of social adjustment which perturbed social gerontologists, but unlike the latter, who sought to bring society into conformity with a new image of aging, marketers encouraged the elderly to see themselves in the context of already approved social and cultural values. Where social scientists generally asked society to adjust to its older population, marketers proposed that older people adjust to and make the best of the given social milieu. The adaptation of the older individual to existing cultural arrangements, argued advertisers like P. J. Kelly, in *Printer's Ink,* was of mutual benefit to the older consumer and to the marketer, for the good social adjustment of this group provided the key to its successful exploitation as a market.[5]

The advertising industry's tendency to exploit the old age market in this manner was tempered by the trend toward "segmentation" in marketing which emerged concurrently within the occupation. *Advertising Age,* Madison Avenue's principal organ, advised manufacturers and sellers to develop submarkets "deeply and intensively," noting that even one percent of the total U.S. market amounted to a segment (1.75 million) well worth tapping. Moreover, as the population grew, most of its respective segments would grow. "We hope there will be more and more marketers catering to the needs of minorities," wrote the editors of that journal in early 1960, "This is one excellent method of insuring that the country doesn't degenerate into a kind of faceless mass of people all conforming to the momentary desires of the great majority."[6]

When advertising agencies applied the principles of segmentation, the aged sector of the overall market represented neither an isolated, neglected group nor yet a group indistinguishable from younger ones though sharing much in common with them. They were, in fact, "senior citizens"—a wholly new group in

American society. Advertising men used this conception as a means of exploiting one market without alienating another. A fig juice promotional for Realemon-Puritan provided an example of the psychological sophistication of this process. It pictured an elderly man with copy that informed the reader: "No more tired, logy, 'off' days for this senior citizen! He's discovered Realfig Fig Juice not only tastes good (refreshing, tangy!) it also keeps him 'on the button'—vital, energetic." The process involved the subtle introduction of a common geriatric problem (irregularity) and its cure, which in turn conferred upon the individual "vital" and "energetic" senior citizenhood. And all this because of a product whose "tangy, refreshing" flavor might lead the reader to confuse it with Pepsi Cola. The emergence of this group and these techniques was an encouragement to agencies, like Maxwell, Sackheim-Franklin, Bruck, Inc., to specialize in the senior market. This particular agency reportedly took in $3 million in billing on vitamin, insurance, and health aids advertising in 1961. In the process, it helped to develop and legitimize the techniques of selling to older people.[7]

As the 60s began, *Business Week* noted, the number of retailers taking interest in this 'senior' market was increasing. Marketers, in improving their understanding of the "psychology" of this population segment, looked forward to the exploitation of a "younger" old age market with more energy, more money, and greater inclination to expend both commodities, especially in the areas of housing, leisure products, travel, and health. The *Wall Street Journal* thought that Heinz' second attempt to establish a geriatric food line and Del Webb's Sun City, Arizona housing development typified a new awareness within the business community. In a survey of the consumer products industry, the *Journal* found two thirds of the firms queried "stepping up their efforts to sell a wide range of goods to older Americans." As one observer who wrote in *Today's Health* remarked: "It is no wonder more and more companies are beginning to design products specially for the aged; they recognize a tremendous growth market among older Americans who have put by for the future and intend to keep right on enjoying life." Within a decade, in fact, the purchasing power of this group had more than quadrupled. Some manufacturers sought to tap it in a conventional fashion, like Heinz with its special foods and Bulova Watch Company with large-numeraled watch faces. Others approached this segment in a new way. Sporting goods firms like MacGregor and builders like Webb and Carl Mitnick focused on an older clientele with more vigor and discrimination than retailers had generally given it credit for. One travel concern, Matson Shipping Company, claimed to have "discovered" the over-sixty-five market as a result of the publicity surrounding the issue of medical care for the aged.[8]

The Federal Housing Authority hypothesized that the private home building industry was attracted by the combination of FHA and Veteran's Administration reforms, social security and relief provisions, and state and local welfare services; all of which promised to free more money for improved living arrangements. A writer for the American Medical Association publication, *Today's Health* (which generally carried a good deal of advertising directed to the senior market), reported in late 1962 that "the senior group has matured as a market." With an aggregate income of $32 billion "most of it distinctly spendable," Americans in general, and marketers in particular, were beginning to pay greater attention to this phenomenon. Leonard Z. Breen observed that "the aging themselves represent a growing market in our society—a market for homes, for services, for special foods, for travel programs. In a great variety of ways, they constitute a highly specialized market." Through the medium of advertising, marketers helped to create an atmosphere in which "senior citizenship" could more easily replace "old age." Repetition of this theme would have as much to do with the popular acceptance of the "new" older American as any other force in American society.[8a]

Speaking before the American Marketing Association, Albert J. Wood, president of a market research firm, scolded the assembled admen for their general neglect of older age groups, even though this segment of the population had "the largest super-numerary incomes in our economy." For years, he noted, retailers of home appliances had ignored this market; yet, it was a potentially rich one. Wood suggested that the themes of retirement and leisure provided a good approach to this group. Advertising copy addressed to such a household might read: "Soon you'll be retiring from your job. Will you permit your wife to retire from hers?" In a two-part series, financial columnist Sylvia Porter explored the dimensions of the "vast over-sixty-five market," and remarked that besides housing, travel, and special foods, one researcher had detected a demand for clothing in "larger sizes which are chic and young looking." Here was more evidence that a new older American had emerged—one that provided "a shining opportunity" to retailers aware of the changing image of the elderly population. This group, according to a National Industrial Conference Board study, constituted "an active and significant proportion of our population." The author of this study traced the traditional neglect of the older consumer to two sources: first, a lack of information about the needs and desires of older people; and second, the sense that the aging were a "destitute and dependent group." As researchers in all disciplines continued to gather the necessary information, the negative image of the older person lost support. "The senior citizen," the study reported, "is becoming an increasingly important part of the American scene—a member with a particular way of life, and with many specialized needs."[9]

As the image of the senior citizen impressed itself upon the popular mind, the *Wall Street Journal* reported, elderly consumers were beginning to receive a greater share of the attention of producers and retailers. Thus, a Florida bank sought increased checking account money by eliminating service fees for depositors over sixty-five; a plumbing fixture manufacturer designed faucets for operation by arthritic hands; a growing number of movie theatres offered 40–60 percent reductions on tickets to senior citizens. The prestigious trade publication, *Journal of Retailing,* featured an assessment of the elderly market which em-

197

phasized its potential in light of the retirement phenomenon with its steadily increasing size, its tendency to concentrate in urban areas, and its improving economic status. Perhaps, the authors of this article conceded, this was not an easy market to sell; but its size and economic power made it worth every effort. As they sold themselves on the importance of the over-sixty-fives, admen also made Americans aware, if only by repetition, of a whole class of active, fun-loving, nonstereotypical oldsters. Marketers C. A. Nolan and R. F. Warmke, for example, alerted advertising agencies to the "senior citizen" potential in the leisure, hobby, food specialty, and travel industries, without mentioning the more traditional geriatric markets—drugs, cosmetics, and audiovisual aids. Wilbur J. Cohen argued that the combination of a booming economy and President Johnson's "War on Poverty" had helped open up these free-time markets, especially among older Americans. Already possessed of plenty of free time, senior citizens were now beginning to achieve an economic status, thanks to medicare and social security boosts, that encouraged retailers to develop this leisure market.[10]

Richard Pelzman, president of Senior Services Corporation, was a leader in this movement to serve a "booming" senior (which he defined as over fifty-five) market. His optimism derived from a survey of 377 people aged fifty-five and over by the Center for Research in Marketing which suggested that there was in fact an older people's market, most notably for special diet foods and clothing (particularly in style and fit), and in these areas, the elderly would not be offended by age-oriented advertising appeals. Speaking before the Society of Cosmetic Chemists in 1966, Pelzman attributed $50 billion in annual discretionary buying power to this group and urged more systematic cultivation of a class of citizens which currently spent $250 million a year on travel, owned 35 percent of all common stocks, owned their homes by a ratio of three to one, and enjoyed the steady income cushions provided by social security, private pensions, and now, Medicare. His company specialized in testing products in this market and eventually contemplated production and sales of those which proved viable. By unabashedly appealing to older Amercians (the marketing label Pelzman had chosen was "Golden Years"), he told an Advertising Institute symposium in New York City, a firm could gain the generally unattached loyalty of this group, and "grow rich as it grows old. Testifying before a U.S. Senate Subcommittee on the consumer interests of the elderly, this tireless champion of the senior buyer went straight to the nub of the older market's problem. As long as the later years were associated with debility and dependency, older people would remain outside society's normal flow. "What is needed," he declared, "is a new and positive appraisal of the aging American." In encouraging a new appraisal, marketers could thus do a social service and make a profit as well. Seconding Pelzman's view of the need for a new image of aging, Prof. John A. Howard of Columbia University School of Business told the Senators that no product could be sold unless it could get shelf space. A positive, dynamic image of the elderly would definitely free more shelf space, since retailers would then see older people as an active market for their wares. An investigation of market potential by *Forbes Magazine* in 1969 revealed the surprising fact that older women spent more on cosmetics than younger women; yet cosmetics manufacturers ignored the older woman in their advertising campaigns. Clothing manufacturers also dismissed older women as a "one-dress-per-year" market. But, *Forbes* pointed out, over-sixty-fives accounted for $40 billion in annual disposable income. Like the youth market, which had been created by marketers within the past ten years, the article concluded, similar developments were about to take place with respect to the elderly market.[11]

When the Twenty-Second Annual University of Michigan Conference on Aging (1969) chose to focus on the "Problems of Older Consumers," it was clear that gerontologists had noted the escalating interest of retailers in the aged. Moving to educate their client group to fraudulent business practices and to curb the susceptibility of older people "to any promise of easy reversal of ills or recovery of lost powers," the conference evoked the concept of "consumer sovereignity" as preached by Irving Ladimer of the Better Business Bureau and by syndicated columnist Sidney Margolus. By 1970, retailers were actually reported to be looking to senior citizen purchasing power to improve a sagging overall market. In view of recent 30% social security benefit increases and the immediate lump payment of two months' retroactive increase, *Business Week* saw an initial one billion dollar increase in disposable income and an extra 300 million per month thereafter. According to one governmental economist, old people could be expected to spend the extra money right away, providing the impulse to a general improvement in the retail market scene. As one California marketer declared in *Dun's Review:* "These people are really the 'now' generation. They have to live for now because they don't know how long their now will last.[12]

As the decade for the 1960s drew to a close, the advertising industry had come to appreciate the potential of the older consumer group and, in the process, helped to create what *Reader's Digest* advertising director Charles Hepler called "the second youth market." This segment of the population, Hepler told the Advertising Club of Indianapolis, "thinks young and likes youthful, colorful advertising," but brings to the marketplace "broader interests and responsibilities, more knowledgeable tastes, much more income, and the power to decide how and where to spend it." Charles F. Adams of the McManus, John and Adams Agency was even more assertive: "The 'generation at the top' is a vibrant, monied, energetic and vital part of America with the most awesome purchasing in the history of the American marketplace. . . . It isn't the 'blue hair and bifocals set' anymore."[13]

A specific instance of how the attempt to create a "senior market" altered, for the better, one stereotype of aging, involved the study of older drivers by the Denver University Law School. Study director, Judge S. E. Finesilver, called the findings pivotal in refuting current popular thinking about the "senior driver" and "a beacon of hope for curing a profound inequity; namely, the gross underestimation of the senior driver." Shortly after publication of these data, *Dun's Review* reported that the Colonial Penn Insurance Company had found "gold in the golden years" by selling significant amounts of a commodity not traditionally associated with the over-fifty-fives–health, accident, and automobile insurance. According to Colonial Penn's chairman, J. S. MacWilliams, revenues from auto insurance alone had doubled annually since these policies were introduced in 1967. Colonial Penn's success, *Dun's Review* noted, had made it a strong issue on the stock exchange: "What Wall Street likes most is that Colonial Penn is not just exploiting someone else's market; it has created its own."[14]

Perhaps the best way to appreciate the evolving influence of marketing on the image of the older American requires a look at one particular industry over the 1950–1970 period. The housing industry serves as an especially useful test case of the means by which advertising attempted to identify and establish this market. As early as 1951, the Flordia State Improvement Commission surveyed the State's older citizens and found that a large minority preferred to consort exclusively with their age peers (45 percent). Similarly, data from such experiments in congregate living in Waltham, Massachusetts (public housing), La Jolla, California (church financed), Salhaven, Florida (labor union administered), and Youngtown, Arizona (private builder), were beginning to challenge some long held gerontological opinions. Looking over such data a decade later, sociologist Irving Rosow assailed the "firm ideological convictions" of gerontologists against age-specific housing. Not only was there evidence of its beneficial influence in many instances but, on the pragmatic side, it was economical to build—a consideration in view of the growing but still meager economic resources of the elderly. Architect William C. Loring joined such critics as Rosow in a pair of articles written for the prestigious *Architectural Forum* in 1960–1961. Until very recently, Loring noted, little research had been done on the housing preferences of older people. Out of current researches, however, emerged the portrait of a group which was as varied in taste and desires as was the rest of society. All older people did not want to live near children nor did they uniformly wish to stay in familiar surroundings. If a majority did stay close to traditional settings, there was evidence that this was more often a result of psychological fears of lost status in a new environment rather than an attachment to the familiar. Apparently, moving out of the house represented the passing of one more status symbol. This resistance to moving, however, could apparently be tempered by merely introducing to the elderly the range of possibilities open to them in the area of specially designed, detached dwellings. "Sociological guidelines" offered by Loring to enhance the attractiveness of these environments for the elderly included maximization of privacy within the dwelling unit coupled with a maximization of opportunities for sociability without (i.e., common rooms, circulation patterns designed to encourage contact with others, etc.).[15]

Addressing the Society of American Planning Officials in 1951, Florida Improvement Commissioner, W. E. Keyes, referred to the data which showed older people favoring age specific environments by a two to one margin over either mixed or exclusively youthful environments. This, he argued, demonstrated the need for new residential designs; housing which would provide "a happy, healthful life for retired workers within their means." One Florida builder had already completed the first units in a contemplated 6000-unit "leisure city." As the journal *American City* described it, this development had been designed with the expressed desires of retired civil service workers, teachers, police, firemen, and servicemen in mind. Prospective builders were growing increasingly aware that, as *House Beautiful* put it: "We are changing our attitude toward retirement. . . . Our former concept of a retired man as a semi-invalid, who putters about aimlessly from day to day, has become obsolete." The responsibility for this new view of retirement, the magazine continued, belonged to the "new science of geriatrics." The geriatricians, in showing that the aged "need to be active, need to feel there is a necessity for what they are doing," had suggested an entirely new real estate market—the smaller, more conveniently designed retirement house. Specific inducements to real estate promoters, observed a housing symposium sponsored by the American Public Health Association, included the growth and extension of pension plans, the increasing interest of employers in retirement preparation for employees, and the changing size and composition of the family unit.[16]

Suggesting a potential market was one thing; demonstrating it to a hard-headed, profit-oriented industry, quite another. The National Savings and Loan League, for example, conceded the demand for specially designed "senior housing." Changes in physical capacity and family situation meant that, in many cases, the houses owned by older people had become too large and too difficult to maintain. League president R. W. Greene outlined the response to this phenomenon by observing that during the past six years "the greatest number of home purchasers have been older veterans." Nonetheless, he expressed the disinclination of the League to make loans to older people for the purpose of purchasing such housing and cited gerontological arguments against residential concentration of the elderly. Doubtless, the unmentioned factor of the high credit risk attached to older persons was also influential in the League's response. Still, Bryn Mawr professor of economics Hertha Kraus, addressing the American Academy of Political and Social Sciences in 1952, marked a "new sympathetic response to the gradual discovery of the housing needs of our senior citizens." A greater proportion of this emergent concern, she continued, needed to be channeled into low and mid-priced private dwelling units for that overwhelming majority of older people who preferred independent, noninstitutional living.[17]

Even as the need was increasingly recognized, the problem of underwriting the needed construction was commented upon by various interested parties. In a paper delivered before the Southern Institute of Gerontology in 1952, for example, architect Henry Churchill talked about the economic problem involved. "The housing industry," he declared, "simply cannot provide its product at a price that will meet the lower market brackets, for reasons which are perfectly well understood." Dependence upon private enterprise then, would be "unrealistic" according to Churchill. What lender, he asked further, would extend long term, low interest loans to a group with a finite life expectancy? Financial expert Norman Strunk also noted the economic difficulties faced by the older home buyer. While mortgage lenders did not follow a conscious policy of denying all home loans to older people, it was nonetheless more difficult for the older than for the younger mortgage applicant. The terms typically offered the older mortgagee, as opposed to the younger included a larger cash down payment, greater emphasis on amount of income, pledges of life insurance to lending institution, and more often, the cosignature of children. As the New York Governor's Conference on the Aging put it: "Because of costs involved in construction, financing, management and operation, private housing built for profit is unable to charge rents low enough for elderly people with low and moderate incomes." The market, nonetheless, was there if financial barriers could be reduced.[18]

Through the 50s influential voices increasingly spoke of the "burgeoning" or "booming" retirement housing market and cited some statistics compiled by social scientists to justify various public initiatives in the field. By 1975, the market would comprise twenty-one million people, or ten percent of the total population, seventy percent of whom owned homes that no longer suited their needs; the same percentage received assured incomes from social security and/or pension plans. Such data, apparently, had more effect upon the private than upon the public sector. Although the Federal Housing Administration showed little enthusiasm for the idea, profit-seeking developers indicated increasing interest in the retirement housing market. Indeed, homebuilders, speaking through the National Association of Home Builders, complained loudly about the FHA's lack of interest in freeing money (through its Federal National Mortgage Assistance or "Fannie Mae" program) for the financing of low income and senior citizen housing. These markets, the NAHB stated, would become the most attractive if financial arrangements could be worked out.[19]

Speaking at The University of Michigan's Annual Conference on Aging in July 1952, E. C. Doyle of the Builders' Association of Metropolitan Detroit apprised the assembled social scientists of the private housing industry's interest in the elderly citizen. Older people, he admitted, were a difficult market, lacking economic strength and hence of limited profitability. Should, however, mortgage and financing money be made available, the demand for such housing would quickly bring builders into the field. Doyle thought the key was to educate Americans generally to the need of their older fellow citizens for adequate housing. Once this goal was made clear, biases against the provision of money for senior citizen or retirement housing would fall away, and free enterprise would build the necessary housing. The "socialistic" alternative of public housing would not be necessary. Seconding Doyle, James F. Peacock of the NAHB told the delegates: "Builders are accustomed to challenge. . . . But homes for the aged also mean a market that our product and service have not reached. To treat this problem on the level of business, we are looking for any new market." By 1956, the NAHB was openly advising its constituency that the over-sixty-fives constituted a "hot market," comprehending large numbers of people with sufficient amounts of either cash or credit to be able to afford new housing. In fact, lending institutions had taken a new position on loans for senior citizen housing in response to the building industry's clamor and increasingly favorable governmental actions. On a practical level, banks now observed that the average life expectancy of the sixty-five-year-old was longer than the average seven- or eight-year mortgage repayment period. Individual builders, like the Mackle Brothers of Florida, were likewise pleased with recent financial trends. "We've always felt," one of the Mackles was quoted, "that a builder has a social responsibility to himself to make a profit."[20]

Among the social, political, and economic elements involved in promoting retirement or senior citizen housing, none had greater impact than the large builders—most notably Del E. Webb, Inc. and Ross Cortese's Rossmoor-Leisure World, Inc. Such organizations not only built houses; they built markets for those houses as well. This market consisted of a new breed of American—the "active" retiree. Once convinced that this market was viable, men like Webb and Cortese approached the problem of exploiting it with an energy, skill, and lack of dogmatism at once admirable, and disturbing, to less self-interested social scientists. Their success and influence can be attributed to two factors. First, their concerns were nationwide and had long experience in industrial and governmental contract work. Thus they had the technical skills and the capital necessary to embark upon a large scale, high impact building program. Second, both were master salesmen who thoroughly researched their markets before entering, then once committed, employed shrewdly all the tools of the advertising trade to promote sales. Indeed, Webb was credited by one of the more critical observers of the retirement community phenomenon with originating many of the positive euphemisms for old age and older people that currently encumber our everyday language—"Golden Years," "Rewarding Years," "Friendly Years," "The New Leisure Set." Prepared to be skeptical of any venture that promoted itself with the slogan "Lucky enough to be fifty or more?" Calvin Trillin of the *New Yorker* paid a ten-day visit to Webb's Sun City, Arizona retirement community. He came away somewhat less disposed than originally to scoff at the patented Webb "active" retirement formula: activity + friendliness = happiness.[21]

In 1955, a Webb marketing vice-president, Thomas Breen, noticed a novel housing development located just 16 miles from Webb's home base, Phoenix, Arizona. Called "Youngtown," this community had flourished since its completion in 1954, despite the fact that it barred residents under the age of sixty. Breen was enough intrigued by this phenomenon to carry out some research on the potential of similar projects. By administering batteries of tests to retired people, he sought to learn as much as he could about the housing needs and desires of the elderly.

Based on the results of this sophisticated process of data collection, Webb committed $2 million to the construction of his first Sun City retirement housing project in 1959. This project was advertised as incorporating "everything which Del E. Webb's extensive research revealed you want most."[22]

More than the shelter of a custom-built house, Webb's chief selling point stressed the attributes of the total environment. Trade publication *Burrough's Clearinghouse* called Sun City "the town that changed the nation's viewpoint on retirement." If it was not exactly that, it did contribute a good deal to this changing viewpoint. "We've always sold a way of life," said James Detrick, Webb's advertising manager; "The homes are secondary." According to sixty-seven-year-old Louis Inwood, president of the Sun City Homeowner's Association, it was the "way of life" which most people bought. "We're active as the devil," he told the *New Yorker's* Calvin Trillin: "Most of us are so damned busy we have to put priorities on our time." In his advertising (the average information packet sent out by mail cost about one dollar), Webb emphasized Sun City's self-government and the more than ninety different clubs and affinity groups which it supported, as well as its facilities—a community center, a country club, a golf course, swimming pools, and a shopping center. Even among those Sun Citizens who did not take much interest or part in the "active" life of the community, preferring their own pursuits and hobbies or, in some cases, simply doing nothing, there appeared to be a general satisfaction "with what they consider decent weather and a pretty good bargain in housing." As Breen put it, the major sources of contentment among residents was the absence of the "fear of being shouldered aside by younger men . . . [and] the camaraderie of shared age and past achievement."[23]

Sun City's young activities director, Tom Austin told Trillin: "We're not philanthropists—sure, we're a business concern—but we've become involved. We're involved in human lives, trying to help old people achieve happiness, help them fulfill dreams." Trillin had to admit, if grudgingly, given his initial biases, that

Sun City had to a great extent succeeded, despite the caveats posed by gerontologists against age segregated communities. Asked about the prevailing view that older people were better off remaining in the communities in which they had lived prior to retirement, Louis Inwood responded bluntly: "As a theory, it's fine. But in practice no one is going to do any listening to them. . . . I'm an outcast because I'm 67 years old. I think the whole bunch of us are outcasts who have found a way of living without impinging on anybody, or bothering anybody." Nor was Inwood alone. In a piece for *Esquire,* one generally critical intellectual concluded, on the basis of his first-hand observations: "Webb's complex of noiselessly functioning 'facilities' appears to make nearly all its tenants as happy as they can get, improve their self-esteem, and actually increase longevity. To put it simply, Sun City is a success."[24]

Although George Wright was over sixty-five and retired, a writer for *Readers' Digest* remarked, he showed "no intention of being shelved like some obsolete piece of machinery. Instead, this former factory manager has sold his house and plunged into a bold experiment in 'country club' retirement at Walnut Creek, California, across the bay from San Francisco." In Ross Cortese's Rossmoor-Leisure World community, George Wright hoped to turn his retirement into something interesting and eventful. His move to Walnut Creek reflected his adherence to "the new philosophy: retirement is not a cessation of life; it is not endless lonely hours in front of the TV set; but it has another, rewarding phase—a combination of recreation and meaningful activity." Perhaps one of the more memorable indications of this philosophy in operation appears in the "Leisure World Theme Song" which urges swinging widows to "tint your hair and keep it curled./And stalk your prey at Leisure World." Cortese's entry into the field of retirement housing was, he told an interviewer, based upon the potential salability of this new philosophy: "As life expectancy is increasing and people are retiring earlier, it seemed to me that a significant number of mature people would want to move to totally new environments which offered leisure pursuits and plenty of contacts with people their own age." Like Webb, Cortese worked hard to translate this philosophy into a demand for his product. *Fortune* called him "a smart and successful packager and seller of a total environment," and attributed his success to a sensitivity to the needs and desires of his potential customers—that is, white, middle class, middle-aged people of average educational attainments. "To find out what older people wanted," *Fortune* reported, "Cortese talked to businessmen, union leaders, doctors, the clergy, and groups of senior citizens." Based on this, he set the lower age limit of his prospective clientele at fifty-two, citing this as the age when many people seem to want to make a fresh start. It is on this basis that he has continued to sell houses.[25]

Webb and Cortese's impact upon fellow builders was quite strong. The *Wall Street Journal,* quoting one retirement magazine editor, stated that between 1958 and 1963 the number of retirement housing facilities had grown from a "handful" to more than 750, scattered all over the nation. The effort to attract older persons to retirement havens in the south and west had quickly exhausted the "adventurous oldster" market—set at about 2 percent of all over-sixty-fives by Professor James Gillies, a UCLA economist and planner—and enterprising builders like Robert Schmertz of Robilt, Inc., began to build their projects closer to the eastern origins of so many retired consumers. Schmertz' Leisure Village in the New Jersey swamplands, for example, offered everything that Sun City, Arizona did (except the climate) and was 3000 miles closer to home. The FHA, which had been generally cool to the idea of senior citizen housing, was also affected by the successes of the large builders, predicting "a tremendous expansion of for-profit old age housing projects over the next few years." In recognition of the bullish inclinations of the housing industry, the President's Council on Aging reported in 1964 that the Federal Government "recognized the need among the aged for a wider choice of places to live and has cultivated the construction of different kinds of housing facilities for older people."[26]

The actual number of older people directly affected by the efforts of builders, like Webb and Cortese, was actually quite small. Office of Aging Director Donald P. Kent, speaking in 1965, criticized a "country club concept of retirement that cannot possibly help millions of less fortunate elders who must exist on the lowest incomes." Moreover, the detailed research on housing preferences carried out by the Rutgers investigators in *Aging and Society* suggested that older people tended to remain in familiar settings after retirement, both for social and economic reasons— that is, access to friends and ownership of their residences—and were for this reason immune to the "new philosophy" appeals of Sun city or Leisure World. In his contribution to *Aging and Society,* planner John Madge dismissed these communities as havens for a relatively small number of affluent retirees. The true impact of the retirement village phenomenon on America's elderly, however, did not depend upon the number of individuals housed, but rather upon the way in which such housing was marketed. To sell novel products, markets had first to be isolated and defined—hence the "bobby sox" and "teen" markets—and often the influence of these creations was more pervasive than the buying habits it stimulated.[27]

Even beyond creating the notions of "active" retirement and retirees as marketing ploys, the builders in question also provided new social environments—however limited their actual impact—within which many long-held gerontological theories could be tested. It was soon apparent that these tests did not always confirm traditional opinion. Thus, an attendant result of the retirement village phenomenon was the dismantling of some heretofore cherished gerontological pieties. Webb's blunt spoken Vice President Breen, for example, listed some of the "basic" assumptions of gerontology which he felt his experience in the field had contradicted. Among these, he included the convictions that older people do not like to be appealed to on the basis of their age; that they need sustained contact with younger people; that they all need frequent cultural and intellectual stimulation; and finally, that they need to feel productive. Such convictions,

Breen argued, were erroneous "because we do the things society tells us to do for societal reasons, and not out of the feeling that we really want to. What's productive," he concluded, "is what's productive by society's standards. And the way of living of the Sun Citians raises questions about the validity of those standards." Like many social gerontologists, Breen felt that altering societal expectations offered the best means of improving the lot of older people in American society; but unlike them, he carried no missionary's burden and felt no sense of ministry to those who could not afford the solution he offered. Nonetheless, examples of places, like Sun City, were gradually converting expert opinions to the view that "many old people are better off where they can find a good many other old people with similar interests and where they do not feel shunted aside in favor of the young."[28]

In reference to the senior housing "boom," Dr. Edward Allen, a psychiatrist and secretary of the American Geriatrics Society, observed: "In a retirement village people can find serenity when they identify with others of a similar age. They speak the same language, have common experiences and areas of communication. . . . From the psychological and psychiatric point of view, they can socialize more comfortably." The respected gerontological psychologist, R. W. Kleemeier, admitted that his thinking had been altered by his observations of life in a Rossmoor facility. "Group living in congenial surroundings," he concluded, "is not repellant to a great segment of our older people." Sociologist and Office of Aging Director Donald P. Kent, though rejecting the retirement village concept as a practical large scale solution to the housing and social complaints of the majority of older people, was moved to preach against excessive dogmatism. Speaking before the National Conference of State Executives on Aging in May 1965, he cautioned the assembled professionals to avoid "projecting on to them [older people] our own wishes and hopes, or assuming something is so because we say it is so." Researchers specifically investigating the question of age-specific versus age-general environments in the housing of the retired older citizen found hard data to support the assertions of construction magnates. Work by gerontological investigators, like sociologist Mark Messer and psychologist Irving Rosow, suggested that age-specific environments were, in fact, functional in facilitating adjustment of aging and retirement by providing older people with a normative system of their own. Gordon L. Bultena and Virginia Wood challenged their fellow gerontologists to begin questioning the segregation-is-bad reflex. On the basis of their comparative study of age-specific and age-general residential communities in Arizona, Bultena and Wood claimed that adjustment to the phenomena of retirement and old age was actually less stressful in the segregated than in the integrated communities.[29]

Perhaps, a writer in *Life* magazine noted in 1970, the exclusiveness of retirement communities offered a more immediately applicable means of adjusting to the facts of old age and retirement that those generally advocated by the gerontologist (i.e., age integrated and intellectually stimulating environments). Increasingly, old people indicated great satisfaction with the idea of living among their age peers, puttering around their gardens, and playing shuffleboard. Marketers approached the problems of image and aging from a different angle than the social gerontologists. Instead of confronting society at large with the need to grant new, acceptable roles to older citizens, marketers had rather approached the older population itself, sold them roles which did not require the approval of the larger social structure and stimulated thereby the self-adjusting capacities of the aged individual. Their efforts were, within limits, highly effective and at a much lower social cost than many of the interventions demanded by the gerontological profession. One of these efforts was the retirement community model. The useful influences of this model, besides the environment it provided for the older person, included the imposition of restraint upon certain long-held views of aging as well as the creation of an active and positive, if generally middle-class-biased, shallow, and commercially oriented image of the elderly.[30]

Like the youth market, the senior market was largely the creation of Madison Avenue. Based on survey data of the most sophisticated kind, unencumbered by traditional gerontological beliefs and powered by the ever present desire for expanding markets, the advertising industry was highly influential in shaping the senior citizen concept. This concept, in turn, affected society's general appreciation and expectations of the aged. As advertising expert Dorothy Cohen put it: "Advertising can tie a product attitude directly to the expression of value-oriented needs in order to help give clarity to the individual's self-concept. Thus a change in value expressive attitudes may be performed by portraying a more desirable self-concept for the consumer." Without questioning the potential for abuse inherent in such power, the by-products of successful senior citizen marketing included heightened self-esteem and an altered social awareness of the attributes of the average older American. Regardless of motives involved, the effect of advertising upon the image of the aged has been too strong to ignore.[27]

N O T E S

1. Duff, "Training for Leadership in Working with Older People," *Journal of Educational Sociology* 30 (January 1957): 222–223; Hepner, *Effective Advertising,* 2nd ed. (New York: 1949), pp. 63–64.
2. "Older, Sprightlier Market," *Business Week* (June 19, 1954): 54–57; J. J. Corson and J. W. McConnell, *Economic Needs of Older People* (New York, 1956); "The Maybe Market," *Business Week* (November 5, 1955): 128; "The Market Potential of Older People," *Tide* 29 (November 19, 1955): 30–31; George B. Hurff, "Our Older People: New Markets for Industry," *Journal of Business* 27, no. 2 (April 1954): 131–136; Bruce Barton of BBDO quoted on the increasing importance of old age market in *Advertising Age* (August 13, 1956): 63.
3. "Older People Provide Market for Special Goods," *Science Newsletter* 63 (May 9, 1953): 296; "14 Million Americans Over 65," *Business Week* (February 4, 1956): 86–87; "More Time to Consume," *Tide* 30 (March 24, 1956): 23+; "Tomorrow's Leisure Time Trends," ibid. (April 21, 1956): 33–41; "Expanding Markets: The Oldsters," *Nation's Business,* 45: November. 1957, pp. 38–39, 87; "Marketing in the 60s," *Printer's Ink* 268 (September 11, 1959): 23–31.
4. Heinz unsuccessful campaign discussed in Leon Morse, "Old Folks: An Overlooked Market," *Dun's Review* 82–83 (April 1964): 46; contrasting view of market noted in "14 Million Americans Over 65," op. cit.: 86; Mitnick view cited in "living and

Housing Arrangements," in Senate Labor Committee, *Studies of the Aged*, V. (Washington, D.C., 1957); Nims view noted in "Toward Planned Communities for the Retired," *American City* 73 (January 1958): 110–111; Reed quoted in *Business Week* (June 19, 1954): 57.

5. Martineau, *Motivation in Advertising* (New York: 1957), p. 158; literature on the youth market is extensive, and all the major marketing texts examined treat the younger consumer as a unique and separate group, unlike the elderly who receive relatively little individual attention; see also the special sections of *Printer's Ink*'s annual market survey issues devoted to this youth market; Kelly, "People Make America," *Printer's Ink* 259 (April 3, 1957): 39–40.

6. *Advertising Age* (February 8, 1960): 12; P. G. Peterson, "Need for Brand New Marketing Methods in the Changing Markets of the Sixties," ibid. (August 14, 1961): 63–66.

7. Realemon advertising campaign reported in *Advertising Age,* November 2, 1959; agencies specializing in senior market noted in R. B. McIntyre, "Newspaper Ads Sell Folks Needing Facts," *Editor and Publisher* 95 (October 20, 1962): 19.

8. "How the Old Age Market Looks," *Business Week* (February 13, 1960): 72–78; "Selling the Elderly," *Wall Street Journal* (June 24, 1960), 1:1; Howard Whitman, "Planning Your Own Security," *Today's Health* 39 (June 1961): 22–25.

8a. White House Conference on Aging, *Background Paper on Housing* (Washington, D.C.: 1960); R. H. Kelly, "Senior Market is Maturing Fast," *Today's Health* 40 (November 1962): 68; Breen, "Aging and Its Social Aspects," *Journal of Home Economics* 54, no. 8 (October 1962): 685–689.

9. *Advertising Age* (March 20, 1961): 36; Porter columns from *New York Post,* June 26–27, 1961; see also "Social and Personal Aspects of Clothing for Older Woman," *Journal of Home Economics* 53, no. 6 (June 1961): 464–468 and "Clothing Preferences of Women 65 and Over," ibid. 54, no. 8 (October 1962), pp. 716–717; F. Linden, "Consumer Markets: The 65s and Over" (2 parts), *Conference Board Record* 19 (November 1962): 30–31. Increasing strength of older market noted in academic marketing texts, C. H. Sandage and V. Fryburger, *Advertising Theory and Practice,* 6th ed. (1963), and Woodrow Wirsig, *Principles of Advertising* (1963).

10. *Wall Street Journal,* September 26, 1963, 1:5; December 30, 1964, 1:6; Charles R. Goeldner and H. L. Mann, "The Significance of the Retirement Market," *Journal of Retailing* 39–40 (Summer 1964): 43–52. On a purely economic level, according to Bureau of Labor Statistic data, the over 65 market was not rated that strongly—see "The Elderly: A Not So Rich Market," *Printer's Ink,* 284 (August 23, 1963): 3; Sidney Goldstein, "The Aged Segment of the Market, 1950, 1960," *Journal of Marketing* 32 (April 1968): 62–68. Nolan and Warmke, *Marketing, Sales Promotion and Advertising,* 7th ed. (Cincinnati: 1965), p. 137; Cohen, "Improving the Status of the Aged," *Social Security Bulletin* 29 (1966): 3–8.

11. L. Morse, "Old Folks: An Overlooked Market," *Dun's Review,* 82–83 (April 1964): 45–46, 88; Pelzman's entry into the aging market reported in "Never Too Old to Buy," *Business Week* (May 23, 1964): 170–171; " 'Senior Citizens' Market: Is it Really There?" *Sponsor* 19 (March 23, 1965): 34–42; cosmetics speech reported in *Advertising Age* (September 26, 1966): 164; symposium remarks quoted in *Merchandising Week* 98 (October 31, 1966): 8; see also Special Senate Committee on Aging, *Consumer Interests of the Elderly, January 17–18, 1967* (Washington, D.C.: 1967), p. 234; Howard, ibid., pp. 128–132; "The Forgotten Generation," *Forbes* 103 (February 15, 1969): 22–23, 29.

12. "Ann Arbor Conference Focuses on Problems of Older Consumer," *Aging* (August-

September 1969): 5–6, 9; "Will the Elderly Rescue the Retailers?" *Business Week* (April 25, 1970): 32–33; "There's Money in the Old Folks," *Dun's Review* 95 (March 1970): 75.

13. Hepler quoted in *Advertising Age* (February 26, 1968): 12; Adams remarks from *Editor and Publisher* 102 (February 15, 1969): 16.

14. Senior driver study reported in *Best's Review* 69 (March 1969): 42–44; "Older Drivers 37% Safer Than Average in 30 States, AOA-Backed Survey Shows," *Aging* (March–April 1969): 9–10; "Insurer of Oldsters," *Dun's Review* 96 (December 1970): 51–52.

15. Flordia State Improvement Commission, *The Sponsored Neighborhood Village Idea in Florida* (Tallahassee: 1951); "Housing for the Aged," *Journal of Housing* 13 (February 1956): 49; Margaret Hickey, "Better Living for Elder Agers," *Ladies' Home Journal* 74 (June 1957): 23+; "Toward Planned Communities for the Aged," *American City* 73 (January 1958): 110–111; Rosow, "Retirement Housing and Social Integration," *Gerontologist* 1 (1960): 85–91; Loring, "A New Housing Market: Older People," *Architectural Forum* 113 (December 1960): 110–113; "Design for a New Housing Market," ibid. 114 (March 1961): 119–121, 184; see also W. F. Smith, "The Housing Preferences of Elderly People," *Journal of Gerontology* 16 (1960): 261–266.

16. "Should the Aged without Families be Segregated," and "Neighborhood Villages for the Aged Proposed" *American City* 66 (December 1951): 7 and 163, respectively; "The Guest House in the Garden," *House Beautiful* 94 (July 1952): 42; American Public Health Association, *Housing an Aging Population* (New York: 1953), p. 43.

17. Federal Security Administration, *Man and His Years* (Washington, D.C.: 1951), pp. 159–180; "Lenders Oppose Segregation of Housing for the Aging," *Architectural Record* 112 (November 1952): 310; Kraus, "Housing of Older Citizens," *AAPSS Annals* 279 (January 1952): 128–129.

18. Churchill quoted in *Living Through the Later Years: The 2nd Annual Southern Conference on Gerontology* (1952); Strunk quoted by Julietta K. Arthur, *How to Help Older People* (Philadelphia and New York: 1954); New York Governor's Conference, *Charter for the Aging* (Albany: 1955).

19. Senator John Sparkman, "Housing Older People: A Growing Market," in Senate Labor Committee, *Studies of the Aged and Aging,* 5 (1957): 32, of document "Housing and Living Arrangements"; "14 Million Americans Over 65," *Business Week* (February 4, 1956): 86–87; NAHB statement from *Advertising Age* (February 2, 1959): 42.

20. Doyle and Peacock quoted in Wilma Donahue (ed.), *Housing the Aged* (Ann Arbor: 1954), pp. 49, 70; Alfred Apsler, "A Town for Old Folks," *Rotarian* 87 (September 1955): 39–40; Tris Coffin, "Retirement Housing Offers a New Market," *Nation's Business* 44 (May 1956): 14–17; M. Abramson, "A New Life—At a Leisurely Pace," *Today's Health* 36 (December 1958): 23–27, 55; see also the promotion of the market by the building supply trade, exemplified by the Douglas Fir Plywood Association, *Advertising Age* (December 5, 1960): 91; the observation of a growing interest among builders in the older market in the WITCOA, *Background Paper on Housing* (March 1960).

21. For biographical and career information on Webb, see "Spreading Webb," *Time* 79 (January 26, 1962): 86; Trillin, "Wake Up and Live," op. cit.; the marketing aspect of senior citizen housing and its impact on popular thinking theoretically treated by Carl Gersuny, "The Rhetoric of the Retirement Home Industry," *Gerontologist* 10, no. 4, pp. 282–286. Trillin, "Wake Up and Live," *New Yorker* 40 (April 4, 1964): 120+.

22. The "Youngtown" development described in "Housing for the Aged," *Journal of Housing* 13 (February 1956): 49; Breen's activities covered in "A Place in the Sun,"

215

Time 80 (August 3, 1962): 46–50, Trillin; "Wake Up and Live," pp. 120 et passim.

23. "A Place in the Sun," op. cit.; Trillin, "Wake Up and Live," op. cit.; "Sun City," *Burrough's Clearinghouse* 48 (February 1964); Paul O'Neil, "For the Retired: A World All Their Own," *Life* 68 (May 14, 1970): 45–54.

24. Trillin, "Wake Up and Live," loc. cit.; Christopher Davis, "Death in Sun City," *Esquire* 66 (October 1966): 143–147.

25. "Old Folks At Home," *Newsweek* 61 (February 24, 1963): 84–84; Paul Friggens, "Where Life Begins at 65," *Readers' Digest* 88 (January 1966): 157–162; Peterson, *New Life Begins at Forty,* p. 165; "Life Begins at 52," *Fortune* 74 (September 1966): 164; the homogeneity of the retirement community is described by one writer in terms of condition of youth (depression years), politics (Republican), and entertainment preferences (Lawrence Welk); see O'Neil, "For the Retired," loc. cit., pp. 46–47.

26. *Wall Street Journal* (December 5, 1963), 1:1; Gillies testimony from Special Senate Committee on Problems of Aging, *Hearings, January 9, 1964,* 149, 88th Congress, 2nd Session (Washington, D.C. 1964); Schmertz' Leisure Village described in *American City* 79 (April 1964): 102; FHA Position change noted in *Wall Street Journal* (June 24, 1960), 1:1; President's Council on Aging, *On Growing Older* (Washington: 1964), p. 110; a realistic assessment of appeal of the retirement village is Theodore Irwin, "Should Your Parents Move to a Retirement Village?" *American Home* 66 (January–February 1963): 8+.

27. Kent quoted in Cooley, *The Retirement Trap,* p. 104; Riley and Foner, *Aging and Society* 2, chap. 6 ("The Residential Setting"), and 2 (Madge, "Aging and the Fields of Architecture and Planning").

28. Trillin, "Wake Up and Live," op. cit., pp. 172, 177, 120.

29. Irwin, "Should Your Parents Move to a Retirement Village?" loc. cit. Kleemeier quoted in Friggens, "Where Life Begins at 65," loc. cit., p. 161; Kent's remarks printed in *Aging* (June 1965): 28; Messer, "The Possibility of an Age Concentrated Environment Becoming a Normative System," *Gerontologist* 7 no. 4: (1967), 247–251; Rosow, *The Social Integration of the Aged* (New York, 1967); Bultena and Wood, "The American Retirement Community: Bane or Blessing," *Journal of Gerontology* 24 no. 2: (1969): 209–217.

30. O'Neill, "For the Retired," loc. cit., 46; see also the expressions of satisfaction in the active life of the retirement village resident quoted in "Florida Philosophy: It's Never Too Late to Be Young," *Look* 23 (April 14, 1959): 50–52.

31. For an example of the kind of survey projects undertaken by the ad industry, see BBDO, *Are You As Young (Or as Old) As You Feel? A Five Year Comparision of Attitudes Toward Age* (ca. 1974), which was designed "to acquire knowledge concerning which age groups people identify with, since this kind of information is vital to creating effective advertising." Dorothy Cohen, *Advertising* (New York 1972), p. 390.

9

Changing the Face of Retirement: Programs and Policies

As we observed at the close of Chapter 2, a phenomenon most closely related to the emergence of the new senior citizen image has been the gradual adoption of policies designed to prune the labor force of its older members. The enactment of the Social Security Act of 1935 and the growth of private pension plans within various larger industries during the later 1940s and 1950s helped to institutionalize retirement in American society. The availability of retirement permitted industry to infuse new blood into constantly changing production systems (or, in many cases, to replace men with machines), and labor to provide increased employment opportunities for the younger memebers of the work force without breaching the key union principle of seniority. By 1950, the struggle between labor and management over the shape of retirement policy had been resolved, with employer control of retirement policy conceded by labor in return for "adequate pensions." The actions of both labor and management in fixing retirement policy had been based on bread and butter motives. As earlier noted, management sought control over retirement age as a principal feature of a "manpower policy" designed to adapt labor force size to economic conditions, and labor wanted to ensure that younger members of the rank and file had sufficient job opportunities without violating seniority guidelines by making postretirement income lucrative enough to overcome older worker reluctance to retire. From the outset of this business–labor compromise on retirement policy, many argued that there was more to successful, well-adjusted retirement than sufficient or "adequate" income. Money was indeed an important element, these critics conceded, but it was not the sole one. Gerontologists, certain businessmen, and various labor leaders all pointed out that the responsibility of an industrialized, production oriented society toward its older, retired members did not end with seeing that they had sufficient income after leaving the labor force. Society, as represented by those who employed and those who spoke for the older worker, had the duty to supply not only their material, but social and emotional needs as well.

Gerontologists were among the earliest proponents of psychological as well as economic preparation for retirement. Most of them, in fact, tended to resist the very notion of retirement. The dominance of "activity" theory, moreover, guaranteed that those few who did recognize that retirement was an unavoidable fact of life, would define it by using all the criteria, save that of remuneration, applicable to work. The gerontological notion of retirement preparation, from the very outset, was based on the older person's need for continued activity and social involvement. Sociologist Elon H. Moore, for example, writing in the *Journal of Gerontology* in 1946, advised that his colleagues recognize that, with social security coverage expanding, the increasing resort by business to private pension plans, the growing technological complexity of the production process, and the numbers of nonworking older people, both voluntary and involuntary, could not fail but grow. It was time, he insisted, that social thinkers accept the notion of retirement—he proposed sixty as an optimum age—and turn their efforts to investigating the social-emotional problems which it appeared to trigger, with an eye to facilitating their resolution. Educational programs, he declared, provided one route by which the social planners could ease the adjustment of older, but healthy and active, workers to the inevitable loss of the work role.[1]

The idea of occupation as a major source of human satisfaction was crucial to any understanding of the problems faced by the retired person, according to sociologists Michael Wermel and Selma Gelbaum. They accepted the trend among employers toward fixed retirement as a tool for opening up employment opportunities for younger workers in the contracting postwar labor market. Although they continued to question "whether it is wise or kind" to retire workers against their wills, they suggested that adjustment problems were not solely the fault of a heartless employer. Society itself was fanatically devoted to the "work ethic." Thus, anything that removed a healthy individual (no matter what age) from a work role, would have not only economic, but psychological and social, implications for him as well. Society, in their view, had to bear a share of responsibility for the phenomenon of unsuccessful retirement. To meet that responsibility, it had an obligation to provide its retired older citizens with alternative opportunities for satisfying the needs once fulfilled by employment. As this obligation came to be more widely accepted, "retirement preparation" would become more common.[2]

Psychologist George Lawton, a strong advocate of such preparation, referred to the typical emotional response to loss of the work role as "retirement shock," which he defined in terms of listlessness, depression, guilt, and physical and mental decline. Lawton was not sanguine about attempts to arrest the drift toward retirement of older workers in industry. Instead of expending energy in such quixotic efforts, he felt that all those interested in the welfare of the elderly would be better advised to concentrate on preparing people for retirement. "Aging successfully," he wrote, "is a matter of aging successively—preparing now for later stages and making the most of each stage as it arrives." Lawton envisioned an educational process begun early in life to prepare each citizen generally for an eventual departure from the labor force in tandem with the development of more specific retirement planning and counseling services immediately prior to retirement, including follow-up investigation to determine the success of the adjustment process.[3]

What was needed now, these vanguard gerontologists argued, was a general recognition that retirement was an accomplished fact. Instead of futilely debating its merits and demerits as policy, the energy and enthusiasm of the profession ought to be invested in making it work. Thus Ollie A. Randall, a long time social worker in the field of aging, emphasized that preparation for retirement was important—both financially and "with respect to the almost more important personal resources." Far from being against retirement, Randall saw it as a potentially rewarding period of life, provided we determined "as early in our careers as possible, what interests and activities can keep life real for us apart from the interests and activities of our careers." Moreover, she noted, the issue of continuing education and preparation for retirement was becoming more imperative each day as a result of shrinking employment opportunities for the older person. The challenge, then, was simple: to make the last one-quarter to one-third of life a period of "personal profit in terms of real living" and to prove "that life can have a quality to be eagerly awaited and emulated by those who will follow us, justifying faith not in the figures of the actuary, but in the old promise of the poet, 'The best is yet to be.' " Joining Randall in her realistic outlook was a fellow New York City social worker, Harry Levine, the Welfare Department's Director of Special Services to the Aged. In a review of Clark Tibbitt's *Living Through the Older Years,* Levine explicitly challenged current assumptions about retirement and posed some questions for further investigation by gerontologists. "While it is generally accepted that employment is highly desirable," he asked, "is it necessary? Should the older person be given the opportunity to enjoy not only the product of his labor but the cultural heritage of the ages and perhaps *add* to it?" Even if, an amendment to Levine's view might read, the older person had to be trained to appreciate this "cultural heritage."[4]

The dauntless team of Tuckman and Lorge, surveying a sample of older garment workers, at the request of the International Ladies' Garment Workers Union, reported on the "economic, psychological, cultural and social factors" which they declared contributed to the workers' resistance to retirement. Such factors combined to define work as a "way of life," they continued, noting that the best means of breaking down employee reluctance, when retirement was inevitable, was to create an image of retirement as being a valid, alternative "way of life." Instilling such an image ought to be a primary objective of any labor-management effort to prepare older workers for loss of the work role. "Role," in fact, was a very important concept in early gerontological attempts to enunciate the ideal of retirement preparation. Thus, Robert Havighurst, The University of Chicago sociologist, writing in a special "Aging and Retirement" issue of the *American Journal of Sociology* (January 1954), expanded upon the concept of "role flexibility." The process of aging, he argued, was featured by the loss of many roles, most notably the occupational role. Successful aging could be enhanced if the individual were stimulated to intensify his identification with the roles that remained, or to assume completely new ones. "The problem for social science and for adult education," he concluded, "is to learn the conditions under which the capacity [role flexibility] may be acquired, and to discover ways of helping all kinds of people to increase it." A cocontributor to this collection, Professor L. C. Michelon of the university's Industrial Relations Department, reported upon his empiric observations of retirees living in a Florida trailer park in an effort to determine the elements of the "personal value structure" which he felt influenced adjustment to retirement. Among other factors, Michelon found that preretirement attitudes toward leisure and nonwork related interests apparently had a strong bearing upon the capacity for adjustment. Where favorable attitudes existed, he wrote, the adaptive process seemed to be much more easily completed.

Could not such attitudes, he asked in conclusion, be inspired? "Changes in a person's value structure might best be achieved through preretirement training and counseling ... not ... to make the positive meanings of work negative, but rather to neutralize them with a better appreciation of retirement opportunities."[5]

Dr. Robert Monroe, a Boston geriatrician and founder of the Age Center of New England, Inc., a private gerontological research institution, also took a broad view of retirement preparation. He rejected the money-buys-happiness mode of thought which seemed to shape the general labor-management view of their responsibility toward retired employees. "Retirement benefits don't necessarily give satisfaction," he told a *Business Week* staff writer; "There may be money to live on, but money doesn't mean a thing if there's nothing to live for." Achieving the goal for which retirement preparation was intended—that is, facilitating individual adjustment to the nonworking status—in a society which revered work and denigrated age, many gerontologists felt, depended upon their success in breaking down the all too frequently blind allegiance to the work ethic. This allegiance verged upon being a national compulsion. Thus, anything that could help minimize the feelings of guilt and social rejection, stemming from the termination of one's work life, had a part to play in preparation for retirement programs. George E. Johnson, vice president of the Teacher's Insurance and Annuity Association, took much the same position in a 1955 University of Michigan collection of essays on education and aging. Chiding business and labor for their excessively laissez faire attitudes toward the noneconomic aspects of retirement preparation, Johnson cautioned: "A retired worker should not be made to feel cast off and laid on the shelf." Thus, the basic theme of a retirement preparation plan developed by the University of Michigan's Woodrow W. Hunter in 1955, according to a report in *Nation's Business,* was simple—get the worker "to think of retirement as a bonus rather than the end of useful life." The industrial community, social gerontologists argued with mounting conviction, had very real responsibilities in this regard.[6]

Having argued the need for retirement preparation, social scientists in the gerontological specialties described a number of ways in which this might be carried out. The method best suited to those companies which regarded retirement preparation as an individual matter involved the provision of materials—books and pamphlets on the subject in plant libraries, articles/special departments in plant newspapers, or, where specifically requested, individual counseling on finances. This seemed to the gerontologist the least desirable, since it offered the least guidance and placed the burden of action upon the individual employee. The necessity for retirement training was specifically rooted in the failure of most workers to make postoccupational plans on their own. Hence, such unstructured, discretionary approaches on the part of management could not be very effective. A second type of program employed the individual counseling method. Under this scheme, a member of the company's personnel staff would interview each prospective retiree at some point (usually five years) before retirement with the intention of alerting him to his approaching severance date and stimulating him to think about the need to plan for this event. Although preferable to the first method, individual counseling had its drawbacks. To be effective, such a program required the employment of specially trained personnel as interviewers; a requirement that many smaller companies could not meet because of its cost. It also tended, on the whole, to emphasize financial questions to the exclusion of social and psychological counseling—and if applied heavy-handedly, it might be considered overly-interventionist by the employee and result in his resistance to it. Finally, there was the formal group style retirement training program which made use of the classroom model of education.[7]

This latter option was the one with which the gerontologists of the 1950s and 1960s were most familiar, and toward which they were most partial. Given the academic environs—most notably The Universities of Chicago, Michigan, California, and Cornell University—within which much of the research on retirement was being done, and out of which, many of the gerontologists operated, it is not surprising that they tended to promote formal, group style, training classes, with syllabi, lectures, discussions, and periodic evaluations. Beyond being a method with which most gerontologists were comfortable, they felt that structured retirement training courses allowed for an orderly and thorough coverage of the nonfinancial aspects of retirement. A psychologist, Leonard Goodstein, rejected the do-it-yourself approach to retirement preparation on the grounds that most of the available popular literature—assuming that the average older worker were self-motivated enough to read it—was overly optimistic and tended to gloss over the problematic areas of retirement. Thus, he argued: "The need for extensive, well-conceived retirement counseling programs seems obvious." E. B. Schultz of Cornell University, developer of the Tennessee Valley Authority retirement preparation program agreed. "The task of our society," he was quoted in a Ford Foundation report, "is to provide a new enthusiasm for retirement." The academic model was best suited to the achievement of this goal, he continued, since this job was "a complicated process . . . [which] involves much more than informing a worker about his pension rights and warning him of some of the difficulties inherent in retirement."[8]

One key benefit of such formal courses was a group reinforcement—the effect on the individual of the knowledge that in his fears and uncertainties he was not alone—which weighed heavily in the gerontological preference shown for this mode of conditioning. Headed by trained leaders, such multifaceted courses left nothing to chance. Once the invitation to attend such a class was extended and accepted, the program itself took over and systematically dealt with all the problems (social, physical, economical, and psychological) raised by retirement. The formal group program also lent itself best to the graduation concept of retirement by providing an identifiable *rite de passage* (i.e., graduation dinners, award of course completion certificates, etc.) from the status of the worker to the status of retiree. This style of program was also not without flaws—it could be complex in organization and substance and thus beyond the capacity of the average industrial worker. It required trained leaders; and it could be begun too late (usually figured to be less than two years before retirement) to accomplish its intentions. But none of these obstacles were insurmountable, and gerontologists from the Labor and Industrial Relations units at the various universities, working under foundation grants constantly modified the content and duration of the formal courses. Charles Odell, director of the UAW's Older and Retired Worker's Department, and a strong advocate of retirement training courses summed up the arguments for them by describing the joint UAW–University of Chicago program in operation at different union plants, concluding: "If we accept as a matter of course the need to invest twelve to sixteen years in formal education for work, why is it asking too much to expect society including labor, management and government, to invest 24 man hours of educational effort in each older worker before he retires? It is to be hoped that ... government, labor, industry and the related fields of social welfare will also agree and join in this badly needed and relatively inexpensive educational and preventive service."[9]

With gerontologists increasingly adverting to the "problem" of retirement and proposing solutions in the form of various "retirement preparation" devices, certain elements within the business and labor communities began to take the broader view being urged upon them. More and more, this vanguard group recognized that it was inhumane to turn the older worker out of a job without at least attempting to ease the emotional stresses which, social science critics of industrial policy insisted, retirement brought on. One individual with close ties to both the business and gerontological communities, the TIAA's George Johnson, was able to point out the blind spots of each of these groups in the debate over retirement. Writing in a 1951 issue of the *Journal of Gerontology,* he first expressed his support for chronologically fixed retirement ages. While conceding that such practices ignored the facts of individual capacity and preference, and that they might indeed, as gerontologists claimed, have adverse emotional and physical effects if not countered in some way, he nonetheless defended fixed age retirement on the grounds that the orderly administration of retirement plans demanded them. Chronological criteria were the only ones available upon which the retirement decision could at present be based. He rejected the "biologic age" criteria advanced by certain gerontologists, arguing that no one was even agreed as to what these criteria were, let alone how to measure them. Another frequently espoused alternative—the "tapering off" plan, which provided for a gradual reduction in work load between the ages of fifty-five and seventy-five—was simply unworkable, save in the cases of the self-employed (who did not face compulsory retirement systems in the first place) or those working for concerns in which continual intraplant transfers were feasible. There also existed the possibility of the "work qualification" test. However, Johnson pointed out to the advocates of this plan that no one had as yet developed any accurate or unbiased tests. Other suggested plans—worker determination, employer determination, review boards—were all subject to objections on the grounds that each provided substantial opportunities for unfairness and bias, depending upon which group dominated the process. What remained—fixed age retirement—emerged as both the fairest and most easily administered plan. Those who argued for an end to fixed retirement, citing older people's positive attitudes toward work and their negative attitudes toward retirement, also had a point. It was precisely upon this point, Johnson felt, that the neglected responsibility of labor and management (and to a large extent gerontology) was brought into sharp relief. Attitudes toward work and retirement, he argued, could be changed; no less an authority than Otto Pollak of the SSRC had asserted this belief. Thus, the formulators of retirement policy could probably end such criticisms once and for all by including in the retirement system some mechanism for encouraging older workers to enjoy the leisure of retirement as they had always enjoyed the status conferred by work.[10] In fact, noted a writer in *Business Week* in April 1951, most older workers were "pathetically unprepared for retirement." Even where postretirement income was adequate, many retired persons failed to adjust to their new status because of an inability to make plans for a life without nine-to-five employment. With growing frequency, management was being subjected to the criticism that it had "killed Jones" by retiring him against all his inclinations. A management consultant firm made much the same point in a 1953 promotional pamphlet: "As an integrated part of society industry is becoming increasingly aware of the need for its participation in plans for ameliorating the status of the aged, especially since its widespread adoption . . . of pension plans with provisions requiring compulsory retirement, adds thousands yearly to the inactive list of older citizens." Apart from the humanitarian regard for older workers that such a policy reflected, there were practical reasons for it as well. Elizabeth Breckinridge, secretary of the Illinois Commission on the Aging, listed some of these incentives in a 1953 Commission publication. These included high morale and hence greater productivity among older workers, good public relations for the company, and an an end to popular resistance to the notion of retirement. Having already begun to experiment with retirement preparation programming, Standard Oil of New Jersey saw yet another reason to urge businessmen to consider establishing similar programs. "If industry can convince the aging industrial population that it is doing something concrete about their uncertain future, socialistic remedies might well wither for lack of support." Thus, getting older workers out of the labor force as quietly as possible, guarding against older worker discontent on the assembly line, and eliminating the poor public relations images fostered by the "killed Jones" syndrome were incentives to both labor and management to look more closely into the "retirement shock" phenomenon; with the added incentive for business to keep government out of this area of employee relations.[11]

In an obvious response to such urgings, an increase of industrially sponsored retirement training or counseling structures, in both number and sophistication, marked the decade of the 1950s.

227

One of the earliest of a continuing series of surveys, designed to determine the extent to which the retirement preparation phenomenon had become institutionalized within industry, was undertaken by the indefatigable team of Tuckman and Lorge. During 1950, these two pollsters prepared a detailed questionnaire designed to collect information on pension plans, feelings of older workers toward retirement, and degree of corporate commitment to assisting employees with counseling or preparation programs, and sent it to the 113 largest United States concerns in *Poore's Register*. Of the 70 responses, the researchers found growing corporate concern over the problems of retirement adjustment faced by retired workers. Of the polled businesses and industries, 37 percent reported having some kind of a program in operation and 9 percent were seriously considering adoption of such a plan. The plans ranged from token affairs to elaborate educational programs, with most attention given to finances and health, and least to psychological preparations, changing social situation, and housing/living arrangements.[12]

Looking at individual retirement programs, one of the earliest, most commented upon, and most widely monitored was that instituted by Standard Oil at its Bayonne, N.J., refinery in 1950. The idea for the ESSO program, *Business Week* reported, emerged after an ESSO executive, Morton Pierson, had returned from a conference on the problems of retired workers. Impressed with the potential gravity of the situation, Pierson directed a company survey of 1000 recent retirees living in New Jersey. The results were not encouraging. "Retirement shock" was rampant. An inability to cope with free time, he concluded, was responsible for this high rate of maladjustment. Indeed, the best adjusted among the sample, Pierson found, were those who had taken new jobs. A concurrent survey of ESSO employees, two years or less away from retirement age, revealed that these workers were heading for the same postretirement fate, and that an "appalling lack of plans" was the rule among the corporation's older workers. Describing the thrust of the program in a special pamphlet, the company declared: "Old age is not necessarily senility, and retirement from business is not necessarily retirement from society. Continuing activity on the part of every individual who is able is vital to the health of the individual and the welfare of the community and its industries." Yet, the ill-prepared retiree in physical and mental decline, because of the poverty of his social life, was an all too common phenomenon. So ESSO, long active in the field of financial planning for its employees, turned its attention to the social aspects of retirement, to giving "real help and counsel to the individual in thinking through his problem." The familiar key to ESSO's program—as in industrial retirement preparation programs in general—was stated as follows: "It [ESSO] feels that retirement is something earned by faithful service, a form of 'graduation' into a new phase of life rather than a 'casting out' process. Retirement should be the opportunity for the employee to enjoy the fruits of his labors in freedom, leisure and relaxation as well as an opportunity to serve himself, his family and his community in ways not open to him during his working career." Like the gerontologists who sought to upgrade the image of the older person, many industrial leaders sought to engineer a new view of retirement.[14]

Although one of the most visible of such schemes, the ESSO plan was one of the growing number of such programs put into operation during the 1950s. At McCormick and Company, an executive in the industrial relations department described that company's program as the means by which employees were reconciled to the mandatory retirement policy. A first interview with employees was held at age sixty, another at age sixty-three, a letter on financial options followed by another interview at age sixty-four, and finally, a last session three months prior to the retirement date. While the emphasis here was on financial aspects (pension, social security, and insurance benefits), some effort was reportedly made to stimulate nonfinancial planning. A booklet was given to all those approaching retirement, and postretirement contact (greeting cards, letters, Christmas baskets) maintained by the company. McCormick and Company, this officer declared, recognized its moral responsibility to older and former employees, but it also saw its action as a blow against governmental intervention in the labor market to outlaw compulsory retirement schemes, regulate pension funds, and so forth. Yet another retirement program was developed by Standard Oil of California. Besides the example of the ESSO model, the California company was specially sensitized to the problem of retirement adjustment because of the abnormally high (56 percent as compared to 36 percent nationally) proportion of over sixty-fives in the state's population. Although unmentioned as a factor, George McClain's recent pension crusade upon behalf of California retirees doubtless played a role in the corporate decision to establish an elaborate training program to assist ex-employees in dealing with the problems posed by limitless leisure. Beginning at age fifty-five, this plan was company-wide, multi-faceted, flexible, and long range in its approach to the issue of personal adjustment.[15]

An interesting approach was that utilized by the Johnson and Johnson Company of New Brunswick, New Jersey, in 1962. Its program, which used individual counseling sessions as its means of contact, was remarkable chiefly for the fact that the employee was introduced to it at the age of thirty. Past experience with counseling efforts which began at age sixty had convinced management that they had been introduced too late to have any effect upon either financial preparation or psychological orientation. As the company's chief of employee relations explained the program's early activation age: "We were aware that an employee might not be too interested in retirement when he was still in his 30s. But if he heard us talking about it, and if he gave it some thought, he would not be startled when we brought the subject up the next time." Each succeeding decade of the worker's employment received a different programmatic emphasis. During his thirties, the employee's attention was occasionally called to the issue of pensions and other financial topics; in his forties, similar informal discussions of health maintenance and the biological declensions of age, supplemented by the company's medical officer's continuing encouragements to financial planning; during his fifties, two formal two-hour sessions emphasized health and finances again, though now in more specific and urgent terms; and finally, in the sixties, four 2-hour meetings provided him with an individualized estimation of retirement income and a thorough explanation of his options, with questions being entertained and answered. Two other, more formal corporate efforts were those of the Scoville Manufacturing Company of Waterbury, Connecticut, and Mead, Johnson and Company of Evansville, Indiana. Each encompassed eight-week courses dealing with such topics as finances, health, living arrangements, legal affairs, and potential uses of leisure time. They were presided over by officials of the company and/or the union, as well as occasionally by outside experts. The aims of such counseling was to "take the fear out of retirement," by assuring each employee of his financial security (within limits imposed by pension level) and by attempting to give him a leisure orientation.[16]

The creation of retirement preparation programs within industry did not, of course, immediately end criticisms of the retirement system. The motives—especially those of management—which spurred expansion of the retirement training/counseling phenomenon were still subject to question. Looking at the wave of managerial involvement in retirement preparation in the mid-1950s, Harvard business professor, Charles Perrow, expressed no doubt that this was in part an indication of business' willingness to fulfill an obligation to long-service employees. He also quoted one industrial spokesman who had declared that "unless we take steps to work it [retirement security] out for ourselves, we may very well find some government agency making an effort to help us—and such help is always expensive." Then too, these programs contributed to the image of corporate responsibility and promoted both good public relations and good labor relations by projecting an air of management concern for older and retired workers. Critics singled out such incentives as these when condemning preretirement programs. Existing programs, they argued, were little better than cosmetic facades designed to permit both business and labor to continue their policy of ejecting able-bodied older employees from the labor force and were never intended to be effective in facilitating adjustment to life without employment.[17]

One such critic labeled the retirement preparation phenomenon, management's response to a growing recognition that the policy of compulsory retirement was both unfair and unwise, and called retirement training programs "elaborate effort [s] . . . to persuade workers to *like* getting paid without working." Professor Perrow, a more neutral observer, agreed that the "social engineering" objectives of these programs tended "to create unreasonable expectations by describing ideal retirements. This, he thought, could lead in some instances to postretirement disappointments and thus could impede rather than facilitate personal adjustment to retirement. Educator Martin Tarcher assailed business for a "window dressing" approach to the issue of retirement training. If business leaders were seriously to undertake the job of readying older employees for their departure from the work force, he argued, they would have to call into question the sanctity of the work ethic. Since business and industrial enterprise derived great benefit from an unrestricted acceptance of this ethic, he continued, there was a deep-seated reluctance on the part of program sponsors to suggest that work might not be, after all, a social and emotional necessity. The end result was a high percentage of ill-considered and wrongly motivated efforts to ready employees for the day when they would be excessed from the work force. What was needed, Tarcher concluded, was a commitment on the part of business to meet its moral obligations to its older workers, to "shake off the many dogmas and sacred cows . . . that encourage conformity and inhibit controversy" and to create "a more humane and human work environment . . . [with] more time and opportunity for learning, social experience and responsibility."[18]

On the whole, however, comments and evaluations tended to stress the usefulness of retirement training as a means of easing the adjustment difficulties of retired persons. Thus, a hard-driving businessman, forced by ill health to retire from a rewarding and successful career, explained that his involuntary retirement had left him "astounded at [his] limitations . . . [and] lack of inner resources." Although he finally made the adjustment, it was only after a grim and depressing struggle. How much easier it could have been, he declared, had he only been alerted in advance to the difficulties introduced by the termination of active employment. What was needed was a "systematic, serious effort . . . to impress on people the importance of such preparedness, or to assist them in finding the answer themselves." When Edith M. Stern, a writer in gerontological psychology, reviewed ESSO's pioneering effort in this area, she emphasized its positive aspect. In a chatty, informal piece in *Nation's Business,* Stern asserted that, based on her observations, all those exposed to ESSO's counseling program were "getting on fine" in retirement, even though prior to this exposure two-thirds of these same men and women had vague plans or no plans at all for their retirement years. Stern was especially struck by the advantages of the ESSO service's presentation of retirement as a "graduation," as something earned after a lifetime of work. Indoctrination in this particular viewpoint, she felt, seemed to be the biggest single reason for the positive attitude of Standard Oil employees toward approaching retirement. The action of the Oil and Chemical Workers Union, ESSO local, in calling for reduction of the minimum retirement age to sixty, was significant too, with its intimations that workers were no longer perceiving retirement in threatening terms.[19]

Another advocate of counseling services, writing in The University of Chicago's *Journal of Business,* noted that the average retiree faced not only the let-down of losing his occupational role, but a culture that was at worst hostile, at best indifferent, to the aged. Hence, adjustment problems would be severe on two separate—the personal and social—levels. "But enough evidence is accumulating which shows that a carefully planned and properly conducted retirement planning program in a company can be of great help," she declared, citing the examples of such programs as that operated by the Prudential Life Insurance Company, and the packaged course developed by The Universities of Chicago and Michigan. With the possibility of retirement training increasingly raised and commented upon, the personnel department of Owens-Illinois Glass Company discovered that the demand for the institution of such a program was strong. Surveying their employees, the company's executives found a strong desire for some sort of retirement preparation assistance. Of the respondents: 90 percent thought discussion of retirement plans with a personnel officer would be helpful; 80 percent expressed interest in formal meeting on the subjects of health and finances; 67 percent agreed that spouses should participate in the preparation course; and nearly all favored some continued contact with the company—through involvement in social events or via company letters or house organs. This very demand indicated an awareness of the need for preparedness, as well as a favorable attitude, among employees toward the importance of retirement training efforts in assisting their personal and social adjustment to the post-occupational years.[20]

Gerontological evaluations of retirement training—with special attention to the formal, academic style programs, such as those developed at Chicago and Michigan—reflected a growing belief in their efficacy and an indication of professional commitment to them. Nor was this result unexpected. The retirement training phenomenon was not only an expression of the profession's belief in the importance of education as a means of altering attitudes; it was also a solution which suited well the "activity" bias of most gerontologists, since the goal of such programs was to introduce new social roles and to expand old ones, thus keeping the older person socially involved after withdrawal from the working world. The achievement most frequently mentioned in gerontological evaluations of formal preparation courses was their softening effect upon the image of retirement. This effect was produced, commentators insisted, not because (as critics frequently charged) the programs presented an unrealistically positive view of retirement, but because such programs provided a source of information about retirement, its pitfalls, and its potentials not heretofore available to the older worker. A writer in one business magazine presented this accomplishment most succinctly when he observed: "The devil the employee knows is less frightening than the devil he doesn't." Another welcome effect of such programs was the way in which they stimulated older workers to begin making postretirement plans. The graduate of one such course, wrote University of Illinois professor and syndicated columnist, Robert J. Peterson, declared that his participation in such a program "aroused my interest in starting at once to prepare for retirement . . . not only about financial security . . . but also about challenging and interesting activities which could be pursued in retirement." Besides reducing the oppressive influence of the work ethic and encouraging realistic planning through the provision of accurate information about aging and retirement, such programs promoted adjustment by bringing together men and women with similar problems, helping them to develop similar interests, and promoting enduring friendships among them. Other benefits cited included higher morale and heightened productivity among older workers; increased interest in the educational process, which led in turn to further learning experiences; improved health and reduction in corporate insurance costs; and greater response to available early retirement options.[21]

Supplementing these impressionistic appreciations, gerontological investigators amassed considerable statistical evidence of the beneficial effects of formal group training courses. Probably the most concentrated evaluations were carried out in conjunction with the training programs developed by The Universities of Chicago and Michigan. (The Chicago course, in fact, had a built-in evaluational component, the "Retirement Preparation Inventory.") A favorite statistical method was the submission of batteries of agree/disagree statements to workers before, and again after, exposure to such a course, and the comparison of the two sets of responses for significant change. One early effort, carried out by The University of Chicago in 1956, on a sample of graduates of the university's "Making the Most of Maturity" course, measured the effect of the series on responses to ten statements on such topics as finances, housing, retirement prospects, health, leisure, and so on. Prior to participation, the average favorable response to these statements was 55 percent; after completion, this average had risen to 72.6 percent. On two key issues, for example, the effect was particularly impressive. With respect to statements about the adequacy of financial preparation and avocational interests, the percentages of favorable responses had risen, respectively, from 44 percent to 81 percent and from 50 percent to 81 percent. A year later, a similar test was applied to ninety-six enrollees in The University of Michigan's "Preparation for Retirement" course, all members of the Upholsterers' International Union. Program developer W. W. Hunter reported that a retesting after the completion of the course indicated a significant favorable shift on fourteen of the twenty statements in the battery, and that 42 percent of the sample had demonstrably begun making and implementing plans as a result of what they had learned.[22]

Another, more statistically sound method of evaluation, was the testing of preretirement program graduates against control groups of nongraduates; noting differences in attitudes or responses traceable to exposure or nonexposure to such a program. A national sample of retirement preparation course graduates and nongraduates was tested during the mid-1960s for the degree of retirement satisfaction—high, medium, or low—as a function of participation in a retirement preparation program. The most satisfied among the retirees (26 to 35 percent) were more likely to have graduated from such a course; the least satisfied (29 to 38 percent) were less likely to have done so. Even more elaborate was the longitudinal survey, carried out at Inland Steel Company by gerontologist Philip Ash, in which he began with a sample of fifty-five year olds, and followed them through to retirement. Everyone in this group was exposed during this period to Inland's own formal retirement preparation program. A control group (those employees who had not had retirement training) was selected from among Inland employees who had retired before the study began. All tests of retirees' attitudes toward retirement, expected and actual satisfaction in retirement, and the degree of planning undertaken reflected a positive relationship to program participation. Most interesting was the evidence of a changing image of retirement. While only 26.9 percent of the old (pre-1951), untrained retirees responded positively when asked if they felt retirement to be a reward, the same question gained the affirmative responses of 63.8 percent of the sixty-year-old and 66.7 percent of the sixty-four-year-old segments of the sample. Another question about retirement as a deserved rest suggested that preparation had a mellowing effect on the work ethic. Thus, only 30.5 percent of the older retirees believed this was a fair definition, and 52.2 percent of the sixties and 41.7 percent of sixty-fours agreed. (This decline in percentage of agreement between sixty and sixty-four was attributed to the common wisdom that resistance to retirement was highest among those closest to it.) Given the general acceptance of a positive correlation between planning and ease of adjustment to retirement, a persuasive conclusion was that offered by a Fordham University study of a number of retirement preparation courses in which program effectiveness was "clearly evidenced in the large proportion [71 percent] of participants who subsequently have taken positive action on one or more phases of retirement."[23]

Retirement preparation courses were one of the factors helping to change not only the image of retirement (from one of social limbo to one of deserved leisure filled with new experiences) but also of the elderly, who were the retired. In a somewhat less direct way, business and labor leaders added their efforts to those of biomedical and social scientists, educators, media people, social workers, and marketers in an attempt to redefine the later years in positive, relevant terms like "activity," "independence," "integrity," and "leisure." To what extent all these groups were successful is the theme of the final chapter. Because "image" is not the sort of thing one can quantify, we will remain focused primarily on retirement, on the assumption that the new characterization of retirement at earlier ages among older people serves as an indicator that older people have grown less defensive, less negative about their social status. In acting within the framework of this newly won status—as swinging retirement villagers, members of political pressure groups, or merely as contented pursuers of favorite avocations in retirement—the elderly have themselves contributed to a more understanding and benign regard throughout all age groups.

N O T E S

1. Moore, "Preparation for Retirement," *Journal of Gerontology* 1 (1946): 202–210.
2. Wermel and Gelbaum, "Work, Retirement and Old Age," *American Journal of Sociology*, 51 (1945–1946), pp. 16–21.
3. Lawton, "When Should a Man Retire?" *New York Times Magazine*, April 27, pp. 12, 52–54.
4. Randall, "Retirement—Dead or Alive?" *Independent Woman*, 27–28 (1948–1949), 366–367, Levine review in *Survey*, 85 (1949), 624–625.
5. "Garment Workers Resist Retirement, Columbia University Study Finds," *Personnel and Guidance Journal*, 31: May 1953, 545; Havighurst; "Flexibility and the Social Roles of the Retired," pp. 309–311; and Michelon, "The New Leisure Class," *American Journal of Sociology*, 59, no. 4 (January 1954) pp. 371–378. Similar analysis offered by Havighurst in his 1953 volume, with Ruth Albrecht, *Older Persons* and in 1954 with E. A. Friedmann, *The Meaning of Work and Retirement* in which the "equivalency of work and play" theory is put forth. See also for additional evidence of the inclination toward retirement preparation among social scientists, G. H. Crook, *The Older Worker . . . Attitudes Toward Aging and Retirement* (Berkeley, Cal.–University of California Institute of Industrial Relations, 1958); Michael T. Wermel and Geraldine Beideman, *Retirement Preparation Programs: A Study of Company Responsibility* (California Institute of Technology, 1961).
6. Monroe quoted in "How to Ease into Retirement," *Business Week,* April 2, 1955, 66–69; Johnson essay in W. Donahue (ed.), *Education for Later Maturity* (1955): 239–250; Hunter's program explained in "Planning for Leisure Helps Production," *Nation's Business*, 45: October 1957, 69–70+.
7. Various options described by WICB, *Retirement of Employees* (1955); Geneva Mathiasen, "Preretirement and Retirement Aid and Counseling," in Senate Labor Committee, *Studies of the Aged and Aging*, vol. IV (1957); Wemel and Beideman, *Retirement Training Programs* (1961); "Putting the Old Out to Pasture," *Business Week*, October 10, 1964, pp. 78–80; and "How to Employ Your Employees for Retirement," *Business Management*, 29–30: August 1966, pp. 53–66.

8. Goodstein, "Personal Adjustment Factors and Retirement," *Geriatrics,* 17 part 1: January 1962, pp. 41–45; Schultz quoted in Ford Foundation, *Golden Years?* (New York, 1963).

9. Descriptions and considerations of various formal programs include M. J. Mack, "A Retirement Planning Program [University of Chicago]," loc. cit.; "Retirement Conditioning and Training Under Union Sponsorship [University of Michigan]," *Monthly Labor Review* 80 (1957): 846–848; "A Labor Union Approach: A New Approach: A New Life in Retirement," *AFL-CIO News,* February 1958; W. W. Hunter, "Preretirement Education [Universities of Chicago and Michigan and UAW programs]," *Geriatrics* 15 (1960): 793–800; Hunter, *Leadership Training for Preretirement Education* (Ann Arbor, Michigan, 1960); University of Chicago Industrial Relations Center, *Time for Living* (Chicago: 1960); E. B. Schultz, *The TVA Preretirement Program* (HEW Patterns for Progress series, no. 5, 1961); H. M. FLint and T. Ruhrig, *Planning for Retirement: A University-Labor Program* (Hew Patterns for Progress series, no. 16, 1964); George A. Bray, "What Illinois Bell Learned from Its Retirement Training Program," *Personnel* 41 (November 1964): 32–47; Odell, "An Urgent Need: Education for Retirement," *American Federationist* 73 (September 1966): 21–24.

10. Johnson, "Is Compulsory Retirement Ever Justified?" *Journal of Gerontology* 6 (1951): 263–271; similar arguments from Jean Campbell of the Bureau of Labor Statisitics in "Retirement and Employment Problems of the Older Worker," *Monthly Labor Review* 73 (1951): 695–699 and "The Pension Problem in the United States," ibid. 76 (1953): 245–248.

11. "Retirement: A Bore or Fun?" *Business Week* (April 14, 1951): 32–38; EBASCO Services Inc., *Encouraging Effective Preparation for Retirement* (New York: 1953); Breckinridge, *Effective Use of Older Employees* (Chicago: 1953); ESSO, "Preparation for Retirement" (1950); see also "Planning for Leisure Helps Business," *Nation's Business* 45 (October 1957).

12. Tuckman and Lorge, "Retirement Practices in Business and Industry," *Journal of Gerontology* 7 (1952): 77–86.

13. NICB, *Conference Board Reports: Retirement of Employees* (Studies in Personnel Policies, no. 148, 155); Cleveland Welfare Foundation, *The Retired Worker and His Place in the Community* (Cleveland: 1955); Charles R. Naef, *Preretirement Programs in New Jersey* (New Brunswick: 1960); see also U.S. Civil Service Commission, *Retirement Planning, a Growing Employment Relations Service* (Washington, D.C.: 1960) for a note on the Federal Government's experiments with retirement preparation programs.

14. "Retirement" A Bore or Fun?" loc. cit.; ESSO, "Preparation for Retirement," (1950); Robert Roessle (Director, ESSO Preretirement Programming), "Good Retirement Adjustment: Influences and Attitudes," ESSO Mimeo, n.d. (ca. 1956).

15. F. J. Bell, "Retirement Planning—A Case Study," in American Management Association, *Preparing Employees for Retirement,* AMA Personnel Series, no. 142 (1951), pp. 9–16; Standard Oil (California) plan reported in "Preretirement Plan," *Business Week* (August 29, 1953): 163–164.

16. Johnson and Johnson Co. program in "Retirement Planning: One Company's Program," *Management Review* 52 (August 1963): 53–55; Scoville's, "A Company and a Union Cooperate to Provide Preretirement Training," *Aging* (September 1965): 5; Mead, Johnson's in H. G. Earle, "Taking the Fear Out of Retirement," *Today's Health* 45 (February 1967): 64–67.

17. Perrow, "Are Retirement Adjustment Programs Necessary?" *Harvard Business Review* 35 (July–August 1957): 109–115; see also American Management Association's *Preparing Employees for Retirement* (1951) for a similar statement of the advantages of retirement preparation to sponsoring companies.

239

18. J. L. Springer, "What is the Right Time to Retire?" *New York Times Magazine,* February 15, 1959, 80–81; Perrow, loc. cit.; Tarcher, "The Role of Business in Education for the Aging," *Adult Leadership* 8–9 (May 1960): 17–18, 33–34; examples of overly upbeat corporate approach such as the Allis-Chalmers Inc. pamphlet *Looking Forward to Years of Pleasure . . . A Guide to Your Retirement* (Milwaukee, 1960) can be found in the vertical files on retirement at the National Committee on Aging Library in Washington, D.C.

19. Walter Willard, "When You Retire, Then What?" *Hygeia* 25 (1947): 518+ (part I) and 613+ (part II); Stern, "Back to School to Retire," *Nation's Business* 40 (February 1952): 45–46+.

20. Margery J. Mack, "A Retirement Planning Program," *Journal of Business* 27 (April 1954): 169–175; the Owens-Illinois survey noted in Appendix A to NICB, *Retirement of Employees* (1955), p. 47.

21. General comments on the benefits of these programs from Donahue, ed., *Education for Later Maturity,* p. x (Peterson quote); Schultz, *TVA Preretirement Program;* Flint and Ruhrig, "Planning for Retirement"; Bray, "What Illinois Bell Has Learned . . . ," loc. cit.; "How to Prepare Your Employees for Retirement, *Business Management* 29–30 (1966); Administration on Aging, *Preretirement Counseling, Retirement Adjustment, and the Older Employee* (Washington, D.C., working paper no. 18, 1960).

22. University of Chicago, *Making the Most of Maturity* (Chicago: 1956); "Retirement Conditioning Under Union Sponsorship," loc. cit.

23. E. F. Lundgren, "Needed Retirement Counseling Programs in Business," *Personnel Journal,* 44 (1965), pp. 432–436; Ash, "Pre-Tirement Counseling," *Gerontologist* 6 no. 2 (1966): 97–99, Studies Evaluation—Final Report—Pre-Retirement Counseling Programs" (mimeo, n.d., ca. 1968).

10

Retirement, Leisure, and the Swinging Senior: The Measure of Success

In our earlier consideration of the changes in the definition of retirement between the 1945–1950 and 1965–1970 periods, the trend toward earlier, voluntary retirement was a sign that the prospect of leaving the working world no longer evoked the dread it once did. Obviously, the growth of private pension funds, both in number and in generosity of benefits, was an important factor in reducing a once-formidable reluctance to retire among older workers. Gerontological arguments for greater attention to the sociopsychological needs of the retired had born fruit as well. For a number of reasons, as we have noted, business and labor leaders were increasingly encouraged to set up retirement training courses during the 1950s. These programs were designed to foster new, positive definitions of the retirement years by taking account of, and attempting to meet these sociopsychological needs. Then too, there was the new view of the average older person—healthy, active, and involved—which, we have argued, was promoted in a number of ways by a number of actors, from grade school teachers to Madison Avenue marketers. This "new" older person was an individual with the personal resources, not only to come to terms with the loss of the work role, but to enjoy the advantages and opportunities afforded by the resulting accession of leisure time as well. Thus we can regard positive changes in attitudes toward retirement as a further indicator of how well those involved in the effort to alter public thinking about the process and prospect of aging had succeeded in their task.[1]

One general social trend deserving mention here was the widely acknowledged growth of a "leisure ethic." This was the "affluent" society's answer to the "work ethic" forged by a developing industrial society, and it comprehended as much the shorter work week and the labor saving appliance as the increasing recourse to retirement. Inaugurating a "life and leisure" section as a permanent part of its format in 1954, *Newsweek* apologized for not having recognized sooner the importance of this aspect of life. "The leisure life of Americans," wrote publisher Theodore I. Mueller, "is news, too—as much news as their politics, the conduct of their foreign affairs, or, perhaps, their business. . . . Leisure activity has become a more basic part of everyday living." The same year, the *Saturday Review* editorially reconsidered H. G. Wells' 1913 novel, *The World Set Free,* in which freedom from the constant necessity of work liberated man to develop his finer sensitivites and create a utopia, expressing the conviction that, to a large extent, Wells' utopian dream "coincides with American life in 1954." However, in an implied criticism of the gerontologists' activity bias, the editorialist cautioned, Americans had to be able to accept leisure as Wells contemplated it—that is, as true freedom from compulsion, rather than merely a switch from the compulsive pursuit of vocations to the compulsive pursuit of avocations. In whatever terms one saw the leisure ethic, there could be no doubt that this new view of free time contributed to the comfortable adjustment of older people to life without work.[2]

Despite the continuing insistence of gerontologists during the 1950s that the only happy older people were busy older people—

busy preferably at their occupations or, at the very least, at pursuits described in terms which made them sound like unpaid labor—there was increasing evidence that leisure, in the sense of freedom from work, was becoming a highly prized commodity among retirees; at least among retirees writing pieces on retirement for mass circulation periodicals—and helping thereby to diffuse their own discoveries even more widely among the reading public. The first year of retirement was the most difficult period, observed one recent retiree. "Nothing can be quite as devastating to retirement happiness, nor even to health and longevity, as the feeling of inutility, of unimportance . . . in the busy world," he wrote: yet from his own experience he had discovered that "retirement . . . can be rich and compensating if we have the wisdom to look upon it as a positive, not a negative step . . . an advance, not a retreat." The key to receiving this wisdom, noted another writer, was preparation based on the recognition by each working individual that old age "isn't just a bare possibility. It is inevitable." Advancing age brought with it separation from one's occupation, lowered income, and reduced social prestige; the earlier a person realized these facts and readied himself to face them, the more it would be "possible at last to cope with old age and make the 'golden age' more than just a phrase." One forty-five year old school teacher expressed an almost exaggerated appreciation of the relationship between advanced planning and retirement satisfaction by reporting that, twenty years ahead of the day, she was beginning to prepare for her retirement. "I'll be engrossed in so many spheres of living," she promised, in a textbook exposition of "activity" theory thinking, "that I won't need to fear it when the day comes." Retirement was her "final opportunity" to enjoy life, and she intended to make the most of it by undertaking activities designed "to bolster one's ego with a sense of accomplishment." According to a physician writing in Today's Health, this growing popular disposition to look forward to, and plan for, retirement constituted "one of the most encouraging features of our modern civilization." He believed that positive expectations made for

243

positive experiences. Beyond that, staying socially active and keeping busy were the keys to contented retirement. Numerous other writers stressed these and similar "activity school" principles of preparation for the end of one's work life. Make plans, stay active, look to the future, do what makes you feel useful— these were the popular prescriptions offered through the medium of various special and general circulation magazines during the 1950s and early 1960s.[3]

One did not, however, have to be a partisan of the dominant gerontological wisdom to write about successful retirement. If leisure meant the chance for involvement and activity to some, to others it was a deserved rest and a license to be happily idle. One recent retiree, for example, lashed out at those "well-meaning advisors" who urged the elderly to retire to a hobby or join some "do-gooder" movement as the only way to stay happy in retirement. The hobby business, he retorted, was a "racket" which robbed people of true leisure by making them feel guilty if they weren't busy, while "do-gooding," if honestly taken up, was a full-time struggle, not a leisure activity. "Leisure is a man's fifth, and often final freedom," he declared, "and he should be willing to fight for it—to fight his family and friends, if necessary. He should take up arms against this false, subversive modern culture that says a man should be ashamed not to be busy, ashamed to enjoy his leisure." As the 1950s gave way to the 1960s, the concept of leisure matured to the point that older people began to feel comfortable with it, and like the retiree quoted above, to resent being told what to do by experts. The writer E. B. White minced no words in this regard. "I believe in work," he told the readers of *Holiday* magazine, in March 1956, "but I don't believe in work-for-the-night-is-coming. . . . As to leisure, it is as valid as a business . . . I spent a solid year once experimenting with idleness and finding out exactly what it was like to occupy myself with absolutely nothing at all. That year now seems to me one of the most sensible twelvemonth periods I ever put in." Looking at the retirement preparation phenomenon in business, White suggested such course listings as "Lunch Without Purpose," and "Seminar for Basket Weavers," by way of expressing his opinion of such guidance.[4]

Another writer, disparaging the "owl-eyed boys with PhD's in a subject we cannot even pronounce, called Geriatrics" for their tendency to make flat pronouncements about the needs and desires of the retiree. Experience more and more often suggested that the individual was perfectly capable of deciding on his own what was his best course of action. Retired auto-industry executive Ivan L. Wiles, a man whom gerontologists would have selected as a prime candidate for retirement shock, reported that he was in fact "having the time of my life." He had approached retirement, he confessed, with much trepidation, fearful of all the pitfalls which gerontologists constantly charted out for him and, most of all, afraid of idleness, but his decision to define retirement as an earned rest, a graduation, had given him the psychological boost he needed to get over the initial resistance to it. Once out of work, he made the amazing discovery that he enjoyed it. Looking at those of his colleagues still on the job, he asserted: "I can't help feeling sorry for those insiders who don't have much of a chance to lie in hammocks. Someday, if they're lucky, they'll find out what they've been missing."[5]

Further evidence of retirement's growing respectability consisted in the increasing numbers of "how to" books on the subject. A forerunner of this genre was Raymond P. Kaign's volume, *How to Retire and Like It,* published in 1942. Despite the railing of experts about the destructive effects of retirement upon the average, work-oriented individual, Kaign, himself a retired YMCA personnel director, took the position that "Keeping on the job until you drop in your tracks may be heroic, but it is not necessarily good sense. The later years of life may be filled with satisfaction, usefulness, and happiness even without sticking at the old task forever." The key ingredient for satisfactory retirement, he felt, was careful planning in both the social and financial spheres. If one readied himself for retirement by anticipating the various noneconomic problems he would face, the inevitable process of adjustment could be greatly eased. The writers who followed Kaign echoed his conviction that retirement, if properly prepared for, constituted the apex of life. Ten books on the subject of retirement published during 1948–1957, repeated this theme in greater or lesser detail. These authors tended to be flexible in their view of retirement preparation and to stress the importance of self-analysis in the process of adjustment. As one of the writers, Paul W. Boynton, noted, retirement was "similar to a job" in that one had to work at it if he was to derive any reward from it. These treatments also emphasized the complex of social, psychological, and biological factors which affected adaptation to the workless state and attempted to alert prospective retirees to them. On the practical side, virtually all of them stressed the need to cultivate leisure skills, since it was generally agreed that no one could simply cease all activity and still be happy. Even so, the range of activities seen as functional ranged from the shuffleboard and canasta for a couple of Florida retirees (George and Jane Dusenbury) to the public service, dollar-a-year type jobs open to retiring executives (H. R. Hall). The mere existence of this kind of book— and there were many more than the selection cited here—at the least implies a demand for such information. The transition from work to retirement was more frequently being perceived as a crucial point in the life cycle. Unsurprisingly, this perception was attended by a rise of interest in the varying means by which outside interventions could help ease one past this critical juncture.[6]

In fact, a great deal of the commonly accepted wisdom about retirement, the adjustment problems it posed, and its ill-effects on physical and mental health had never been tested empirically. Thus, gerontological researchers undertook efforts to determine the validity of the stock correlation of retirement and accelerating degeneration, in hopes of strengthening arguments either against, or for acceptance of, and preparation for compulsory retirement. Cornell University Medical School, with the aid of a Lilly Foundation grant, began in 1951, a seven-year longitudinal study of a sample of people from their sixty-fourth

246

through their seventieth birthdays "to check systematically on the validity of the hypothesis that there are significant differentials in illness and mortality between those who retire and those who continue in gainful employment." Research by sociologist L. C. Michelon suggested that retirement environment was a key factor in adjustment to retirement. He focused on a highly structured Florida mobile home community for older retired individuals and found satisfactory employment of leisure to be a characteristic of residents. That is, it did not appear that retirement was necessarily a time of maladjustment in a community where, because of the diversity of activities "everyone can find something of interest. Such communities cater to people's interests by providing appropriate leisure activities."[7]

Two researchers taking direct aim at the view that held retirement responsible for shortening life spans, set out to test this hypothesis on a sample of retired army and air force officers whose careers had spanned all or some portion of the period 1925–1948, 2,798 of whom had died during this period and 1,432 of whom still lived. Both groups were further stratified into age quintiles. The study proposed to count the number of five-year periods (up to three) past retirement that each individual had survived. If the hypothesis was correct, the mortality rate would be highest among the group passing through the first five-year period. When allowance for the high death rate among the youngest group (50–55), on the grounds that the health reasons which forced them to retire were also responsible for their deaths within five years of retirement, evidence for the normal retirement age groups (60–64 and 65–69) indicated no support for the hypothesis that, in fact, the survival rates among these groups during the first five years beyond retirement were higher than those of the average American white male of comparable age. This study, however, left itself open to some obvious questions about the exclusive nature of the sample used. Gordon Streib was more careful in his selection of a socially representative national sample of 936 over–sixty males with which he proposed to test the old saw about retirement occasioning frustration, maladjustment, and social and political deviancy. His hypothesis suggested that adjustment to retirement ("morale") depended upon a "meaningful nexus" of health, socioeconomic status and work status. His analysis of data measuring morale according to these variables indicated "that a person who is retired but has good health and high socioeconomic status is more likely to have high morale than a person who is employed but lacks either good health or high income . . . the Common notion . . . is not supported by these data, for other factors can overcome the impact of being retired."[8]

In a similar vein, a member of the Chicago Medical Society, addressing his fellows in April 1957, charged that the retirement shock phenomenon so much deplored with the medical and gerontological professions and so widely attributed to compulsory retirement was, in fact, a product of a sudden shift from meaningful work to meaningless leisure. If one potential solution depended upon the abolition of fixed retirement ages, he argued, surely a more practicable solution was the provision of a "stimulating social environment for people who retire at sixty-five." This, he insisted, would be as effective as continued employment in arresting the physical and mental decline which were said to accompany the loss of the work role. Three researchers involved in the longitudinal study, administered by Cornell University during 1951–1958, provided some empirical data to support such conclusions. Opponents of involuntary retirement consistently noted that the highest incidence of personal maladjustment was to be found among the retired. But, asked these young social scientists, did this mean that work was an emotional necessity? "It may be . . . that the chances of retirees finding a satisfactory 'retirement role' has been underestimated, both in terms of the flexibility of the older person and the extent to which the institutional milieu provides or permits the opportunity to do so." The implications of the Cornell study, in fact, suggested that maladjustment derived not from retirement, but from negative preretirement attitudes toward loss of occupational status. The data seemed to indicate that retirement often had a positive effect on personal adjustment, and that it was the false images of retirement among professionals which continued to impede and distort an understanding of its effects. Although research data represented retirement in an increasingly benevolent light, a *Saturday Evening Post* editorial pointed out, in reference to a recent study carried out by The University of Michigan, it did appear to have a negative effect upon wives, who apparently heartily disliked having their husbands around the house all day and feared a "loss of status" within the household as a result.[9]

Finally, a survey of 1,268 occupationally diverse retirees, drawn from 100 different locals, conducted by the AFL–CIO in 1968 on a grant from the Federal Administration on Aging, provided a provocative challenge to the retirement-as-disaster school of thought. Of the sample, 33.3 percent had elected retirement prior to age sixty-five, 31.9 percent had reached mandatory retirement ages, and 30.7 percent had stopped working because of ill health. A substantial majority then, had been involuntarily retired. Moreover, 91.8 percent of them had received no preretirement counseling, and only 34.7 percent reported having made any plans for their retirement years. Traditionally, gerontologists would have charted such a group for social disaster. Yet, according to survey results, 60 percent of the sample called retirement "highly enjoyable," and only 8.2 percent expressed dissatisfaction with their new life styles. Among the gravest problems were, predictably, health (30.9 percent) and finances (30.4 percent); but, from a gerontologist's viewpoint, the relative unimportance of loneliness (2.6 percent) and excess of leisure (5.3 percent) were instructive data. Although health was given as a major complaint, direct questioning on this point yielded self-assessments of "good health" (48.8 percent), "average health" (33.7 percent), leaving a mere 17.5 percent reporting poor health. As to health while in retirement, 51.7 percent reported it unchanged from preretirement status, and 26.3 percent actually thought that it had improved as a result of the decision to stop working, arguing that "retirement brought less pressure, and more time to relax." The leisure activities most frequently mentioned included house maintenance, gardening, travel, lodge or club affiliations, reading, hobbies, visiting friends, watching television, and listening to the radio. Significantly, only 13.3 percent of the sample expressed interest in educational or cultural activities. Of the whole group, 18.5 percent indicated an interest in availing themselves of opportunities to further their education, and a fractional 5.3 percent stated that they would opt for job retraining, if available.[10]

Anticipating such conclusions as these and apparently convinced that over a decade's efforts at redefinition of retirement and leisure had borne fruit, business leaders were expressing, by the mid 1960s, a decreasing zeal for the establishment and maintenance of retirement training programs. In the view of many perceptive and pragmatic executives, retirement had become a cultural fact. Moreover, they saw increasing evidence to indicate that it had become an acceptable, even desirable, status. Because of this, they no longer deemed retirement training necessary. Besides their cost in money and time, such programs, if continually relied upon, threatened ultimately to undermine the work ethic. There was, representatives of management continued to assert, an obligation upon the employer to help his retired workers lead contented lives—both morally and in the more pragmatic public relations sense—but formal retirement preparation courses were no longer considered to be part of that obligation. Subsequent research carried out by Richard Barfield and James Morgan in 1967 at The University of Michigan's Survey Research Center tended to approve this view. Retirement preparation, they found, did bear positively on satisfaction in retirement; but within the sample which had been exposed to such programs, the elaborateness or simplicity of the preparation procedure appeared unrelated to its success. That is, a simple, informal program was apparently as efficacious as a complex, formal one in promoting satisfaction in retirement. An NICB investigation of retirement practices in 1964 (based on 1961–1962 data) noted that the incidence of such programs was the same (65 percent) as it had been in a similar 1955 study; but of the 633 concerns offering such programs, the majority offered only two or three sessions of individual counseling, mostly on financial matters, begun a scant two or three years before retirement age. Of the companies claiming more broad-reaching treatments (i.e., involved with other nonfinancial aspects of retirement) only 10 percent offered group sessions and called upon outside specialists. Of this 10 percent, only one-half supplied reading material pertinent to retirement, and only one-fifth invited spouses to attend. Against the kinds of programs being advocated and developed by social (and the newer "industrial") gerontologists, the NICB findings represented an actual retreat from the "ideal" formal, group session concept of retirement preparation. Similarly, an investigator writing in *Fortune* magazine, in early 1965, polled 284 companies and found only eighty involved in the training of older employees for retirement.[11]

An article in a 1964 issue of *Business Week* confirmed the trend within the business community regarding the sponsorship of preretirement preparation programs. Only one-third of all United States corporations, the article stated, were concerned with retirement orientation, and among these efforts the typical program went into operation three to five years prior to retirement and dealt only with financial counseling and planning. The solutions to all those much investigated sociopsychological problems associated with retirement adjustment were, in most cases, left to the retiring individual himself. Two personnel experts— W. E. Scheer of Blue Cross, Inc., and H. G. Zollitsch of Marquette University Business School—stressed the view that retirement preparation was primarily an individual responsibility and that the employer's only role ought to be administering the pension funds. If assistance was specifically requested, management was bound to respond as an ethical and a practical matter, but the idea of formal retirement preparation was rejected. Zollitsch was especially vigorous in this regard, asserting that management had no competence to administer retirement adjustment classes, since it was an economic rather than a social entity. In sum, these men believed that the company's chief responsibility was to provide an unobtrusively encouraging environment—

251

material in the company library, articles in the company newspaper—and leave retirement adjustment problems to the individual. The faith in the individual worker's ability to put his own retirement plans into effect was especially striking in the case of Standard Oil of New Jersey, one of the earlier remarked-upon pioneers in the field of formal retirement preparation. The once-elaborate group program established by the company around 1950 had by the mid-1960s been abandoned in favor of a limited counseling program, and the provision of do-it-yourself materials—pamphlets, magazines and books—to those older workers requesting company assistance. A survey of associated Standard Oil plants in New Jersey had concluded that close guidance was no longer necessary; that a number of social interventions (including retirement preparation) over the past decade had lessened the negative connotations of retirement, making it not only more respectable, but more desirable as well.[12]

To this point, we have talked about the changing perceptions of retirement and leisure as monitored from various quarters—gerontologists, popular writers, and representatives from the business and labor communities. The most significant evidence that society had positively reevaluated retirement, leisure, and the later years, was the actual response of the older worker to the increasingly available option of early retirement. The availablity of this option alone suggests a demand for it, although it originated in a UAW-auto industry plan to thin out the industry's work force by encouraging older workers to retire early through the use of generous "supplemental benefits" to the normal pensions. The extra money which this plan provided was doubtless a powerful incentive to early retirement; yet early retirement was also becoming popular in other industries, like big steel, where pensions were less generous. Moreover, the enthusiasm with which early retirees adapted themselves to the "leisure ethic" could not be explained solely in material terms. One of the pioneers of industrial gerontology, Harold L. Sheppard of the Upjohn Institute on Employment Research, saw no reason to be startled by this fact. "In a society that stresses personal independence as much as ours," he wrote, "it should not be surprising that many workers would prefer more time of their own, instead of receiving all of the benefits of increased productivity through increased income and equivalent benefits." Twenty years of effort in renovating social attitudes had also played an influential role in forging an image of retirement which made 'thirty years and out' a legitimate demand among workers as young as fifty-five throughout the labor force.[13]

Looking at the thirty years' service, age fifty-five retirement won by the UAW, one federal official remarked, in reference to the plan's effect on the civil service: "I don't see how we can stop the 55–30 plan next year. . . . Workers in other industries are sure to get benefits similar to those of auto workers." As the magazine *Financial World* predicted, with 13 million workers between the ages of fifty-five and sixty-five, most of them covered by insured pension plans, early retirement would become increasingly popular. Retirement, a survey by the National Institute of Life Insurance indicated, was not only economically feasible; it was becoming socially desirable as well. At The University of Michigan, the study of a phenomenon that had seen over one-half of all recent retirees leaving work before the age of sixty-five, despite the reduction in social security benefits which such action carried, found "more and more aged men who are well enough to work . . . but who prefer the leisure of retirement." Although retirement income was still the most important variable, this survey of both national and UAW samples found that the optimistic view of retirement as a meaningful and desirable status was also of crucial import.[14]

The trend towards early retirement, coming as it did during a period of rapid economic growth, provoked some concern within the Johnson administration. Another impressive piece of evidence of retirement's new popularity was the comment of Otto Eckstein of the President's Council of Economic Advisors that, in the present expansionist situation, "no social purpose is served by hastening the retirement of experienced workers possessing the productive skills that our economy will need." Secretary of Labor Willard Wirtz also expressed disagreement with the trend, as did Harvard economist John Dunlop. There was a crucial difference in the administration policies of Johnson and those of Truman twenty years previous, in that the latter's had been addressed to discrimination against older workers, while the former's focused on the increasingly successful incentives to voluntary retirement won by labor and concurred in by management. "At a time when the economy offers the American workers strong inducements to stay in the labor force," reported *Business Week,* "large numbers of auto workers are retiring as soon as they become eligible." In the first six months of the UAW's early retirement plan, ten thousand of the thirty thousand eligibles had elected to quit work, thus providing "leisure for the declining years of the production line veteran," and creating "jobs for younger workers and the unemployed." Surveys also showed that initial fears of 'sunlighting'—that is, the reentry into the labor market by early retirees—were unfounded; when UAW workers quit, the majority of them quit for good.

EARNED INCOME	NO. OF CASES[a]		PROPORTION SATISFIED WITH RETIREMENT
None	297	(62.26%)	76.7
$1–999	18		72.5
$1,000–1,999	18		81.8
$2,000–2,999	16		68.2
$3,000–3,999	61		67.7
$5,000–7,499	44		75.2
$7,500–9,999	17		57.1
$10,000 or more	6		87.5

Source: Barfield and Morgan, Early Retirement: The Decision and the Experience (Ann Arbor: 1969), 135.
[a] For 477 auto workers who were retired when interviewed.

The idea, moreover, was spreading. According to *U.S. News and World Report,* "early retirement has become a way of life in the auto industry and there are signs that the idea is catching on in other fields."[15]

The retirement plan of the United Steel Workers offered perhaps a more realistic test of the new-won social respectability of retirement, since there was no "supplement" to the pension rate to encourage steel workers to opt for early retirement. As a USW spokesman put it: "You have to look at the individual worker's situation. If he's tired and his job is hard, or if he thinks he has a lousy foreman or hot, rotten conditions, he'll probably quit. If he can live on very little, he'll quit." The most impressive data continued to come from the UAW where, according to the journal *America,* more than ten thousand auto workers under that age of sixty-five had been induced to leave "well-paying jobs, with lots of juicy overtime, for a life of leisure." It is not surprising that the best survey of employee response to early retirement to date has come out of the auto industry. In addition to their initial survey of 646 retired workers (608 men, 38 women) in 1967, Barfield and Morgan made a follow-up survey in 1969 to give a longitudinal dimension to the data, reissuing their first study with an addendum entitled *A Second Look* (1974). From the outset, the two researchers conceded the importance of economic factors to the early retirement decision. In the 1967 report, a multivariate analysis of the sample showed that the higher the ratio of retirement income to working income and the higher the benefit level, the more likely the decision to elect early retirement. Again, a man with assets sufficient to produce an annual income of $3,000, a paid-off mortgage, one or no dependents, and at least $1,500 in life insurance was almost certain to retire early.[16]

PREDICTOR	NUMBER OF CASES	PROPORTION (IN PERCENT)
Ratio of Expected Retirement Income to Current Family Income[a]		
0.00 (no available pension income)	92	39.8
0.01–0.19	75	43.9
0.20–0.29	65	64.3
0.30–0.39	91	71.8
0.40–0.49	77	69.6
0.50–0.59	70	66.2
0.60–0.69	40	79.6
0.70 or more	26	80.0
Not ascertained	110	49.2

PREDICTOR	NUMBER OF CASES	PROPORTION (IN PERCENT)
Pension and Social Security Income to Which Respondent and Spouse Is Entitled When Interviewed[a]		
Less than $1,000	178	40.7
$1,000–1,999	34	53.9
$2,000–2,999	70	56.3
$3,000–3,999	91	58.0
$4,000–4,999	235	76.2
$5,000 or more	38	72.2
Potential Income from Assets that Respondent Held When Interviewed[a]		
None	76	54.9
$1–499	126	56.9
$500–999	160	54.9
$1,000–1,999	209	59.2
$2,000–2,999	53	54.4
$3,000 or more	22	80.8

Source: Barfield and Morgan, ibid.

[a] These variables could explain more than 0.5 percent of the total sum of squares by a single divison of the whole sample.

How the decision was made, however, was only part of the issue: Barfield and Morgan also delved into the ramifications of that decision by trying to determine to what extent 777 already retired subjects (none for more than two years) were satisfied with the option they had chosen. Again, they found economic factors to be important. Expressions of dissatisfaction (9 percent) were strongest among those with mortgages outstanding, more than one dependent, a low income from pension and social security, and little or no life insurance. Yet it was also true that a "great majority" of this group declared ill health to be the chief source of their discontent. Health, in fact, was in all probability the reason they had elected early retirement under otherwise economically disadvantaged circumstances. Moreover, income earned after retirement seemed to bear no relationship to satisfaction or dissatisfaction—another implied restriction upon the significance of purely financial interpretations.

PREDICTOR	NUMBER OF CASES	PROPORTION (IN PERCENT)
Age Mortgage (if any) Paid Off		
No mortgage at time of interview (including renters)	388	77.7
Under age 65	22	75.4
65–70	32	56.3
70 or older	19	64.5
Ratio of Current Income to Previous (i.e., preretirement) Income		
Less than .30	14	87.5
0.30–0.39	27	64.1
0.40–0.49	44	75.0
0.50–0.59	66	75.0
0.60–0.69	74	81.2
0.70–0.79	58	79.4
0.80 or larger	124	80.3
Not ascertained	70	55.9
Potential Income from Assets		
None	29	62.1
$1–499	75	61.7
$500–999	162	79.0
$1,000–1,999	160	75.9
$2,000–2,999	32	83.6
$3,000 or more	20	95.6
Pension and Social Security Income of Respondent and Spouse		
Less than $3,000	23	57.1
$3,000–3,999	53	66.4
$4,000–4,999	207	71.6
$5,000–7,499	172	82.6
$7,500 or more	22	78.6

	NUMBER OF CASES (1967 RETIREES/ 1969 RETIREES)	RETIRED BY 1967	RETIRED 1967—1969
Whether Respondent Has Worked for Money Since Retirement			
Has worked	65/47	70%	71%
Has not worked	311/263	69%	69%

Source: Barfield and Morgan, ibid.

The kind of noneconomic "predictors" that bore upon satisfaction, Barfield and Morgan observed in a comparison of 1967 and 1969 data, included how well retirement life accorded with preretirement expectations of it, the subjective or self-perceived assessment of living standard in retirement versus that while still working, the extent to which an individual planned for his retirement, and the level of activity (hobbies, civic work, etc.) maintained.

	NUMBER OF CASES (1967 RETIREES/ 1969 RETIREES)	RETIRED BY 1967	RETIRED 1967—1969
Whether Postretirement Conditions Have Been as Expected		Percentage of Satisfaction	
Exactly as expected	60/57	93	91
About as expected	242/197	73	70
Somewhat as expected	73/53	45	48
Not at all as expected	11/9	7	7
Postretirement Family Income			
Less than $4,000	83/28	59	65
$4,000–$4,999	71/55	66	62
$5,000–7,499	163/161	72	74
$7,500 or more	45/42	80	63
Perceived Change in Living Expenses Since Retirement			
Much lower since retired	20/16	54	71
Lower since retirement	107/90	68	79
Unchanged	139/142	77	65
Higher since retirement	116/68	61	57
Perceived Change in Living Standard Since Retirement			
Better after retirement	21/18	89	81
Unchanged	268/238	72	68
Worse, but adequate	43/30	55	74
Worse, and inadequate	43/25	44	40

	NUMBER OF CASES (1967 RETIREES/ 1969 RETIREES)	RETIRED BY 1967	RETIRED 1967—1969
Perceived Effect of Inflation on PostRetirement Living Standard		**Percentage of Satisfaction**	
Substantially adverse	83/44	59	55
Moderately adverse	89/77	69	57
Slightly adverse	93/80	66	82
No effect	100/91	81	67
Amount of Eleemosynary Work Done Since Retirement			
More than before retirement	142/97	73	72
Same as or less than before retirement	42/40	68	71
None since retirement	203/182	64	64
Amount of Leisure Activity[a] Undertaken Since Retirement			
More than before retirement	211/159	81	78
Same as before retirement	33/32	63	55
Less than before retirement or none	145/127	52	58
Amount of Social Interaction (with children, relatives, friends) Maintained Since Retirement			
More than before retirement	205/177	74	68
Same as before retirement	136/114	70	74
Less than before retirement	48/30	37	41
Amount of Interest in Newsworthy Events Maintained Since Retirement			
More than before retirement	197/171	76	70
Same as before retirement	141/127	68	67
Less than before retirement	48/21	40	54

Source: Barfield and Morgan, ibid.
[a]Defined as hobbies, sports, crafts, travel, etc.

259

Finally there were direct questions about retirement asked of the two samples to determine subjective reactions to retirement. Barfield and Morgan asked retirees to express their feelings about retirement as they moved further into it; if they would advise others to opt for early retirement; whether they felt that they had retired at the right age; whether the end of the early retirement supplement (at age sixty-five) had caused financial difficulties; and whether health status had changed since retirement.

	NUMBER OF CASES (1967 RETIREES/ 1969 RETIREES)	RETIRED BY 1967	RETIRED 1967—1969
Feelings about Retirement as Respondent Moves Further into the Retirement Period		Percentage of Satisfaction	
Enjoying much more	54/35	89	100
Enjoying more	216/178	81	75
Feelings unchanged	52/47	63	68
Enjoying less because of problems not associated with health	45/31	30	21
Enjoying less because of problems	16/11	4	0
Whether Respondent Would Advise Others to Retire at a Similar Age			
Would advise similar age	290/247	75	74
Would not advise similar age	49/41	43	46
Whether Respondent Felt He Had Retired at the Proper Age			
Had retired at proper age	353/283	73	71
Had retired at wrong age	22/24	24	43
Whether End of Negotiated Early Retirement Supplement Has Caused Financial Problems[a]			
Has caused problems	63/14	60	54
Has not caused problems	69/32	71	56

	NUMBER OF CASES (1967 RETIREES/ 1969 RETIREES)	RETIRED BY 1967	RETIRED 1967—1969
Perceived Change in Health Since Initial Interview in 1967		Percentage of Satisfaction	
Health better in 1969	69/78	79	77
Health unchanged	231/188	72	66
Health worse in 1969	86/55	50	56
Perceived Change in Health Since Retirement			
Health better since retirement	131/107	84	81
Health unchanged	186/171	65	63
Health worse since retirement	71/42	46	53

Source: Barfield and Morgan, ibid.

In concluding their report of the resurvey and comparative data, the two researchers asserted that auto workers "are overwhelmingly happy with their lot" and that the factors bearing strongest upon satisfaction were the ability to remain active and involved, and the maintenance of good health and financial security. Suggesting that economic factors were only one of many determinants, Barfield and Morgan emphasized the finding that "early retirees who have passed sixty-five, and thus lost their early retirement supplement, were not significantly less satisfied than those younger retirees still receiving the full pension amount"— despite the fact that this loss substantially reduced total income. Such a conclusion had not, the authors observed, been appended to the original (1967) study simply because none of the subjects then surveyed had been in retirement for more than two years; thus the high degree of satisfaction expressed might have been only a reflection of the novelty of the situation. Resurvey, however, showed that satisfaction continued at a high, if slightly reduced level. In 1967, 75 percent reported their retirement satisfactory, 12 percent had mixed feelings, and 9 percent were unsatisfied; in 1969, the two-thirds of that initial group available or willing to be resurveyed responded as follows: 67 percent satisfied, 19 percent mixed feelings, and 12 percent unsatisfied (with one-half of this latter group citing ill health as the main reason). There remained the arguments that the early retirement supplement provision, along with special factors—generational and racial antagonisms—at work within the union made the UAW situation unique. Yet, with the resurvey behind them, Barfield and Morgan denied that the phenomenon of early retirement represented only flight from a bad situation, concluding, that despite such arguments: "We remain convinced that, for many people, the satisfactions of a life free from the demands of work are both pervasive and abiding.[17]

Older, retired persons, as Barfield and Morgan among others pointed out, were increasingly capable of living perfectly happy existences apart from family and younger people in what Margaret Mead has called "golden ghettoes." What of the "centrality of the work role," and the paucity of "alternative social roles" for older, nonproducing individuals? If these were significant factors, would not the retirement experience quickly lose its savor, regardless of individual financial security? Would not these idle old people experience crises in self-indentity and self-respect as well as physical decay? Evidence on these points was accumulating, and a great deal of it ran counter to classical gerontological thinking. Indeed, the apparent successes of early retirement in the auto industry led one Ford executive to predict that, in the near future "we will measure a man's status by how early he can retire—a kind of reverse English on the Protestant Ethic." The popularity of early retirement, pollster Louis Harris suggested, meant that retirement was losing its negative connotations, and that "people in the United States no longer look on retirement as a signal that a person is washed up, doomed to become dormant, and relatively unproductive." Instead, the cessation of the work role was more and more perceived as an opportunity to enjoy a life of leisure. "Even if they must live on reduced incomes," Harris found, "there are many opportunities now open to them for exciting experiences in education, art and group activities, and there will be more of these opportunities each year." From three Southwest retirement communities, reported *Newsweek,* came the suggestion "that retired persons may be far more retiring than the experts suspect." If there was one gerontological truism, it was that to stay healthy, old people needed to remain both active and productive. Yet, when the owners of the Horizon Land Corp. sought to provide residents in three of its senior citizens' projects with two days per week of work on new housing units, the program failed. According to Horizon's President Joseph Timan, this labor pool "just didn't want to be tied down to a work schedule, even part time. It interfered too much with their leisure fun"[18]

Although individual old people quoted 20 years earlier had been uniformly negative on the subject of life in retirement, the post-1965 subjects seemed to share no such bias; indeed, the comments of retirees tended to be highly favorable to their status. One auto worker, retired at the age of sixty-two on an annual income of $7,632 (pension plus supplement plus early social security benefits), told an interviewer: "With all this money available, I don't think I'd be justified in working." He demonstrated none of the much discussed symptoms of "retirement shock." After explaining his intention to return to his native Italy and visit it for an unspecified amount of time, he expressed the opinion that between television, his yard, and his flowers, "I'll always find something to do." A sixty-one-year-old coworker was likewise worried by the prospect of retirement: "I plan to do very little now. What's the sense of retiring and then getting a full time job." Discussing the motives for his early retirement, Michael Guzak, a former Chrysler employee, declared: "I was tired of taking orders. Now I go to bed when I want to, get up when I want to and do whatever I please. I've never regretted retiring." Comparing the "idyllic" retirements of two individuals, one from the auto and one from the steel industries, *Business Week* declared them representative of retirees of the future. Neither of the two men lived in a retirement village. Gus Tisdale, a sixty-three-year-old bachelor and former auto worker, lived in a three-room Detroit apartment, while a sixty-two-year-old ex-steel worker Robert Lantz lived with his wife on a seventeen-acre farm in western Pennsylvania. Their respective life styles could not have been more different—urban and highly social versus bucolic and individualistic—yet each emphasized their satisfaction. Tisdale stressed the active aspect: "I don't have time to get everything done. Some days I have to make a list of what I want to do or else it will never get done." Lantz, on the other hand, accentuated the freedom: "You can sit, you can drink beer at a beer garden, you can fool around the yard, you can visit neighbors or go shopping. You can go anywhere you want to go, and do anything you want to do." Nor were their preparations for retirement similar. Tisdale took advantage of the UAW early retirement pension supplement plan, while Lantz, with a much less generous pension, planned carefully and saved judiciously in order to achieve his retirement goal.[19]

In the last analysis, men like Tisdale and Lantz indicate how far society has gone toward redefining the concept of retirement. Twenty years earlier, neither of these men would have dared to take the step of voluntarily relinquishing the work role. In all probability they would have resisted the notion of compulsory retirement as well. Even had income not been a problem (and in 1950, it typically was), the very idea of an aimless existence would have been repugnant to both of these serious, hard-working men. Yet, by the late 1960s, such representatives of the working class were living in contented retirement, whether pedaling a bicycle around the streets of Detroit or raising vegetables in a garden in western Pennsylvania. The efforts to create such new, acceptable retirement roles have proceeded along a number of fronts during the twenty-year period which this study has covered. Often in ideological conflict, as we have noted on repeated occasions, the various elements have nonetheless all contributed something to the degree of success enjoyed in making over the concepts of old age and retirement. The Tisdales and Lantzes are the evidence of this success. There is, indeed, a long way yet to go in upgrading the status of older people in America; but the progress over the past twenty years gives us hope that at least some of the distance remaining can be covered.

N O T E S

1. "Does It Pay to Retire?", *U.S. News & World Report* 37 (July 30, 1954): 82–84; "A Rush is on to Retire," ibid. 38 (May 20, 1955): 43–43; "Should You Be Forced to Retire at 65?" ibid. 43 (September 13, 1957): 94–97; on the importance of finances to retirement adjustment see R. J. Peterson, "Will You Have Enough Money When You Retire?" *Ladies' Home Journal* 74 (June 1957): 159+; "The Startling Impact of Pension Funds." *Business Week* (January 31, 1959): 88–105; the "supplemental" benefit to pensions offered by the UAW contract to encourage early retirement (discussed in Chapter 2) is likewise an important indication of the importance of monetary provision as a legitimate social intervention.

2. "Life and Leisure" section incorporated by *Newsweek* (August 9, 1954); "Utopian Nightmare," *Saturday Review* 37 (August 21, 1954): 22; some useful applications of the leisure ethic to retirement have already been cited in other contexts—particularly Friedmann and Havighurst's *The Meaning of Work and Retirement* (1954); Michelon's "The New Leisure Class," loc. cit. (1955); and more recently, Margaret Mead, *The Changing Cultural Patterns of Work and Leisure* (1966).

3. A. E. Bryson, "The First Year is the Hardest, *American Home* 45 (April 1951): 120–123; V. Cohn, "The Rainy Day Nobody Saves For," *Woman's Home Companion* (March 1952): 44, 127, 148; Laurie Von Tungelen, "I'm Getting Ready to Retire," *Coronet* 33 (December 1952): 87–90; E. F. Richardson, M.D., "Retirement—Tonic or Slow Poison?" *Today's Health* 31 (May 1953): 18–19; E. Caudill, "We Are Eager to Retire," *American Home* 50 (October 1953): 124–127; "How to Retire," *Changing Times* 8 (February 1953): 39–43; H. E. Moeller, "The Luxury of Retirement: Can You Afford It?" *American Mercury* 78 (April 1954): 37–38; J. F. Smith, "Three Paths to Retirement," *Rotarian* 85 (August 1954): 12; A. H. Schneider, "Old Age is What You Make It," *America* 92 (March 2, 1955): 589–591; "What Will You Do When You Retire?" *Changing Times* 10 (March 1956): 17–19; Dr. Harry M. Johnson, "How To Retire and Be Happy," *U.S. News & World Report* 42 (February 1, 1957): 38–40; "What Will It be Like When You Retire?" *Changing Times* (March 1960): 7–12; Gereon Zimmerman, "The Secrets of Successful Retirement," *Look* 25 (March 14, 1961): 26–35.

4. Raymond A. McConnel, "I Refuse to Be Organized," *Christian Century* 17 (November 24, 1954): 1428; in a similar vein, see Peggy Paepper, "Occupation: Retired," *American Home* 53 (March 1955): 42+; White, "A Strategem for Retirement," *Holiday* 19 (March 1956): 84+.

5. Bruce Bliven, "A Few Words from the Shelf," *Harper's* 213 (September 1956): 46–49; Wiles, "Life without General Motors," *Fortune* 60 (October 1949): 126–127; see also the story of four successful retirements by people otherwise unprepared, at least by gerontological standards to stop working, by L. C. Spicer in *Ladies' Home Journal* 74 (June 1957): 160.

6. Kaign, *How To Retire and Like It* (New York: 1942); C. W. Crampton, *Live Long and Like It* (New York: 1948); Raymond Giles, *How to Retire and Enjoy It* (New York: 1949); I. Saloman, *Retire and Be Happy* (New York: 1951); P. W. Boynton, *Six Ways to Retire* (New York, 1952); Kathyrn Close, *Getting Ready to Retire* (New York: 1952); Geroge Preston, *Should I Retire?* (New York: 1952): Joseph Buckley, *The Retirement Handbook* (New York: 1953); H. R. Hall, *Some Observations on Executive Retirement* (Boston: 1953); Geroge and Jane Dusenbury, *How To Retire to Flordia* (New York: 1954); G. R. Hart, *Retirement: A New Outlook* (New York: 1957).

7. Cornell study announced in *Journal of Gerontology* 6, no. 2 (1951): 172; Michelon, "The New Leisure Class," *American Journal of Sociology* 59 (1954–1955): 371–378.

8. C. A. Mahan and T. R. Ford, "Surviving the First Five Years of Retirement," *Journal of Gerontology* 10 (1955): 212–215; methodological criticisms of this article noted by C. L. Hosmer in a subsequent piece, ibid. 11 (1956): 204; Streib, "Morale of the Retired," *Social Problems* 3 (1955–1956): 270–276.

9. Dr. Ben Bosches quoted in "America is Backward in Caring for Oldsters," *Science Newsletter* 71 (April 1957): 237; a preliminary Cornell Report stressing these findings noted in "Idle but Happy," *Scientific American* 194 (February 1956): 60; W. E. Thompson, Gordon Streib, and J. Kosa, "The Effect of Retirement on Personal Adjustment: A Panel Analysis," *Journal of Gerontology* 15 (1960): 165–169; "Now It's the Wives of Retired Men Who are the Problem," *Saturday Evening Post* 234 (November 11, 1961) p. 102.

10. Survey details reported in "Labor Union Survey of Members Reported," *Aging* (August-September 1968): 15.

11. Barfield and Morgan, *Early Retirement, The Decision and the Experience and A Second Look* (Ann Arbor: 1974), pp. 133–147; the growing acceptability of retirement and the lessening influence of the work ethic upon attitudes of workers approaching retirement in the mid-1960s noted by one gerontologist, G. L. Maddox, "Retirement as a Social Event in the United States," in McKinney and Devyver, eds., *Aging and the Social System* (New York: 1966); NICB, *Corporate Retirement Policy and Practices* (Studies in Personnel Policy No. 190, 1964); see also 1967 survey "75% of Firms Honor Retiring Employees," *Administrative Management* 28 (May 1967): 66; and G. W. Boehm, "The Search for Ways to Keep Youthful," *Fortune* 71 (March 1965): 152.

12. "Putting the Old Out to Pasture," *Business Week* (October 10, 1964): 78–80; Scheer and Zollitsch, quoted in "Is a Program of Counseling for Retirement the Responsibility of Management?" *Personnel Administration* 48 (January 1965): 48–50. Interestingly enough, two other people interviewed on this question—both of whom were very much in favor of formal retirement preparation—favored less formal retirement training programs; see comments of W. F. Wagner, a labor relations consultant, and Yvonne Karbowski, a placement officier in the Nebraska Division of Employment in ibid. Argument that the environment had grown more supportive to individual adjustment chances made by gerontologist Wayne Thompson, "Preretirement Anticipation and Adjustment in Retirement," *Journal of Social Issues* 14 (1959): 35–45.

13. The UAW's arguments for early retirement given by C. F. Odell, "The Case for Early Retirement," *Industrial Relations* (May 1965): 3; Sheppard, "Implication of Technological Change for Leisure," in J. M. Kreps (ed.), *Technology, Manpower, and Retirement Policy* (New York and Cleveland: 1966), 179.

14. On seductiveness of early retirement within civil service and the socioeconomic factors contributing to it. see the statistics provided by E. F. Messer, "Thirty-Eight Years is a Plenty," *Civil Service Journal* (October-December 1964): 6–8+; quote from federal official from "Geriscope," *Geriatrics* 19, part 2 (December 1964): 29A–30A; "Early Retirement—A New Factor," *Financial World* 126 (August 31, 1966): 3–4+; Richard Barfield and James Morgan, *Early Retirement: The Decision and the Experience* (Ann Arbor, Michigan: 1969); a good compendium of opinion of early retirement, both lay and expert found in "Early Retirement and the Individual," July 26, 1967, hearings of the *Senate Subcommittee on Retirement and the Individual,* 90th Congress, 2d Session.

15. "Early Retirement: The White House Takes a Dim View," *U.S. News & World Report* 59 (November 8, 1965); 99–100; "Early Retirement Plan Meets Golas," *Business Week* (March 5, 1966): 120; "Second Test for Early Retirement, ibid. (July 2,

1966): 74–75; table from Barfield and Morgan, *Early Retirement* (1974), p. 135 (Table 9–1).

16. "Is Early Retirement Popular?" *U.S. News & World Report,* 62 (April 3, 1967): 62–64; "The Decision to Retire: A Canvass of Possibilities, *Monthly Labor Review* 89 (January 1966): iii–iv; "The Attraction of Retirement," *America* 114 (April 16, 1966): 540; according to a writer in *Dun's Review,* it was rank and file Pressure that sent union leadership to the bargaining table with demands for early retirement; see "Dilemma of Retirement, 81; Barfield and Morgan, *Early Retirement* (1974), p. 135.

17. Barfield and Morgan, ibid., *Early Retirement* (1974), pp. 115–117; 135–137; 322–334.

18. "Early Retirement Meets Goals," *Business Week* (March 5, 1966): 120; Harris Poll cited in "A New Day Dawns for Older Americans," *Aging* (May 1966): 2, 24; "Beats Working," *Newsweek* 66, part 1 (September 27, 1965).

19. "How Workers Like Early Retirement," *U.S. News & World Report* 59 (October 18, 1965): 96–100; "Is Early Retirement Popular?" ibid. 62 (April 3, 1967): 62, 64; "Getting an Early Start on Those Golden Years," *Business Week* (April 27, 1968): 104–106.

Index

American Medical Association
(AMA), 25, 26, 40, 70–71,
137, 196
American Psychological
Association, Division on
Maturity and Old Age, 109,
111, 147
American Public Health
Association, 113, 203
American Public Welfare
Association (APWA), 143,
173, 177, 178, 180–183
American Sociological Association,
111
American Teachers' Association,
133
Anderson, John E., 147
Anderson, Joseph P., 170
Andrews, E. V., 169
*Annals to Social Contributions by the
Aging,* 107
Annual Conference on Aging, 1951,
112
Anti-Semitism, and stereotypes, 78
Archetypes, 24
Architectural Forum, 201
Arden House Seminar on Casework
with the Aging, 174
Arnhoff, Theodore, 86
Arthur, Robert A., 154
Ash, Philip, 236
Atlantic Monthly, 30
Attitudes, inventory on, 104
Austin, Tom, 207
Authoritarian Personality, The
(Adorno et al.), 118
Authoritarianism scale, 118, 119

B

Baltimore Department of
Education, 135
Banay, I., 58
Barfield, Richard, 250
Barfield and Morgan, 255ff.,
260–262
Barkin, Sol, 47
Barron, Milton L., 77, 78
Bassett, John, 52, 53

Beame, Abraham, 26
Beattie, Walter M., Jr., 179
Beckman, R. O., 160
Beery, Wallace, 157
Bellow, S., 159
Bell Telephone Company, 58
Best Years, The (Pitkin), 51
"Best Years, The," 152, 153
Better Business Bureau, 200
Bloom, Murray Teigh, 9, 10
Bonds, war, sale of, 16
Bortz, Edward L., 70
Bowen, Georgene, 172
Bowles, Chester, 169
Boynton, Paul W., 246
Brandeis University School of
Social Work, 181
Breckinridge, Elizabeth, 173, 178,
179, 227
Breen, Leonard Z., 196, 210, 211
Breen, Thomas, 206
Breslow, Lester, 87
Brody, Selma, 151
Brookings Institution, 191
Brown, J. Douglas, 44, 106
Brown, Rollo, 20
Broyard, Anatole, 159
Builders' Association of
Metropolitan Detroit, 205
Bulova Watch Company, 196
Bultena, Gordon L., 60, 61, 212
Bureau of Old Age Assistance,
Massachusetts, 167
Burgess, Ernest W., 3, 102, 105,
107, 110, 111
Burrough's Clearinghouse, 207
Business Week, 7, 56, 191, 192, 195,
200, 222, 226, 228, 251, 254,
263

C

California Chamber of Commerce,
42
California State Conference on the
Problems of Aging, 136
Cameron, Paul, 122
Campbell, Clarence W., 47
Cane, Melville, 21

Frank, Lawrence K., 3, 19, 74, 75, 110
Fraser, Douglas, 57
Freedman, Joseph, 140
Fremont-Smith, Frank, 72
French, Carroll E., 43
Freud, Sigmund, 166, 173
Friedmann, E. A., 116
Friendless, Isolated, Needy, Disabled (FIND), 185, 186
Fuchs, Dora, 167

G

Gallup poll, on old age, 50
Gelbaum, Selma, 219
General Electric, 44
Gerontological Society, 4, 5, 48, 51, 55, 109
Gerontology: in curriculum, 139; development of, 97, 98; term origin, 67
Geriatrics, 148
Gillis, James, 209
Gilmore, Kenneth, 25
Ginzburg, Raphael, 77
Goldberg, Rube, 22
"Golden ghettoes," 262
"Golden Years," 199
"Golden Years, The," 160
Goldhammer, H., 102
Goldwater, Barry, 26
Good adjustment, 120
Gordon, Ruth, 158
Grand Rapids survey, 89ff.
Grant, Cary, 157
Great Depression: retirement in, 6; unemployment in, 37
Great Society programs, 25
Green, William, 47
Greene, Graham, 159
Greene, R. W., 203
Greenfield, Josh, 159
Greenleigh, L. J., 110
Griffen, John, 167
Growing Old: The Process of Disengagement (Cumming and Henry), 98, 117

Gumpert, Martin, 4, 16, 20, 71
Guzak, Michael, 263

H

Hall, G. Stanley, 2
Hall, H. R., 246
Ham and Eggs, movement, 41
Handbook of Gerontology (Tibbitts), 115, 116, 122
Harold and Maude, 158
Harris, Louis, 262
Harry and Tonto, 159
Hartmann, Heinz, 173
Hatton, Raymond, 157
Havighurst, Robert, 74, 75, 79, 80, 102, 107, 108, 110, 111, 116, 131, 136, 221
Hayes, Gabby, 157
Hayes, Helen, 156
Heinz Foods, 192, 195, 196
Henry, Ray, 161
Henry, William, 98, 117–123
Hepburn, Katherine, 157
Hepler, Charles, 200
Hepner, Harry W., 191
Hertel, Frank J., 17
Higher Education Conference, 1965, 139
Hillboc, H. E., 69, 70
Hinman, Frank L., 3
Hodson Community Center, New York, 167, 168, 175
Hoge, E. B., 178
Holiday, 244
Holland, Weare, 30
Hollender, Marc, 169
Hopkins, Harry, 18
Horizon Land Corp., 263
Hoskins, R., 74
House Beautiful, 202
Housing: age-segregated, 114; industry, 196, 201ff.
Howard, John A., 199
How Public Welfare Serves Aging People (APWA), 178, 179
How to Retire and Like It (Kaign), 245

273

Philco Television Playhouse, 154, 155
Philibert, Michel, 123
Physical condition, of aged, 88ff.
Physical Health Index, 90
Piaget, Jean, 166, 173
Pierson, Morton, 228
Pinza, Enzio, 157
Pitkin, Walter, 51–52
Playhouse 90, 154
Pollak, Otto, 99–103, 105, 226
Poore's Register, 228
Porter, Sylvia, 197
Posner, William, 141, 160, 174
Pregnancy, concepts, and aging, 59–60
President's Council on Aging, 150 209
Preston, Caroline E., 58
Princeton University Industrial Relations Survey, 44
Printer's Ink (Kelly), 194
Problems of Aging, The (Cowdry), 3, 68, 73
Problems of America's Aging Population, The, 108
Product development. *See also* Marketers; examples, 191, 192; retirement-leisure theme, 197
Progressive Era, gerontology, 165
Protestantism, and retirement, 35–36
Prudential Life Insurance Company, 234
Psychoanalytic process, 169
Psychological needs, of elderly, 108
Pullman, 36

R

Radio. *See also* Media; on aged, 149ff.
Randall, Ollie, 74, 131, 143, 172, 220
Reader's Digest, 200, 208
Readers' Guide to Periodical Literature, 67
Realemon-Puritan, 195
Realfig Fig Juice, 195

Reed, Vergil, 193
Relief, image of, 183
Retirement, programs-policy. *See also* Pensions; activist, approach, 244; activities, 250ff.; adjustments in, 232ff.; attitudes, 235ff., 260, 261; compulsory, 38, 39, 45, 49ff., 232, 246, 264; criteria for, 226–227; and earnings, 254ff.; in life cycle, 101; preparation for, 218ff.; and productivity, 10; reasons for, 8; shock in, 219, 228; and social utility, 6; systems, formal, 9; and unions, 46; voluntary, 9
Riesman, David, 76, 77
Riley, John W., 59
Riley, Matilda W., 28
Robert Montgomery Presents, 155, 156
Robinson-Rabson, Grace, 17
Rockefeller Foundation, 108, 180
Role, and retirement, 171, 221
Role of the Aged in Primitive Society (Simmons), 75
Romanticism, nineteenth-century, 15
"Room Upstairs, The," 156
Rosenfelt, Rosalie, 123
Rosow, Irving, 212
Rossmoor-Leisure World, Inc., 206, 208
Rudolph, Mae, 27
Rusk, Howard, 20
Russell Sage Foundation, 89, 109, 180

S

Salhaven, community, 193
Saturday Evening Post, 40, 249
Saturday Review, 242
Scheer, W. E., 251
Schmertz, Robert, 209
School, as institution, 129
Schultz, E. B., 224
Science, 85